CHANGE POWER

Capabilities that drive

corporate renewal

DENNIS TURNER

MICHAEL CRAWFORD

Business & Professional Publishing

Published by Business & Professional Publishing
Unit 7/5 Vuko Place
Warriewood NSW 2102 Australia

First published in 1998

The National Library of Australia
Cataloguing-in-Publication entry

Turner, Dennis, 1926- .
    Change power : capabilities that drive corporate renewal.

    ISBN 1 875680 73 X.

    1. Organizational change. I. Crawford, Michael. II. Title.

658.406

Printed and bound in Australia

10 9 8 7 6 5 4 3 2 1

Edited by Ruth Matheson
Text design by Alice Graphics
Cover design by Deborah Clarke
Publisher: Tim Edwards

Distribution in Australia by Woodslane Pty Ltd. Business & Professional Publishing books are available through booksellers and other resellers across Australia and New Zealand. For further information contact Woodslane Pty Ltd on ph (02) 9970 5111, fax (02) 9970 5002 or e-mail info@woodslane.com.au

FOREWORD

When Dennis Turner first told me he would be collaborating with Michael Crawford on a major research project, the result of which is *Change Power*, my first reaction was one of considerable surprise.

Dennis came to the Australian Graduate School of Management in the University of New South Wales after a distinguished career as a senior executive of private and public sector organisations. His 'no nonsense', results-oriented and practical approach to teaching and research reflected this background. Michael Crawford, on the other hand, is a highly skilled consultant who has built on his scientific background and rigorous doctoral training in taking a quantitative analytical approach when tackling management problems.

On reflection, it could well have been this special combination that was required to shed new light on the important and difficult subject of change. Change is unavoidable. Yet while the rewards of successful change are great, as examples such as Woolworths locally and General Electric internationally show, few companies achieve their change targets without significant setbacks. Much of the earlier research tended either to tell stories about change or provide narrow but not terribly useful statistics.

Dennis Turner and Michael Crawford have combined both approaches in order to help understand why so many change efforts fail and how these difficulties might be overcome to achieve success. They carefully identify and analyse the capabilities required for effective change. Their insight is that these change and reshaping capabilities are quite different to the capabilities required for achieving ongoing operational performance. In their own words: 'Being good at running a business today has little relationship to the ability to change it, and vice versa'.

The book builds on this insight, identifying the different capabilities required for change versus operations. It not only provides evidence as to why these capabilities are important but also illustrates how different companies have developed and relied on these capabilities in order to change successfully. Their findings have great practical and theoretical value.

Frederick G. Hilmer AO

CONTENTS

PREFACE

T HIS BOOK IS THE RESPONSE TO A CHALLENGE. Why do some organisations
change successfully and many others fail? The issue is of central importance both to managers and the community in general. Seven years
ago we set out to see if we could find answers to this question. The journey of discovery was longer and harder than we imagined, but many
people have helped us along the way.

Without the information provided by the 243 senior executives who
completed our survey, we would not have been able to develop the
database from which so much new knowledge flowed. We believe we
have cracked the code of change. We have been able to discover the
fundamental framework for the actions needed to make effective organisational change.

We would like to thank Dexter Dunphy for his unwavering support
for our work from its inception. We are grateful to many colleagues and
friends who encouraged us and added to our understanding, in particular, Fred Hilmer, Roger Collins, Phil Yetton, Alison Turner and
Gillian Turner.

We are indebted to Woolworths, Du Pont Australia, the FAI group,
StorageTek and Tubemakers for access to talk to their executives. Without such help and that of many others our task would have been so
much more difficult.

Our thanks go to our editor Ruth Matheson who has considerably
improved the final text and Cynthia Turner who contributed much by
editing and clarifying earlier versions.

The work was funded by the Centre for Corporate Change, in the
Australian Graduate School of Management, University of New South
Wales, and we appreciate such strong and sustained support.

Dennis Turner and Michael Crawford, Sydney, June 1998

About the authors

Dennis Turner is Professor of Management at the Australian Graduate School of Management in the University of New South Wales. Dennis combines his academic work in teaching and research with substantial earlier experience in chief executive and senior management roles in both the private and public sectors in Australia and the United Kingdom.

Dr Michael Crawford is principal of Corex Pty Ltd, a consulting firm specialising in corporate strategy and the management of strategic change. Michael combines academic achievement in science and management with experience in information technology, systems analysis and management.

INTRODUCTION

W HY ARE SOME attempts by managers to change their organisations spectacularly successful while so many others fail? Are special capabilities needed to change an organisation effectively? Are they the same, or different, from those needed to manage an organisation to achieve high performance? What are the important things we should do, as managers, to achieve successful corporate change?

This book provides answers to these important questions. It will give you an understanding of the few fundamental factors that, our research shows, make the difference between success and failure in corporate change. It will provide a powerful, practical framework to focus your actions on the things that matter most to change success. It will give you new tools and concepts, and help you apply them to your business. It will increase your personal skills and impact in managing change.

Some managers and organisations have found effective ways to achieve the changes essential to their long-term performance. Their organisations grow and succeed. They are not immune from the difficulties and problems that cause failure in others. Indeed, at times, they stumble in their journey. But they develop capabilities, see new opportunities, find new pathways, create and summon fresh energies, and continually renew and revitalise their businesses.

Sadly, there are very many more that do not discover how to make effective change. Our own study of 243 cases of corporate change shows that 67 per cent of firms suffered at least one major setback in their attempts to change, 47 per cent were hit by at least two, and 29 per cent by at least three. Yet, overwhelmingly, in 88 per cent of the cases, the executives felt the intended changes and new directions for their firm were right, and almost all, 92 per cent, felt the changes were not beyond their organisation's capacity to achieve. The reality turned out to be otherwise.

This gap between expectations and achievement is unacceptably large. The consequences and heavy costs of failure are borne by the firm's workforce and management, by its shareholders, suppliers, customers, and often by the community at large. With such high stakes, we need to learn to manage corporate change more effectively. If achieving successful change is so important and prized, why is it so elusive for so many?

Is every change unique?

Change challenges us in an endless variety of situations and forms, whether we manage a small or large organisation, work in the private sector, in a not-for-profit organisation, or in a government-owned enterprise. In some cases the changes we face are small, perhaps affecting just part of the organisation. In others they are major, affecting the way in which the entire organisation works. In some the changes are evolutionary and incremental; in others they are dramatic and transformational. For some organisations, change may require the development of new capabilities or the servicing of new markets, or both. In others it may be the challenge of new technologies, of changing outdated cultures, dealing with unwieldy or unworkable organisational structures, working with incompetent top or middle management, or facing massive redundancies. In some cases change is a response to the need to stave off disaster; in others it is a proactive initiative to take advantage of exciting new opportunities. Such variety and situational differences pose the natural question: 'Is every change unique? Are the answers I need to find to make effective change in my organisation unique?'

In some respects every change is unique. Yet we have found that there are some fundamental forces at work in every form of change in every situation. The knowledge of these forces provides the keys that unlock the structure and secrets of successful change. Action based on these forces provides the power and capabilities that drive effective corporate renewal.

A bewildering array of advice

Most guidance about corporate change is largely anecdotal. We read how Paul Simons in Australia revitalised Woolworths or how, in the United States, Jack Welch changed General Electric or Jan Carlzon in Europe changed Scandinavian Airlines. The many battle stories, some-times written by the generals, make fascinating reading. Among the often conflicting conclusions they draw, there are real pearls of wisdom. But which are the real pearls and which the artificial ones? On what basis can you make a judgment? Various leaders comment on change:

> 'When I try and summarise what I've learned since 1981 one of the big lessons is that change has no constituency. People like the status quo. They like the way it was. When you start changing things, the good old days look better and better. You've got to be prepared for massive resistance.'—Jack Welch, CEO, General Electric[1]

> 'Campbell's people had incredible pride. When I drew attention to the fact that their results sucked then, man, I stirred up a hornet's nest of very proud talented people. They wanted to win as badly as I did.'—David Johnson, CEO, Campbell Soup Company[2]

> When I come in, I like to make change very quickly.'—Al Dunlap (Chainsaw) who effected major change at Australian Consolidated Press for Kerry Packer, and at a number of US corporations[3]

> One thing Girraween [a Du Pont plant in Sydney that achieved signifi-cant successful change] taught us is you can't do things quickly.'—Dick Warburton, then managing director, Du Pont (Australia) Limited[4]

From the consulting and academic world, lots of ideas have emerged that offer guidance. Management by objectives, total quality management, value engineering, re-engineering, just-in-time management, downsizing, outsourcing, benchmarking, best practice, corporate culture, managing values, entrepreneurship, intrapreneurship, leadership, and many others, offer solutions to particular problems. While some of these may be fads, many of these single-focus approaches and ideas have real value. But they do not go to the heart of giving managers a framework and focus for action that works and that can be applied to the effective management of change.

Most managers learn most things by doing—by learning from experience. Learning by doing is often a most effective way to learn, particularly when the game is a continuing or repetitive one and mistakes can be rectified along the way. However, by the time the lessons have been learned about managing corporate change in a competitive world it is frequently too late, for the game has already changed. What managers need is to be able to move confidently and quickly to take decisions and action that will work in their own situation. Such a framework for action and an understanding of the organising principles involved are vital if the rate of change success is to be improved.

Out of the world of magic

In 1992 we set out to try to find a more reliable and objective basis to help managers understand and manage change more effectively. We did so primarily by collecting and analysing data about a large number of corporate changes. We wanted to find out what works and what does not work when firms try to change. And we wanted to know if the things that work are successful across the board, not just in one, two or three firms, but in many organisations, for different kinds of change and in many different situations.

What we have to say in this book, therefore, is not based on our subjective assessment or judgment of what makes change effective. Nor is it based on particular insights that may be gained from the in-depth study of a few successful changes. We use a number of examples of corporate change to illustrate our findings, but our conclusions do not come from these examples. What we say is based on our analysis of measurable data about what succeeds or fails in the corporate change process. It is based on information about organisations going through change, collected from 243 cases of change in both the commercial and government sectors. The comprehensive data collected have enabled us to identify and measure many of the key factors involved in successful organisational change. The scope of these data has allowed us to make some conclusions that are generalisable. We have been able to identify the relatively few vital things that make the difference between successful and unsuccessful change. The database, methods and subsequent statistical analysis provide rigour, robustness and validity to our findings. It is this that gives us confidence that we have found some reliable answers to the questions posed at the beginning of this introduction.

In the real world our beliefs are influenced by an amalgam of factors only a few of which we can subject to robust statistical analysis. When we read findings from such a process of statistical analysis in a topic that interests us there is likely to be a progressive interaction between what emerges from the collected objective data and our own experience of the subject. We check the results of the analysis against the testbed of our own experience. As we unfold our findings and as you test them against your own experiences and knowledge of organisational change we are confident you will find your own experience will add further relevance, understanding and substance to our concepts.

Change Power takes corporate change out of the world of myth or magic where gurus, corporate magicians and charismatic leaders unfold their fascinating stories. It puts it into the world of facts and management responsibility, where it belongs. We realise that management is not just about facts. Myths and magic are part of corporate life, but they provide no reliable basis for transfer into effective management action. Our work provides such a basis for a great diversity of corporate changes in both private and public sector organisations. It provides a framework for management action to help you change your organisation more effectively.

The way this book is organised

The first chapter outlines our findings and concepts to give you an overall picture of what is important to achieving effective change. Chapter 2 explores the actions taken by the chief executive of a retail organisation with a thousand stores, which changed and renewed its business and revitalised its performance. We use this example to illustrate how the concepts and framework for action, which arise from our research, apply to the real world of managers. In Chapter 3 we explain important aspects of the way the research was carried out, and present its key findings in more detail. Chapter 4 explores the concept of organisational states, and how management action to achieve particular organisational states is important to achieving effective change.

The next three chapters, Chapters 5 to 7, describe, more fully, the three key capabilities of Engagement, Development and Performance Management, which are of central importance to achieving effective change. We illustrate these through a number of real cases, to put recognisable flesh on what are abstract though important concepts. These chapters should give you an understanding of the important characteristics of each capability, a sense of what each one actually consists of, and how each capability contributes to effective change. Chapter 8 consolidates the three previous chapters and looks at the application of our general findings, in particular, to cultural change, to change in the public sector, and to mergers, to alert you to some of the key factors that you should take into consideration before you take action.

Our work is focused principally on the effectiveness of change, not on achieving current performance, but we use Chapter 9 to develop a clear understanding of the structure and functioning of capabilities that relate to current performance. Chapter 10 explores the building and embedding of corporate competencies. Our aim here is to analyse and describe the process and its benefits in a way that will be helpful to managers who wish to develop their own organisation's corporate competencies. The final chapter takes you through a personal planning process for action to achieve effective change. In the epilogue we summarise the key ways in which managers can contribute to the leadership of change.

In Appendix A we provide a summary of the sixteen competencies used in the survey questionnaire and their main linkages with the capabilities. Appendix B lists the organisations from which our 243 cases of change were drawn. Also provided are endnotes to indicate the sources of quotations and ideas that have enriched our understanding.

Throughout *Change Power*, we focus on the task of managing the organisation through change. While it is a convenient shorthand to talk about 'managing change', it is in fact an incorrect description. Change is not managed, but rather the organisation is *managed through change*. This difference in focus is important because it goes to the heart of how the people of the organisation, who in the end must achieve the changes, can be influenced to succeed.

A book for managers facing change

Change Power is written principally for managers who are facing the need to make effective organisational change. We offer no quick fix. We have used some new terms because some of our concepts are new. It will take a little time for you to become familiar and comfortable with their use. We are confident that when you finish, you will be able to see your organisation and its business through a new, different and powerful lens, which clarifies the key things you need to do to achieve successful change and long-term performance.

One of the exciting things is that while change looks complex and confusing and a major challenge, and it is all of these, our data and analysis show that there are a few vital areas for action that make the real difference between failure and success. If you focus on them and get them right, you are much more likely to succeed. Our data also say if you ignore them, or get them wrong, you are likely to add to the statistics of failure with which we opened this introduction.

CHAPTER 1

A framework for change

The first day

As Robert Stanley walked into the large department store on the first day of his appointment as its general manager, he felt both a sense of achievement and a slight sense of foreboding. The reasons for feeling good were clear. In many ways he thought he had made it. In his early 30s, he had been appointed to manage one of the group's major stores. It was a key step towards his long-term aim of being the group's managing director.

He was not quite so sure why he felt uneasy. Perhaps it was because the store had not done well for some years and was seen as the group's problem store, though, he told himself, that gave him more scope for improving its performance. Perhaps it was because, as the lift took him up to his new office, the store seemed bigger than he had thought.

He greeted his secretary, Heather, whom he knew from his visits to the store in his previous post as a central footwear buyer for the group.

On his desk was an intray with the recent mail. There was a letter of good wishes from his new boss, the store's director, which gave him a pleasant sense of support, for which he felt a quite sudden but unanticipated need. The last paragraph congratulated him on his substantial pay rise and said he could expect another good increase if the store's results improved. Heather had also left a note explaining that every Monday morning there was a regular meeting at 9 o'clock between the general manager and the 20 department managers to discuss the week's results. Did Robert want to hold the meeting this morning or did he want to cancel it and meet the managers individually?

Robert took a deep breath and looked at his watch. It was now a quarter to nine. 'Of course I'll have the meeting,' he said to himself. 'It's a good way to get to know them and find out what they think.'

Robert was a good communicator and the meeting seemed to go well. He told the department managers something about himself, his hopes for the store and his desire to use their experience and talent in improving its performance. 'Why don't we make a start now?' he asked, when he thought he had established some rapport with the group. 'We all know the results from the store have not been as good as we would like for some years. What do we have to do to make them better?'

There was a long pause. The body language was clear. How far could they trust this new manager? 'Well,' said Robert, 'suppose we thought of the one most important thing we could do to improve the store's performance. What would it be?'

'I think the main thing,' said the women's wear manager, feeling her way cautiously, 'and I'm not criticising your predecessor or the others who have been here in the last few years, is many of our customers have less money and different tastes from those who live where our other stores are located. The stuff we get from the central buyers is aimed at, what I would call middle or upper middle class customers. Our immediate neighbourhood is more working class, so often it's not what customers are looking for. When it doesn't sell, we have to mark it down to get rid of it. The markdowns ruin our profit.'

'Well that's partly true,' broke in the furniture manager, 'but we're also surrounded by lots of middle class suburbs. We have been given the right to do some of our own local buying so we can cater to our local needs as well. I'm doing quite a lot myself now and have been for a couple of years, perhaps more. I don't see why we can't get the best of both worlds. After all there is some real business in the locals. Just look at the business that Jones and Smithson down the road do.'

'I know we can buy some stock ourselves but I don't think it's the goods that are our main problem,' said the hardware manager. 'I think it's more a question of morale. We haven't had a real win for some time. There's a strong rumour the store will be sold if the results go on as now. I think a number of our people have lost a lot of confidence. Frankly, some are depressed. Some of our best people have left to go to places where the grass looks greener.'

'It's much more than morale,' commented the children's wear manager. 'I think people in this room are under such pressure to get results, we just concentrate on the short term. Many of the things we need to do, if we're going to get this place right, are about what it needs longer term. I've been here five years and all we seem to have done is to constantly cut costs to the bone in an effort to make our budget. Take staff training for example and ...', looking around, 'take managerial training in particular. When's the last time we really gave some time and effort to that?'

'And the store generally,' chipped in the cosmetics manager. 'The fixtures and carpet and layout and decor all need a facelift. Also we want a computer system that gives us the information we need to do our job, not the information head office wants.'

'I think all these things matter,' said the china and glass manager. 'But the real issue is,' she paused, 'we need leadership. We need someone who believes we can make it and we need to believe it ourselves. We need to know where we are going. Each department seems to have its own view about who our customers are, and they're not all the same. I'm confused about our image and I'm sure some of our customers are too. I've been here four years.' She hesitated, 'I'm not sure I'm as confident today as when I arrived.'

There was a very long pause. Robert realised every eye in the room was focusing on him. 'Well,' he said, taking his courage in his hands, but feeling far from comfortable, 'I believe we can make it. I know there are lots of difficulties but,' he paused and something seemed to happen inside him. 'A year from now, maybe two years if necessary, I hope our biggest difficulty will be counting up the size of our increases over the previous year.' He was almost surprised to hear what he had said.

There was another long pause. The menswear manager spoke quietly. 'A lot of us have different views,' he said. 'Obviously we have to go on doing our best to get immediate results. Equally obviously we have to change all sorts of things, including many things that haven't been mentioned in this room. I appreciate it's early, but', he leaned forward towards Robert, 'what do you think are the really important things we should do? Where do you think we should start? How should we go about it?'

While most managers do not face these questions on their first morning, and changes come in all sizes, shapes and situations, these same fundamental questions are faced by countless managers throughout the working world. What and how should we change to perform better in the future?

Meeting the needs of effective change

To make effective change the organisation needs to succeed in three important dimensions: the economic, the social and the managerial.

First, the organisation has to meet the economic requirement. Change must enable an organisation to 'deliver the goods', not only in the minds and visions of those who wish to implement the changes, but also in the hard reality of the competitive marketplace.

The firm has to have, or develop, capabilities that will give it competitive advantages in a particular market. It has to identify and create a position in that market in which it can make an economic return. So change involves building new capabilities and finding new directions. And these need to be aligned. A strategic position is not achieved or maintained without the relevant competencies. Competencies that do not provide competitive advantage in a market will not help to achieve or maintain a strong position. Commercial organisations need an economic surplus to survive and grow. Government and not-for-profit organisations, while not focused so strongly on economic outcomes, are finding, more and more, the need to operate under growing economic and financial pressures, sometimes in direct competition with the private sector. They increasingly need efficiency and productivity to perform and compete for scarce public resources, and they have to deliver the expected outcomes.

Secondly, effective change has to be achieved by an organisation working as a social entity to achieve its purposes. While individuals play vital roles in the change process, ultimately the people of the organisation collectively have to bring into being the ideas and intents that will deliver the economic benefits. They have to make the ideas work, using the organisation's resources to achieve the new directions. So organisations need shared purposes, visions and values that support the development of new or improved capabilities and directions, and they need to build cultures that create and sustain beliefs, and develop, encourage and reward behaviours that help achieve them.

This means that change and renewal have to be managed into existence and effectiveness. The organisation, as a social entity, has to be managed through the change, achieving at the same time its immediate performance and its change intents. Both are needed, whether the change is small or large, is short, long or continuous, incremental or transformational. So the managerial task is to manage an organisation and a process and to do so in ways that enable the economic and social requirements of performance to be met.

Finding the answers to what should be done has to be married to producing the action to do them. And solutions for the future have to be achieved while the organisation is still performing to meet its customers' needs today. You cannot close your organisation down while you change it for the future. Change and current performance has to be managed, in almost all cases, simultaneously.

Change in itself is without value. It can be change for the good or equally change for the worse. *What makes organisational change valuable is that it renews the organisation's abilities to perform.* Action to achieve this renewal may focus on many things that are involved in the organisation's operations. The focus of action may, for example, be on the skills of its workforce or its managers, a new technology, its positioning in its marketplace, its structure, culture, resources, or in fact on an endless number of aspects of its business. But changing any of these things is not an end in itself. It is a means to enable the organisation to function more effectively and achieve better performance in pursuit of its goals.

Actions that affect change

Of the factors that affect change, actions are the most visible and the easiest to recognise. They typically provide the illustrations and examples through which most corporate change is described. While actions in all levels of an organisation are important to change and performance, our focus in this book is on management action. Achieving effective change is, in the end, a management responsibility. Those actions, of course, typically affect the actions and work of many others. Actions are what we see management doing, or not doing. Conveying a vision is an action. So is setting priorities, or planning, or providing training, or monitoring a process. There are many such broad actions and some of them take place in many change programs.

Early in our work we explored the actions that managers took in a number of cases to change their organisations and some of these are described later in the book. We rapidly came to recognise that the more specific the actions were for a particular firm, the more likely it was that they were less useful or indeed irrelevant for others. For example, if we looked at management actions at Woolworths, Du Pont's Giraween Sydney plant, the NSW State Library and StorageTek, all of which made very successful changes in recent years, we would see very different actions and emphases. While action to reposition the firm in the marketplace was central to Woolworths and StorageTek, it was not to Du Pont. Though Woolworths sought staff stability, an end to frequent job rotation, and a focus on personal specialisation, the NSW State Library moved towards less specialisation and changes in culture and structure. While StorageTek built its entry into a new market with important specialised external senior recruitment, Woolworths achieved its success with a top team composed almost entirely of insiders. Though training was a factor in all changes, in some it focused on acquiring new technical skills, while in others it focused on personal growth. In some, the training was entirely voluntary; in others it was compulsory. In some cost reduction was very important; in others it was not. At Du Pont, trade union action in developing a 'joint beliefs statement' with the management was the initial key to success, but significant union involvement was not evident in any of the others.

Though all of these specific actions were appropriate and worked for the organisations concerned, they are clearly situationally dependent. In some situations they could clearly be inappropriate and perhaps even counterproductive. Looking at action itself gives little basis for generalised advice that would be useful to all managers. But clearly action is vital to achieving effective change. But in what areas is action vital? What are the fundamental purposes of such action? What kinds of action can be taken to achieve effective change?

To provide useful advice to managers about appropriate actions to take we needed to identify something that is not dependent upon the particular situation of an organisation but fundamental to many changes, in many organisations, in many situations. However, since action in an individual case must clearly be relevant to its particular circumstances, our search needed to discover if something existed which, while common to all change, nevertheless also provides a basis or framework for specific actions that work in the very many different situations in which change takes place. Our research uncovered such a fundamental structure.

What makes action effective?

If you drove to work today, you would have made thousands of decisions and actions in driving your car, without normally having thought consciously about any or many of them. Indeed it is quite possible that as you completed your journey you could not really recall any of the actions, decisions or directions that got you there.

You know a lot about driving cars and what you have to do to get to a destination safely. You have developed your skills to do so and have honed them with constant practice. And you have done it thousands of times in different conditions having learned to manage yourself to get good and safe driving performance. *You have, by now, developed capability as a driver.*

But when you first sat at the wheel of a car to learn to drive, every action you took was preceded by conscious thought. The first time you turned a corner, you wondered how far and how fast you should turn the steering wheel. When you thought about your speed, you looked at the speedometer since you would not have enough experience or knowledge to judge it. If you were braking, you might have started to brake too early, though hopefully not too late! You may well have felt nervous or anxious or not confident that you would be able to stop the car quickly if needed.

The capability you have now developed provides the basis for you to take effective action. You take action every time you get into your car. The higher your developed capability, the more effective your actions will be. You will get the benefit of them every time you drive and they may save your life in an emergency. Capability provides the basis for effective action, not only in driving cars but also in every activity. *The effectiveness of our actions in different situations and under different pressures is thus directly linked to our developed capability in the activity.*

The impact of capability on actions

When we have a capability in a particular activity or area, whether it's in an aspect of managing, like communication or planning, or goal setting, or, as in our example, of driving a car, we know what to do, how to do it and when to do it. Our *personal capability affects our actions* in a number of important dimensions.

Capability helps you to focus your action on the important things. It has a strong basis of knowledge, much of which, by now, in relation to driving a car, you have internalised. You know what's important and relevant to performance and this identifies the areas where action is most needed. Many of the things you do, you do automatically. In an emergency your focus sharpens enormously. You time your actions better. You know when to do things because you know what you are doing and how it works. When you focus on the things that matter to performance in the activity, all your skill, knowledge and resources are used more efficiently. When you develop capability in managing change, your knowledge of what to do enables you to focus on the most important things; you use your skills and resources more efficiently.

When you have capability in an activity your performance becomes more consistent. You can be lucky, once or twice, when you act without having real capability in something, but when you get good at doing something you can do it consistently no matter how often you have to. That is one reason you get to work safely each day. You can replicate your good actions. It doesn't guarantee you will never make a mistake but if your capability is high, your performance will be consistently high. Because of the practice and feedback, and perhaps tuition, which has taken place in learning the particular skill, you can usually do things more accurately and more quickly. Speed is not always needed, but sometimes it is vital for performance and survival. When you have developed capability in making effective organisational change the actions you take will be more consistent and you will be able to take them more accurately and quickly. Some of them may become almost automatic, as they become in driving a car, though, of course your actions will be affected by the actions of others.

As your capability grows so do your confidence and your command of your personal state in action. As a consequence you perform better and can act more effectively when under pressure. As your confidence develops you can integrate the various individual components of knowledge, skill and self-management, which together combine to form a capability. This applies to driving a car, communicating with someone and managing an organisation through change.

So when we have a capability in a particular activity it enables us to act effectively in a wide range of situations and under different pressures. The actions will be different but they rest upon a common capability. If, for example, you have capability in communication, you can use your knowledge and skills well, but differently, in conducting a disciplinary interview, congratulating a winner in a national sales contest, in being interviewed by a hostile media representative or conversing with a partner during a romantic evening. The basic capability will be the same but the actions, words, gestures, eye movements, postures and listening will be different.

In finding out what might be a common structure underlying a number of different actions we therefore focused on the underlying capabilities needed to perform the task rather than on particular actions that managers took. So we collected a great deal of information about the competencies that existed in the organisations represented in our survey as well as information about successful and unsuccessful change and performance outcomes.

This enabled us to identify the capabilities involved in making effective change and achieving business performance. These capabilities provide the basis for effective action.

Confusing terminology: capabilities and competencies

The terms competencies and capabilities are frequently used interchangeably, which often leads to unnecessary confusion. In everyday language there is no difference in the meaning of these two words. In our example of driving we described how what we called our 'capability' as a driver was composed of a number of contributing factors, such as steering, braking or accelerating. For convenience we could call these important but lower level factors 'competencies', simply to differentiate these individual items from the accumulation and integration of them into something bigger, which we called a capability. A capability is the embodiment of a number of contributing but lower level competencies. To minimise confusion over terminology we will follow this practice throughout the book.

Our analysis of our data shows that there are a number of 'competencies' that are associated with one another and cluster together to form a more embracing group, which we have called a 'capability'.

We identified five such capabilities. For example, we call one of these capabilities, Performance Management. That capability is formed from a number of contributing competencies, such as performance control, resource application, planning, financial, integration, and so on. Each of the five key capabilities we have identified encompasses a number of contributing competencies.

In the remainder of this chapter, we provide an overview of the five key capabilities. In Chapter 3 we describe the research process that identified these capabilities. The five capabilities underlie effective management action to enable a firm to meet the two requirements of long-term performance—that is, to perform well in the present and to change effectively for future performance. In later chapters we explain the make-up of each capability and the key competencies that contribute to each.

The five essential capabilities

The five capabilities are split into two fundamental groupings. One group, *reshaping capabilities*, enables an organisation to *change effectively*. The second group, *operational capabilities*, provides the basis for *current performance* and results. Each of these two major groups consists of three capabilities since one capability, Performance Management, is common to both groups.

Our data show that:

- The capabilities to achieve effective change are very different from those needed to achieve current performance.
- A business needs both these two differing sets of capabilities if it is to achieve long-term performance.
- Having one set of capabilities is not related to having the other.
- Being good at running a business today has little relationship to the ability to change it, and vice versa.
- One capability, Performance Management, contributes significantly to both current performance and effective change.

The three reshaping capabilities

Three capabilities provide the basis for action to achieve Change Effectiveness. These are Engagement, Development and Performance Management (see Figure 1.1). These capabilities are needed by organisations *whenever* change is needed. The first, Engagement, is about getting the people throughout the organisation informed, involved, committed and motivated to act to achieve the firm's purpose and future directions. The second, Development, involves developing all the resources—personal, physical, technological and systems—needed to achieve the firm's future directions. The third, Performance Management, involves managing the factors that drive the processes of change.

Each capability is formed from a number of contributing competencies. For example, the contributing competencies that go to form Engagement include those relevant to finding new directions and opportunities, and also those needed to get commitment to them. Engagement is much more than communication or motivation, though these are important to it. It is also about having pathfinding skills—being able to develop, crystallise and articulate new directions to accomplish the firm's purpose and values. It is difficult to get real Engagement without

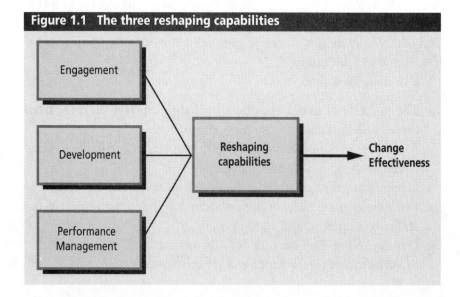

Figure 1.1   The three reshaping capabilities

Engagement

Development → Reshaping capabilities → Change Effectiveness

Performance Management

knowing and being involved in where you are going or likely to go. Similarly, Development capability requires contributing competencies not only in the actual development of resources, but also in skills in identifying those resources that are relevant for the organisation's future direction. Development is not an end in itself but a means to higher future performance. Performance Management likewise includes a range of contributing competencies, including resource application, performance control, financial, planning and integration.

Action based on the three reshaping capabilities meets two vital needs. It *reshapes* the organisation's *operational* capabilities, which will, in turn, provide the firm's *future performance* and results. Secondly, reshaping actions influence the *organisation's state* so that its members collectively understand the intended changes, become committed to them, grow confident in their collective abilities to succeed, and are empowered to take action. Action, not just talk, is vital to effective change—and action across the organisation, not just at the top, or the middle, or at the coalface.

Across the sample of 243 cases of corporate change, as the strength of reshaping capabilities rises, so change success rises. As strength falls, change success falls.

The three operational capabilities

Three capabilities provide the basis for action to achieve Current Business Performance. Since these capabilities enable an organisation to perform well at any point in time they are *always* needed. We called these Biztech, Marketing and Selling, and Performance Management, as illustrated in Figure 1.2.

Biztech: the need for a new word for a new concept

Biztech consists of competencies involved in commanding and understanding the technologies, processes and mechanisms through which the organisation creates and delivers its products and services to its market.

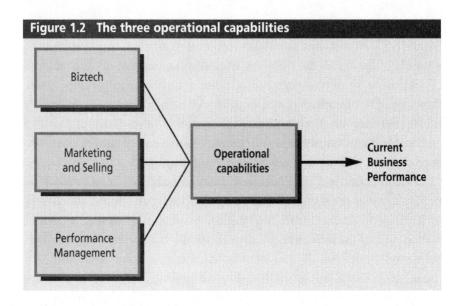

Figure 1.2   The three operational capabilities

Biztech

Marketing and Selling

Performance Management

Operational capabilities

Current Business Performance

Unfortunately there is not an existing word in current use that accurately describes this capability.

Biztech includes core technologies and skills that are very specific to the business—for example, routing logistics for a transport company, or skills in hydraulic systems for a water utility. It also includes other technologies that are not unique to it—for example, information technology, which both of these businesses would use, but which need to be integrated with the firm's core technologies to achieve performance.

However, Biztech is not just a description of physical technologies or technical skills. It includes a management, knowledgeable of those technologies and skills, which is able to harness them and guide their application. It also includes the systems and processes within the organisation that assist in the application of the technologies within the business. As you can see, it includes all those business technologies, related skills, processes and mechanisms needed by the organisation to deliver its products and services to its market.

While the term Biztech will obviously be new to you, we hope its use will help in the understanding of what the capability really is and that you will become comfortable with its use.

Marketing and Selling

The second operational capability is Marketing and Selling. Marketing and Selling lies in understanding the firm's markets and how external events affect them, identifying customer needs and selling the firm's goods and services effectively to them.

Performance Management

The third operational capability, Performance Management, as we have seen, is a strong contributor to change. It also influences and drives the organisation's current performance, to ensure high current results are consistently achieved now and in the future.

The manager's framework for change and performance

Figure 1.3 provides an overview of the capabilities needed for both outcomes, Change Effectiveness and Current Business Performance. It shows the contributing competencies to each capability and provides a brief description of each capability. All of these capabilities and competencies are explored in later chapters. The relationships between the capabilities and the outcomes are also shown in Figure 1.3. Operational capabilities are frequently the major base and focus for management action. Having strong operational capabilities, however, does not, generally, help you to change your business effectively.

Capabilities can be personal and corporate

Capabilities can be personal and corporate. A manager may have personal capabilities in, say, Performance Management or Marketing and Selling. An organisation, similarly, may have a corporate capability in these or any aspect of its business. Corporate capabilities are embedded in the fabric of the organisation—in its practices, processes, systems, structures, culture, values, know-how and technologies. Importantly this is as true for reshaping capabilities as it is for operational ones. While personal capabilities leave the organisation when their owner does, corporate capabilities tend to endure, despite the comings and goings of individuals.

Figure 1.3   The manager's framework

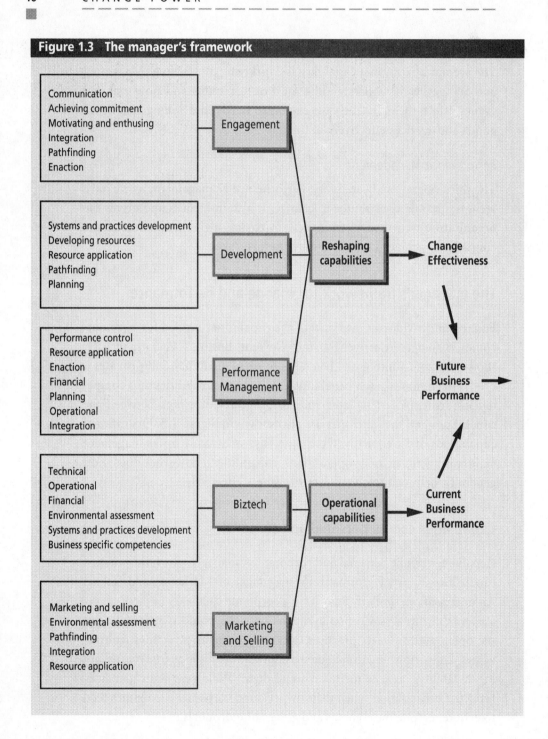

The five capabilities

Engagement—Getting the people throughout the organisation informed, involved, committed and motivated to act to achieve the organisation's purpose and future directions.

Development—Developing all the resources—personal, physical, technological and systems—needed to achieve the firm's future directions.

Performance Management—Proactively managing the factors that drive the organisation's performance to ensure it consistently and effectively achieves what is intended.

Biztech—Commanding and understanding the technologies, processes and mechanisms through which the organisation produces and delivers its products and services to its market.

Marketing and Selling—Understanding the firm's markets and how external events affect them, identifying customers' needs and selling its goods and services effectively to them.

When an organisation has strong corporate reshaping capabilities, many actions that help to achieve change will take place as part of the normal, typical way in which the organisation works. For example, when an organisation has a strong corporate capability in Engagement, actions will take place as part of its normal way of working that will help the people to become engaged in the changes. Likewise, if it is strong in Development capability it will take many actions as part of its normal way of operating to develop and change its resources of all kinds. The same is true for Performance Management. In some cases these actions will occur almost automatically. In others this may not be so because new situations will arise. Nevertheless, the organisation will have in place practices, processes, systems, mechanisms and supporting cultures that will energise and facilitate individual and collective behaviour and action that will provide valuable support for whatever needs to be done.

Where organisations have weak corporate reshaping capabilities, the success of change will depend much more on the personal reshaping capabilities of key individuals. Successful change is still possible but much harder to achieve. The key individuals will have to ensure that actions to achieve Engagement, Development and Performance Management are taken throughout the change in a way that impacts on the whole organisation. This demands much greater effort and personal skills than when those same capabilities are owned by the organisation itself.

Your organisation needs both personal and corporate competencies. But some competencies are more strongly dependent on individuals. While organisations can have corporate competence in pathfinding, which we mentioned earlier as part of Engagement, some aspects of pathfinding, particularly those that require the synthesis of information, knowledge, patterns and trends, are more dependent on personal skills. We later discuss those areas where personal competence is important to effective change.

Organisational states

We have talked about the importance of capabilities to the impact of action but the effectiveness of action is not solely a matter of having the necessary capabilities to act. The level of performance is also influenced by the 'state' of the actor, whether an individual or an organisation. Much research shows that personal capabilities and actions are more effective and have stronger outcomes when an individual is highly motivated to perform, has a strong sense of self-efficacy, and is committed and confident.

As 'states' is a new concept, in the way we use it, a personal example may make it more easily recognisable.

On the day we wrote this section, a 22-year-old Australian woman became the first person to swim the 200-kilometre-wide Straits of Florida from Cuba to the United States. Susie Moroney accomplished what 50 other long-distance champion swimmers had over the years tried, but failed, to do. She swam almost 25 hours non-stop and had prepared herself to swim for 40 hours. She was trained and fit. As she walked out on to the sand a reporter asked her how she had been able to do it.

She replied, 'I concentrated all the time on the distance. I kept happy thoughts in my mind. It was not letting go of the dream of swimming to America.'

In three short sentences Susie was describing aspects of her state and how she managed it. She was focused on her actual performance and how it was going. She knew how far she had swum and how far she had to go. She was managing her efforts and her reserves of energy. She had found a way of controlling her thoughts and emotions to support her non-stop, draining, unrelenting 25-hour effort. In spite of pain and sickness she focused on happy times and concentrated on positive thoughts. She had a vision—'a dream'—of what she wanted to do and she simply would not be deflected from it or give it up. She was strongly motivated to perform. And she was trained and superbly fit. Of course, it was not her state and the management of it alone that enabled her performance. Her capabilities as a long distance swimmer were central and essential to that. But even with those high capabilities, many champion swimmers had failed before her. Susie had to manage her personal state to perform at her best for a very long time under immense pressure. And she did.

At a personal level our actions are what we do, our capabilities are what we are capable of doing, and our states determine how hard and well we try to do what we are capable of doing. Each of these three factors in our performance needs self-management if we are to perform at our best, whether in changing ourselves to do something different, or in performing well at something we already do. So the personal states of individuals, especially in positions of power and responsibility, have an impact on the success of change initiatives.

At an organisational level states are the collective beliefs, feelings, behaviours and prevailing conditions that affect individual and collective action and predisposition to act. As action is central to both change and performance, the states of the organisation are important to achieving both change and performance. So we also collected a great deal of information from our survey sample about their organisational states.

The analysis of the data enables us to identify a number of organisational states that are linked to successful change and business performance. Some states have stronger impact on Change Effectiveness and some on Current Business Performance. For example, states of *commitment*, or *understanding*, or *empowerment*, enhance Change Effectiveness, while a state of *conflict* undermines it. A state of *esprit de corps* is strongly linked to Current Business Performance.

Effective corporate change requires change and shifts in the collective attitudes, behaviours and skills of the *many*, not the few. That is why the concept of organisational states is important. States impact on the many. Management action is needed during change to create the states that help to make the changes successful. While corporate capabilities take time to build, managers can take action, relatively quickly, to help the development of states that enhance effective change and minimise those that make it harder to achieve.

The three factors are interlinked

The interconnecting lines in Figure 1.4 show that the three factors—actions, capabilities and states—are interlinked.

Actions influence the process of building and developing personal and corporate capabilities and organisational states. The *capabilities* provide quality and effectiveness to the actions, and influence the existence and strengths of the states. *States* affect the manifestation of the capabilities and actions that impact on the outcomes.

We will be focusing in *Change Power* principally on what happens within the centre circle, where the impact and interaction between these three factors takes place. We will demonstrate these interconnections and their importance as we go along.

A framework for change

When the menswear manager asked Robert his fundamental questions about what and how to change, Robert unfortunately did not have the output of our research to help him deal with them! In the event, like most managers, he had to learn as he went along. But some managers are skilled in making effective change. They clearly possess some or all of the key personal capabilities. Consciously, or intuitively, they reshape and renew their organisation's operational capabilities and effectively influence the development of organisational states that facilitate effective change. In so doing they may be helped by the existence of corporate reshaping capabilities. Sometimes they help to build such

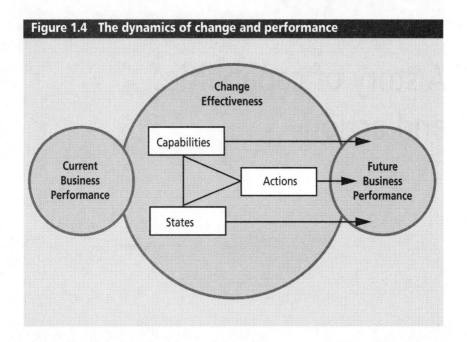

Figure 1.4 The dynamics of change and performance

corporate capabilities so that the organisation becomes less dependent on their personal capabilities and influences its own continual renewal and long-term performance.

While Robert was inexperienced to deal with the situation he faced, the manager we are about to meet in the next chapter was not. This manager—Paul Simons—was a mature and extremely knowledgeable chief executive with a lifetime of experience in business. He had managed substantial retailing businesses with great success. When we first meet Paul Simons in the next chapter, he has just been appointed as executive chairman of Woolworths, a group of nearly a thousand stores with a staff of 70,000. Clearly this is a very different scenario from Robert's one store.

Paul Simons started on the job of changing his organisation at the very first meeting with his senior managers in his new job. We want to use the story of his success to illustrate the application of the concepts we have just explained. Our framework and concepts were not derived at all from an analysis of Paul Simons' actions, but from the analysis of 243 cases of corporate change. Paul Simons' actions, and those of others, in the story of the revitalisation of Woolworths enable us to put recognisable flesh, in terms of corporate change and performance, on the skeleton and structure of the ideas we have just outlined.

CHAPTER 2

A story of capabilities and action

Another first day

PAUL PLACED THE packet of Danish Butter Cookies on the board-room table. Next he put the pack of Razzamatazz panty hose, the pack of three Philips light bulbs and lastly the Nylex garden hose on the table. It was his first meeting with the senior executive team of the retail business of which he had just been appointed executive chairman.

He looked round the table. 'I bought these goods today from Franklins, our strongest competitor. I'd like you to write down what you think is the price difference between our total price for these goods and Franklins' total price.' He then went round the table and noted the expected differences. All had assumed that Franklins, a major competitor, would be cheaper. The biggest expected difference between the totals noted on their pads by the senior management present was just over a dollar. 'The actual difference,' said Paul, 'is $8.20 and these four items cost 54 per cent more to buy in our Woolworths' stores than they do to buy from Franklins.'[1]

It was 1987. Woolworths, an organisation of nearly a thousand supermarket and discount stores with a staff of 70,000 and sales of $5.6

billion, was about to record a drop in its profit from $108 million in 1986 to $2.7 million. It faced a serious situation. It needed to make substantial change. It did so. By 1997, in a mature market that was growing very slowly, its sales had almost tripled. As shown in Figure 2.1, its profit had risen to nearly $450 million. It had also established its position as the leading player in the supermarket food business with a share of over 30 per cent of the fiercely contested Australian food market.

Figure 2.1 shows this major turnaround. What it does not show is that the profit of 1986, the year before the profit collapse, was the sixty-second consecutive year in which Woolworths had increased its sales and profit since it had started life as a small bargain basement operation in the Imperial Arcade in Sydney in 1924. Starting as a small variety store, it had established a major operation that spread from this base into supermarkets, discount department stores and specialty chains.

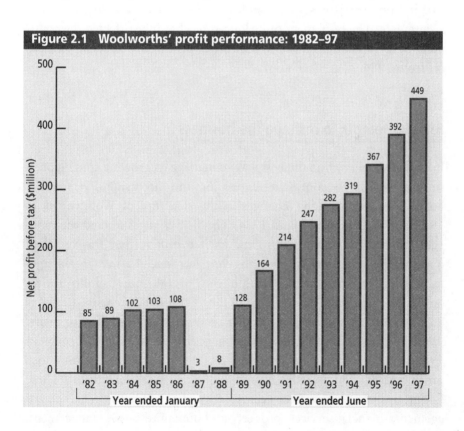

Figure 2.1 Woolworths' profit performance: 1982–97

Woolworths was the first group in Australia to introduce electronic price scanning into its checkout operations. The computerisation of its warehousing was ahead of its time. Its competence in new store construction and planning was high. Its central buying operation was strong. Its systems of store control and inventory management were sound. Its continued sales growth attested to its ability to respond to its customers' needs. In 1986, Woolworths seemed a success story of long-sustained growth in sales and profits. Clearly the firm had proved its operational capabilities beyond question.

But along with the apparently strong pattern of results, there were some emerging problems. Strong price competition in the supermarket area from Franklins put pressure on Woolworths' profit margins, and its archrival Coles grew impressively in supermarket sales and profits throughout the 1980s. Woolworths' own sales growth was coming principally from new stores, not from its existing stores. Old stock began to accumulate. The retirement of its long-time chairman affected the continuity of its top management. Woolworths' profit growth began to taper off from 1984.

Failed attempts to reshape the business

In endeavouring to find the best way to manage its growing trading pressures as well as its continuing expansion and increasing diversity, the board presided over five changes in the structure of Woolworths in 1977, 1979, 1980, 1982 and 1984. The first changes altered the management reporting structure to the chief executive, but this failed to improve the situation. Woolworths then introduced a matrix management system with state managers having overall responsibility for all operations within their states and the divisional managers (such as Supermarkets, Variety, Big W) having a national responsibility for theirs. A further modification failed to get this change working properly. In 1984 a major change was made to establish five largely autonomous profit centres—four in retail groupings and one in manufacturing. These five groups were supported by central corporate services in general management, financial services, property and human resource management.

The establishment of these five divisions was followed a year later by the splitting of Woolworths' major centralised buying operation into separate operations under divisional management.

All of these many significant changes would have been thoroughly analysed and discussed by the board and top management, but they did not in fact deal with the problems. Unfortunately, they added to them. Their combined effect, together with ensuing senior executive retirements and other related changes, moved this successful business towards steady, and then rapid, decline. The continuing strong program of new store expansion masked the developing problems, but only for a time. The infighting that took place with each change, with its rapid succession of winners and losers, new appointments and new policies, focused the energy of its management on internal troubles rather than on serving the customer in a market that was becoming more and more competitive. Woolworths became a game of musical chairs. There was no consistency in policy. The focus was on sales for six months and on margins the next six months. There was little common central vision and there was an autocratic style at the top.

What is compellingly clear, in retrospect, is that the organisation operated extremely effectively for five or so decades before the 1980s. When it attempted to change and reshape itself, it made five attempts in the late 1970s and early 1980s, which were quite unsuccessful. *Woolworths' operational capabilities were sadly not matched by its reshaping capabilities.* Following the traumatic profit crash of 1987, another major attempt was made to reshape the organisation. This time the results were spectacularly successful.

A spectacularly successful attempt to reshape the business

In September 1986, as profits began to crumble, Harry Watts, who had been an executive for 26 years, mainly in the supermarket operations, was appointed managing director. The process of reshaping the corporation began. Nine months later, Paul Simons joined Woolworths as executive chairman and the reshaping process just getting under way was reinforced and accelerated. Within two years, substantial progress was being made. Within five years, the corporation was transformed. Looking at the events retrospectively, there were nine key actions, or programs of action, that were responsible for this major turnaround:

1 A new top team was appointed that consisted entirely of insiders, with the exception of Paul Simons who had had 24 years' experience in Woolworths before rejoining it from Franklins.
2 A new 'fresh food' policy was introduced that positioned Woolworths differently in its customers' minds.
3 Woolworths became price competitive, particularly in relation to Franklins, which had frequently undersold it.
4 The cost structure was reduced, unwanted assets were sold off and head office costs were reduced.
5 Previously separated buying operations were consolidated and the skills of its buyers were upgraded.
6 Services to its customers were increased—in the greater range of goods offered, in the quantity of stock on the shelves and in service through the checkouts.
7 Inventory management efficiency, warehousing and goods distribution to the stores were improved.
8 Communication and teamwork, horizontally and vertically, were improved throughout the organisation.
9 Rewards were increased and tied more effectively to performance.

These actions formed the basis of one of the most effective change programs in corporate Australia.

However, as we noted in Chapter 1, if we tried to use these specific actions as a basis of advice to you about how to effectively change your own organisation, you could well find that many of them would be quite irrelevant to your situation. For example, while Woolworths worked almost entirely with a top team of insiders, you may feel your major need might be to recruit a number of outsiders. While Woolworths sought staff stability after its spate of changes, you may be facing rigidity and complete lack of flexibility in staffing, particularly in management positions.

One of Woolworths' key actions was to change its positioning in the food market and focus on an expansion into fresh food. Your strategic positioning may not be the issue for you, but rather one of better execution of your existing strategy and market positioning. Your cost structure may be under control and you may not face issues of consolidating split operations. Perhaps your issues may be around investing more in research, or facilities, or actually breaking up structures that have become unwieldy.

We could go on down the list of effective actions that Woolworths took and find that very few applied to you and your organisation. Even many of the areas, let alone the actions taken in them, could be irrelevant for you. We could take examples of successful change in many other companies and similarly find that, although the changes had been spectacularly successful, only a very few of the actions taken were actually relevant to you and your business.

However, we will now put the actions that Woolworths took in a different framework. We will look at them as manifestations of the five essential capabilities that we outlined in Chapter 1. This will give you concrete examples of the abstract concepts we described earlier, so that when you look at the evidence in the next chapter, from which the framework was developed, you will have some familiarity with what our concepts mean in terms of corporate realities.

It will also start a process, which we will extend in the subsequent chapters, of thinking about the five capabilities in relation to their application to your business.

In Chapter 1 (Figure 1.3) short definitions of the five key capabilities were provided. These are Engagement, Development, Performance Management, Biztech, and Marketing and Selling. We are going first to look at the three reshaping capabilities and illustrate them in action from some of the things that happened in Woolworths. In the chapters that follow we will take each capability in turn and explore it in greater depth than we can simply by looking at illustrations from one company.

The reshaping capabilities

The three reshaping capabilities are Engagement, Development and Performance Management. They provide the basis for actions to change and reshape an organisation effectively. Our study found that as reshaping capability rises, so change success rises. Conversely as reshaping capability drops, change success drops.

Engagement

We have called this capability Engagement (see Figure 2.2) because it is about getting the people throughout the organisation informed, involved, committed and motivated to act to achieve the organisation's purpose and future directions.

Engagement requires the competencies to communicate, to motivate and enthuse people, to identify and convey new directions for the future of the business, and to achieve commitment and action across the organisation to these new directions.

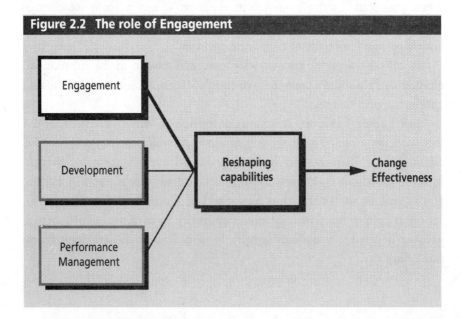

Figure 2.2 The role of Engagement

We will start by looking at some actions that were taken in Woolworths, which demonstrate aspects of this capability.

Engagement at Woolworths: identifying new directions

Our story of the attempt to reshape and revitalise the company, which opened with Paul Simons' first meeting with his senior executives, really begins some two years earlier. At that time, the newly established Supermarket Division, concerned about its problems and its future, established a working group under the chairmanship of Reg Clairs, then one of its state managers, to think through its future strategy.

How would Woolworths best serve its customers' needs? How would the changing demographics, the immigration program, the changing age profile of the country, and shifts in lifestyles and tastes affect the kind of goods the customers would demand? And when and how often would they wish to buy them? How did the current skills of Woolworths meet those potential challenges? What new competencies might be needed? Which ones were Woolworths confident of building? How would they generate the funds to provide all the things they might need to do? These and many other questions needed to be faced and answered if the new strategy for the organisation was to serve its future needs.

The group gathered all the relevant information it could. It consulted widely with people at all levels in the Supermarket Division about ways the division could operate and meet its customers' needs more effectively. It identified what it saw as the strengths and shortcomings of its own operations. It commissioned outside market research on the future shape of the Australian market, and it informed itself about trends in major markets overseas. It spent some time pinpointing how Australian consumers wanted to buy their food and what would attract them to one type of supermarket rather than another. It then developed a comprehensive strategic action plan paying particular attention to how this could be funded within the resource constraints that the Supermarket Division would undoubtedly face within Woolworths' overall operations.

At the same time, therefore, as Woolworths' operations began to falter and profits began to come under pressure, a plan was being put in place for future improvement by a group of its own senior executives, chaired by the man, who, some years later, would become its next managing director. One key recommendation in the wide-ranging document was a plan to alter Woolworths' strategy and differentiate it from its competitors, particularly Franklins, by focusing on fresh food. The plan was, unhappily, put in the pigeonhole.

Two years later the plan came out of the pigeonhole when Harry Watts was appointed managing director. He decided immediately to implement the suggested strategy of positioning Woolworths as 'The Fresh Food People'. This decision was taken before the appointment of Paul Simons as executive chairman, which came a few months later.

A strategic intent in a plan is one thing. Bringing it to life requires a range of actions that ultimately result in the development of new operational capabilities. To reposition itself effectively, Woolworths needed to get the commitment of its management and staff to the new vision, to motivate and enthuse them to achieve it, and to integrate the changes across an organisation with nearly a thousand stores.

Engagement: conveying the new vision to its people

One early major initiative Woolworths took to convey its new vision to its staff was to develop an exciting and significant television advertising program. The television commercials portraying Woolworths as 'The Fresh Food People', which heralded the new vision, are still a strong feature on Australian television more than ten years down the track. From the beginning, the commercials were targeted just as much to the 70,000 employees of Woolworths as to its customers. Harry Watts wanted them to share the excitement he felt about the new focus on fresh food. He wanted them to feel part of it. The commercials featured Woolworths' own staff, not external professionals. Indeed, the scenes focus more on the interest, confidence, commitment and excitement of the staff in selling fresh food than on the products being sold.

The television commercials were a significant part of engaging the people of Woolworths in their new directions. They helped to clarify the direction. The slogan 'The Fresh Food People' appeared everywhere—in stores, promotional materials, vehicles, internal documents, and on radio and television. The focus on the 'people' of Woolworths was also significant. The focus was not only about products and strategies, but also about the staff of Woolworths.

The simple but vitally important fact was that you could not work in Woolworths and not know what its vision for itself and its future was.

The earlier failed changes before 1987 were primarily focused on changing organisational structures. This new approach focused on the position Woolworths wanted in the eyes of its customers and its people.

Engagement: motivating and enthusing

As developing and conveying the vision clarified direction, it became an integrating and motivating force across the organisation. The organisation had become separated and split up by the previous successive structural changes and the ensuing divisional and regional antagonisms that they had spawned. As a consequence, vertical and horizontal communication had substantially diminished. As the company clarified its future directions, and commitment and motivation began to grow, so did communication. But its growth was not instantaneous. The 'tribal encampments' and past fiefdoms took time to die. The growth in interaction took at least two years to grow. Interchange of ideas grew and there was no longer a frontier mentality.

The capability to engage an organisation so that members become committed and actively and coherently involved in its future directions is not just about initial interest and enthusiasm for the new direction. It applies too as change gets under way and commitment has to be maintained. Engagement is maintained by continuing action to reinforce direction and to recognise contributions to it. As business and profits improved, the accolades began to roll in. *Australian Business Magazine* voted Woolworths as having 'The Top 500 Best Growth Strategy' and two years later awarded it 'The Most Improved Company in 1991'. *Business Review Weekly* awarded Paul Simons 'The Businessman of the Year'. Other awards followed.

However, when Simons or Watts went along to accept the prize they did not take, as other recipients usually did, the members of their top team. They took a checkout operator, a shelf-filler, a storeman from the warehouse and a clerk from the buying office. These actions symbolised and communicated, in a way not done before, the importance and involvement of the people of Woolworths. It was a theme constantly pushed by the leaders. They talked about their pride in 'the people of Woolworths'. There was nothing phoney or patronising about it. They believed it. Others knew they believed it. This made all the difference. It was one important factor that motivated and enthused people.

Over time, not overnight, but bit by bit, the people of Woolworths became *engaged* in their hearts and minds and actions in changing and reshaping their organisation's future. They knew its direction. They had had some involvement in shaping it. It was sold to the organisation in general in a positive and exciting way that linked its work, its customers and the new organisational directions. And many actions were taken, of which we will say more, which helped to constantly motivate them to be part of it.

Development

Development (see Figure 2.3) is the capability of developing all the resources—personal, physical, technological, and systems and processes—needed to achieve the firm's future directions.

Development is about effectively investing in the firm's future and is therefore also about understanding that future, and the need, shape and substance of the necessary resources and capabilities to achieve that future. Development actions lay the foundation for the improvement and creation of the firm's future operational capabilities, which will enable the organisation to achieve its changes and new directions.

Development at Woolworths: people and skills

A strategic intent to become the fresh food people required the knowledge, skills and effort of many to bring it to life.

At the time it began to convey its new vision through its television commercials, Woolworths embarked on a major training program to

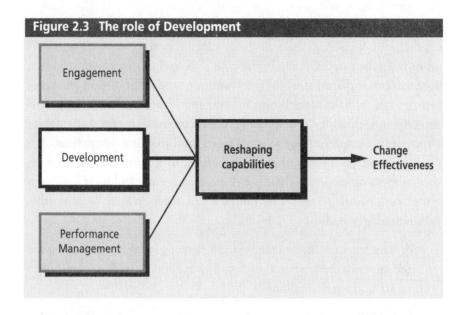

Figure 2.3 The role of Development

develop the competencies of its staff in all aspects of the buying and selling of fresh food. The training did not start half way down the organisation, it started at the very top. Three hundred of the top people were taken to Melbourne for a week's intensive training in fresh food in Woolworths' Safeways organisation. It involved state managers, area managers and store managers. Harry Watts, the managing director, came on the program and so did the NSW state manager.

Part of the purpose of involving all the top managers in the program was to alter mindsets just as much as to teach new skills. It was recognised that top management needed to get close to the fresh food business—partly to change the mindsets of the senior people and upgrade the status of fresh food. Finance was also needed to refurbish the stores. It changed the focus.

Buyers were sent overseas to learn from international operators, particularly Safeways in the United States, with whom Woolworths began to develop closer working relationships. A few specialist buyers were recruited and trained. Buying technology goes far beyond the mere notion of purchasing. It deals, for example, with managing relationships with major suppliers to influence the characteristics of the goods ultimately bought. Woolworths' tentacles stretch into Australian farming, and influence crops in terms of produce characteristics. This affects not only flavour and quality but is also reflected ultimately in packing, presentation and transportability. Contract, and relationship management, as well as food technology, became important business competencies. Buying technology thus provides competitive advantage and enables Woolworths to differentiate itself in fresh food from its competitors.

Our research shows that one feature of organisations high in Development capability is their use of existing people and their low rates of replacing people. It was a striking feature of renewal at Woolworths. As one manager said:[2]

> 'We have the same key executives. The same guy who was leading the NSW supermarkets when they lost $35 million is leading them when they are making $50 million.'

The top team Harry Watts put in place on his appointment as managing director was composed wholly of insiders. Paul Simons was a previous employee 'returning to the fold'. Additional people were needed, particularly in the stores, in expanded new specialist departments, such as delicatessen and butchery, and some of these were recruited but many posts were filled by retraining existing staff. People were told they would stay in jobs for some years, which enabled them to develop skills and be there long enough to be responsible for and judged on results. The game of musical chairs, which was a feature of previous changes, was jettisoned. Developing people is about building their competencies to do their jobs better, or to be capable of doing new or different jobs, which enables them to develop themselves and the business.

Development: systems and processes

Development capability applies to more than people and skill development. A great deal of corporate retail competence is captured in systems and processes. Many of these are computerised and interlinked. These help managers replenish their stocks, control their inventories, exploit opportunities for promotions to gain extra business, and staff their store to meet peak demands. They are vital to buyers in providing information on sales and stocks, helping to identify winners and bad buys at an early stage, and providing forecasts of the patterns of customer demand so that purchasing and deliveries can be more accurately made. They are just as vital for the major warehousing and transportation services required in moving vast tonnages of fresh and packaged food.

Woolworths began a program of developing its systems and practices to improve the integration of the whole process of purchase, delivery, sale and restocking merchandise. This involved a great deal of communication across the business and the way it was carried out helped knit the business more closely together. It also began to link Woolworths more closely with its major suppliers as technology allowed and encouraged major information flows and interaction between them. As one manager said:[3]

> 'The new systems are sold internally by having meetings with people in the states and involving them in the new ideas. Our people are like evangelists.'

Performance Management

Performance Management (see Figure 2.4) is proactively managing the factors that drive the organisation's performance to ensure it consistently and effectively achieves what is intended.

Performance Management is the one capability that relates strongly to both Change Effectiveness and Current Business Performance. While Engagement is concerned primarily with identifying and getting the organisation's commitment to the 'where and whether' of future performance and Development is focused on 'with what', Performance Management is more to do with the aspect of 'how' or perhaps 'how much better'. It is concerned with achieving intended outcomes.

Performance Management capability is contributed to by competencies of performance control, resource application, financial and planning competencies, among others. While Performance Management contributes to change through actions that influence the change process, and

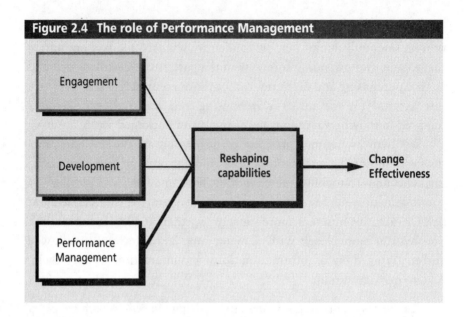

Figure 2.4 The role of Performance Management

the changing of behaviour and resource use, it contributes to business performance by impacting upon the application of the organisation's Biztech capabilities, by keeping the business operations on track and by improving their efficiency and effectiveness.

Part of the process of change is to get people to adapt to new ideas, strategies and methods—to alter the way they do and see things. The feedback on performance, which is a critical part of Performance Management capability, assists people to make these adjustments by giving them understanding of how they are functioning in the changing environment. Performance Management capability also provides the base for action to alter the way resources are used in the firm.

Performance Management at Woolworths: direct action

Performance Management has a strong emphasis on getting things done, on making improvement, on action, not talk. This is often done by improving a process or a system, but sometimes, as in the following example, direct action brings a desired result.

It was difficult for the store manager to believe what had happened during the night. The pallets that arrived in the store every night around midnight were always badly loaded with part deliveries. It was a constant problem. Other managers also complained. Something would be done, he was told. He had heard that one before! A number of times. What he hadn't heard before was that Paul Simons and Harry Watts had together visited his store after midnight and had watched the pallets being unloaded to check for themselves that the problem was being solved. He heard about it when he came into his store that morning. The rest of Woolworths heard about it at much the same time, including those who loaded pallets in the distribution centre.

Performance Management: resource reallocation and use

The more effective and intensive use of resources, and the strong implementation and enforcement of its trading policies, were major features of the reshaping of Woolworths.

Woolworths' previous policy had been one of continued and rapid expansion both in numbers and types of retail outlets. In 1988, after its profit collapse, for the first time in its history, its total retail space was reduced. Stores were sold (135 in all), underperforming assets were disposed of, and the resources were ploughed into the refurbishing of key stores needed for the new fresh food strategy. By 1991, its total trading area of 1.389 million square metres was virtually the same as that of 1987, but by then its sales had risen, in the same period, from $5.6 billion to $8.2 billion and its profit from $2.7 million to $214 million. The focus of its reinvestment and resource reallocation was changed to support its new positioning in fresh food and at the same time Woolworths looked for more intensive use of its assets. Paul Simons said:[4]

> 'I remember talking to someone in our George Street headquarters. He said, "We know we've got big overheads but we've had a good look and are not sure where they are." I thought, I do. You are sitting on them.'

The scale of Woolworths' corporate head office in George Street was dramatically reduced. The state and national buying offices were merged and moved from the city centre to the major warehouse operation in western Sydney—'close to where the action was'.

As well as the more effective use of its capital assets, Woolworths went on to build performance controls into its business with detailed cost reviews of all operations. Besides reviewing all the overhead costs, Woolworths made a line-by-line examination of all operating costs. For a company that, for example, spent $32 million on wrapping materials, many opportunities for large savings presented themselves.

The overall savings in costs were considerable. Saving a dollar in costs when net margin on sales is below 5 per cent is equivalent to making $20 in extra sales. But just as important as cost savings was the direction of the new investment into major store refurbishing and competence development to underpin the strategic repositioning thrust into fresh food.

But small savings, with large symbolism, were also made. Paul Simons brought austerity with him. Gone were first class travel, chauffeur-driven Mercedes and, for senior people, the silver tray tea service.

Performance Management: review and audit

Woolworths also created specialised store review practices and posts. The regular and frequent reviews finished with an agreed action plan for the manager to implement in the next month. The constant movement from knowledge about performance, to action to improve it, was one of the hallmarks of Woolworths' successful reshaping. Another feature was the constant build-up of corporate competencies as the improvements, stemming often from individual actions and skills, were embedded not only in the emerging culture but in systems, processes and practices, many of which, in later stages of the change, became captured in computerised software.

Performance Management: price focus

Woolworths had always had a policy of being price competitive. However, as the pressure for immediate profit had become more and more intense in the years leading up to the profit crash, many store managers and buyers had sought short-term increased margins often at the cost of longer-term growth and competitiveness.

As Paul Simons so dramatically showed at his first meeting with his top team, the firm's stated policy of competitive pricing simply did not exist in practice. And there was no effective action or system of Performance Management to see that it did.

This was changed. The latitude given to store managers to alter some prices was withdrawn. Prices had to be the same in all stores. No deviation was tolerated. Paul Simons constantly checked prices himself on his way into work or when visiting branches. He always personally phoned the buyer when he found prices above those of competitors. Buyers don't like the chairman phoning them personally to talk about shortcomings! It produced a bigger change than all the policy documents. As one manager said:[5]

> 'Paul gave us the shits. He had his nose in everything. But he was right and people recognised it.'

Even with the strong action that Simons personally took in this key aspect of Performance Management, it was probably two years before a consistent policy of keen pricing became recognised by the customer and began to fuel the major sales growth that then took place.

Performance Management: service focus

As a key part of its change process, Woolworths focused its attention on improved customer service. This was not a new policy for Woolworths as such but a new approach to see it was actually carried out. Service not only involves the interaction between the customer and staff but, in a wider sense, between the customer and the whole organisation. Are the goods the customer actually wants on the shelves? Are they keenly priced? Are they fresh? Do the checkouts operate efficiently? Is there help, if necessary, to take the goods to the car? Is the store attractively laid out? Is it clean and well lit?

However, it is in the store, at the point of sale, that those many activities become apparent to the customer. A Customer Courtesy

Service Program was launched and customer service was the first item on the agenda of every meeting.

A corporate requirement was laid down that at every meeting there was always to be a symbolic vacant chair. The vacant chair was to represent the customer. Her likely view was vital.

A new slogan was created:

'If you're not serving the customer, serve someone who is.'

The slogan appeared at the top of every document the firm used internally and it symbolised that customer service was the reason why everyone in the firm was there.

Paul Simons replied, in his own handwriting, to every letter of complaint about service sent to him. Store managers had to talk personally to any complainant, if necessary in their home.

Performance Management: rewards for performance

As Woolworths' results began to improve, it rewarded its people significantly better. The recognition of contributors to the new direction was an important action in the reinforcement of the change. Comments included:[6]

'The rewards are much better. You can get a bonus of 50 per cent on performance.'
'People are better rewarded. They are now judged on performance, which is a major change. Before it was a pretence. It was not carried out.'

Reshaping capabilities at Woolworths: an interim consolidation

The description of a few of the actions taken in Woolworths illustrates the basic capabilities involved and, at the same time, the key areas on which to focus action.

Engagement involved a new vision with fresh food as its major focus, a strikingly successful conveying of that vision not only through its major television promotion but also though improved communications, and the involvement of shop floor staff in the public recognition of progress achieved so that Engagement continued as the changes were underway.

Development was principally provided in the substantial retraining of staff at all levels to provide skills for the new directions together with a policy that slowed down job change to give people accountability and the opportunity to see the results of the application of their new skills. These developments in personal competencies were underpinned and supplemented by substantial development in systems and processes across the whole gamut of operations.

Performance Management involved a more intensive use of space, careful examination of all costs and setting an example in the frugal personal use by senior people of the organisation's resources. New policies and systems controlled prices more effectively, review and audit processes influenced store management, a major focus on customer service buttressed by a series of corporate-wide processes provided an outward orientation for the organisation, and people began to be rewarded on performance.

Reshaping capabilities in your organisation

Engagement, Development and Performance Management need to be tailored to your own situation. However, whatever your situation may be, to achieve successful change you need to:

- *engage* your people in the change to get their understanding and commitment
- *develop* the skills, resources, systems and processes needed for your new directions
- *manage the performance* of the change process and of the organisation through change.

Effective action in these areas will help you achieve successful corporate change.

Importance of the framework for top managers

This framework is particularly important for senior managers. Because our data show the actions of senior management are the most important and have the strongest impact, it is crucial that they take actions in the right areas to achieve the outcomes needed. In many cases this does not occur and powerful actions, and the signals they send, have a negative effect. Effort is too often put into specific problem solving. The fundamental job of top management is to see Engagement, Development and Performance Management actually take place. If they lose sight of how to win the main game and get too involved in matters that are not central to this, they are likely to lessen their potentially positive influence on the change process.

Within the reshaping framework there are two areas where personal contribution by top management can be particularly beneficial to effective change. These are *pathfinding* competence within Engagement capability and *performance control* competence within Performance Management capability. We deal with these in later chapters. In the story of Woolworths the personal contribution Paul Simons made in performance control illustrates the impact of one person's actions even in a very large organisation.

Corporate capability and action

While we have illustrated the reshaping capabilities at work in Woolworths largely through a few of the actions of its senior management, part of the thrust of our work is that organisations can develop *corporate reshaping capabilities*. These become embedded in the organisation's fabric—in its practices, processes, systems, structures, culture and technologies. When this takes place it enables the organisation collectively to influence the continual reshaping of the business and the renewal of its operational capabilities.

If *Engagement* is a strong corporate capability then, whenever the need for change arises, Engagement is more effective because the corporate capability strengthens and underpins widespread, or collective, action throughout the organisation, including the actions of the organisation's leaders. Similarly, if the organisation has a strong corporate *Development* capability, actions are taken as part of the organisation's normal management processes that develop the resources and systems of the organisation for its needed changes. And if there is an existing strong corporate *Performance Management* capability then actions are taken to manage the performance of the change process and the organisation so that what is needed for success is done.

When the organisation is strong in particular capabilities, relevant actions often happen as a matter of course. They are the normal behaviour of the business and its typical actions and responses to situations.

When organisations are weak in any, or all, of the three corporate reshaping capabilities, much more, and sometimes all of the responsibility for action falls on its senior management. This was largely the case at Woolworths when the changes we have described began. It is even more important in this situation for managers to understand on what to focus their own, inevitably, limited energy and action, since they will be without the support of the organisation's reshaping capabilities. The framework of Engagement, Development and Performance Management provides this sharp focus, for distilled into it are the three key areas for action that are necessary to the achievement of effective change.

As managers take effective personal actions, and learn from them, the possibility arises to embed some of this individual and collective experience into the creation of corporate reshaping capabilities to enhance the contribution the organisation can make to the achievement of future change. Corporate capabilities take time to develop, particularly reshaping ones, but we can see early aspects of the development of some corporate reshaping capabilities at Woolworths. They took place largely in Engagement and Performance Management. Communication began to spread not only vertically but also horizontally throughout the organisation and became less and less dependent on a few individuals. In Performance Management, new practices and responsibilities were developed to strengthen audit. The structure of careers within the business was altered with an end to very rapid job rotation and an establishment of personal accountability for results. The reward system was altered.

We will explore fully in Chapter 10 the creation of corporate competencies.

The operational capabilities

The central focus of *Change Power* is *effective corporate change*. Operational capabilities form the basis for actions that relate not to effective change, but to *managing the business for current performance*. The three capabilities principally involved in operational performance are Biztech, Performance Management, and Marketing and Selling. We have already commented on Performance Management. Our study shows that as operational capability rises, current performance rises. As operational capability falls, performance falls with it.

Biztech

Biztech is about commanding and understanding the technologies, processes and mechanisms through which the organisation creates and delivers its products and services to its market. It is composed of those competencies that enable the organisation to create and deliver its products and services, drawing on its own body of knowledge, skills and particular processes for developing, producing and delivering them. The capability draws particularly on technical, operational and financial competencies, but in a combination that always makes them business specific. The Biztech of firms in cement manufacturing, or banking, or of organisations like the Police Service or the local Water Board, is completely different from the Biztech of Woolworths.

If we look at Woolworths as an example of a supermarket chain, its Biztech, in the final analysis, is about buying, the logistics of goods movement, and competencies in selling. Woolworths' competitors all have to buy goods, transport and sell them, but they all try to do this better, and sometimes, differently.

In the case of Woolworths, Biztech would include, for example, competencies such as product specification, contract management, product analysis and testing, packaging and coding, and systems that result in better relationships with and financial management of its vast number of suppliers. Other key competencies for supermarket operators include all aspects of delivery, transport and distribution of goods. The financial control and the handling and moving of perishable goods which, of

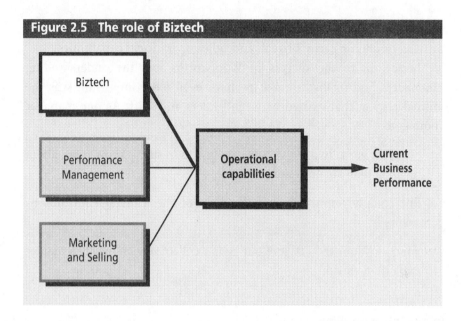

Figure 2.5   The role of Biztech

Biztech

Performance Management

Marketing and Selling

Operational capabilities

Current Business Performance

course, grew dramatically in volume with Woolworths' strategy of positioning itself in fresh food, became a particular area for increased Biztech capability. Woolworths is advanced with its own version of cross-docking, the logistics technology which Walmart pioneered in the United States, and which significantly lowers its inventory holding costs.

Biztech in the selling area includes the siting and design of stores, layout, use of fixtures and lighting, visual merchandising of its goods, space allocations of its merchandise, procedures for restocking and reordering, design and management of pricing procedures and coding systems, technologies of checkout design and operation, and methods for helping customers with their shopping generally. Although many of these aspects of Biztech have a strong technical foundation, they do not work effectively without the human element. Biztech includes this human tacit knowledge and skill at all levels including, from the perspective of this book, the management element.

These are indicative of only some of the specific competencies through which supermarkets deliver value to their customers.

The actions taken at Woolworths, based largely upon the reshaping capabilities of its senior management, impacted upon the people,

CHANGE POWER

systems, processes, resources and culture, with the end purpose of improving or creating new Biztech and other operational capabilities.

Important to the success of Woolworths was the understanding the leaders had of Biztech. But perhaps even more important was the mutual respect that existed between leaders and staff. As one manager commented:[7]

> 'The fact is the two guys at the top of this business know more about retailing than anyone else.'

But equally important was the view of the leaders. Paul Simons commented:[8]

> 'Harry [Watts] and I believe our people collectively know a hell of a lot more than we do.'

Marketing and Selling

Marketing and Selling capability is understanding the firm's markets and how external events affect them, identifying customer needs, and selling the firm's goods and services effectively.

For a retail organisation like Woolworths, Marketing and Selling capability is demonstrated, for example, by the range of goods that is available in the store to meet its customers' needs. This includes aspects such as how keenly they are priced, whether there are interesting new goods, whether there is a wide range to choose from, whether the goods customers want to buy are actually in stock, and so on.

Particular actions that are important to achieving a successful range of goods include collecting information about what the customer wants as well as what they buy, the way such information is used to guide buying and selling decisions, and development of buying and selling skills. So some of the actions we have outlined earlier in this chapter contributed directly to Woolworths' responsiveness to its customers' needs. They created an improved capability in Marketing and Selling.

Woolworths' policy of pricing its goods competitively had eroded under its previous management, as Paul Simons demonstrated at his first meeting with his team. Action taken to make sure that pricing policy was followed efficiently affected more than just the price of goods. When Woolworths was previously uncompetitive it priced many of its new introductions too highly. Computerised programs, which had been designed to track sales and delete 'slow sellers', consistently removed these new overpriced lines from the range. Consequently, Woolworths' range of goods became significantly smaller than its main competitors. It no longer met its customers' needs, who went elsewhere. The corresponding drop in volume in individual lines reduced Woolworths' buying power and this in turn affected its ability to price keenly. It was estimated at the time of Paul Simons' arrival that Woolworths' main competitor was buying some lines about 20 per cent cheaper. When the pricing policy became managed and enforced, goods previously deleted from the range as poor sellers, became, on reintroduction at competitive prices, good sellers. The range expanded rather than contracted. Sales responded as the organisation became more responsive to its customers' needs.

As Woolworths developed its merchandising information systems, the level and quality of knowledge available improved and decision making improved. Woolworths' Marketing and Selling capability became much stronger. Just as reshaping action improved Biztech, it also improved its

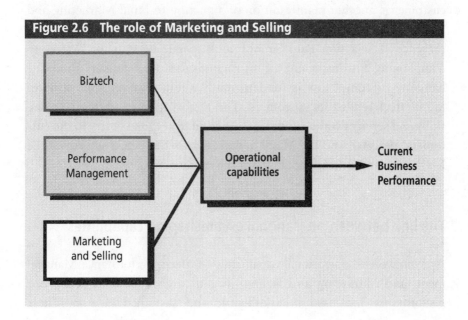

Figure 2.6　The role of Marketing and Selling

Marketing and Selling capability. As it marketed and sold its goods more effectively its current business improved. As one manager said:[9]

> 'Woolworths used to be reliant on manufacturers for its information technology. Today we are in command.'

The combination of better pricing and stronger and more dependable information from new systems gave buyers, transporters and sellers better information. New systems also extended the information link to include manufacturers and other suppliers of goods and services. These actions not only improved Biztech, they also met its customers' needs better.

Training of buyers and sellers, and substantial increases in productivity in warehousing and distribution, increased Woolworths' ability to better meet its customers' needs. As more competitive pricing, better presented stores and improved service began to be reflected in bigger volumes, the buyers were able to buy at lower prices. This in turn enabled more aggressive pricing in the stores. Just as earlier Woolworths was on a downward spiral of higher prices, higher margins and shrinking volumes per store, they were now on a spiral moving in the opposite direction. Woolworths had become more responsive to its market.

The action, we have noted earlier, of the empty chair to represent the customer is another manifestation of an action to build Marketing and Selling capability by giving every internal meeting a customer focus or presence. The action Paul Simons took to handwrite short letters to complaining customers and the instructions to store managers about the handling of complaints is fundamentally about marketing its services more effectively to its customers. The major drive to improve selling skills and services was a fundamental action to respond better to the customers' perceived needs. Many actions across the board improved the Marketing and Selling capability of the organisation.

The link between operational and reshaping capabilities

As Woolworths' operational capabilities—Biztech, Performance Management, and Marketing and Selling—began to change, sales and profit performance increased in a dramatic and sustained fashion. These improvements resulted from actions that it had taken to *engage* its people in its operations and new directions, to *develop* their skills and the systems that supported them, and to change and improve the way they saw and did their work so that *performance was managed* more effectively, in alignment with the new directions.

Woolworths in the future

Woolworths, of course, has to go on reshaping and renewing itself to continue its success. The reshaping may be minor or major depending on what it needs to do to compete effectively in the marketplace. Some of the actions Paul Simons' successors may take may be quite different but equally successful. However, whatever shape these actions take, if Engagement, Development and Performance Management capabilities are no longer underpinning and giving focus, timing, speed, accuracy, consistency and quality to the actions, Woolworths' progress will falter and cease. Part of keeping those capabilities alive is achieved by embedding them in the organisation so they support and leverage the actions future leaders might take. We discuss this process in Chapter 10.

An illustration only

The story of Woolworths illustrates some of the many actions the organisation took to reshape and revitalise itself. Woolworths is not a special example which should necessarily be emulated, although quite clearly the actions taken were very successful. There are many similar examples. We have grouped the actions at Woolworths under the five capabilities we have identified during our research. That structure emerged from our analysis of 243 cases of corporate change. We now turn to that evidence and its creation.

CHAPTER 3

Faith or facts?
The survey findings

M OST COMMENTS ABOUT corporate change are based on personal experience, anecdotes or the examination of a few cases, rather than the analysis of quantitative data from a large sample of organisations. Many of these comments may well have some insights when seen in the context of the particular situation and circumstances of the commentator. For example, in relation to Al Dunlap's comments, which we quoted in the Introduction, about making change quickly, our own data show there is no general relationship between the duration of change and the effectiveness of the change. However there is slight support in our data that when the change attempted is contractionary (primarily cutting costs and resources), it is more effective when it is done quickly. Dunlap may well have specialised in such changes and his comment relates to what works well for him in very specific circumstances and time frames.

This is not unlike the occasional case of the ninety-year-old who gets press coverage for longevity, claiming it is due to a life-long practice of drinking a bottle of whisky and smoking thirty cigarettes every day. This may be so, but we have many sources of reliable tested information about longevity, over a number of different populations, which give us strong reasons not to copy this particular behaviour.

For all its importance, the arena of change management has been relatively short of assessments with an objective foundation. So managers have had to rely on the equivalent of our nonagenarian's recipe for a healthy life, from a number of such individuals, each drawing on different experiences of change and espousing different recipes. Of course, some of these recipes may be valuable, but we have had no objective basis or foundation to separate the wheat from the chaff.

In *Change Power* we have set out to avoid these problems through the type and extent of data we use and the way they have been analysed. It is important in looking at the data and their analysis to see them as only a part, though a vital one, of enriching our understanding of change. For all of us our beliefs and insights are influenced by many factors, only some of which we can subject to robust statistical analysis. Some that cannot be analysed are very important. When we are presented with collected objective data about a matter that interests us, we test and check it against our own experience and insights. Often the data help to consolidate our experience, or enable us to see it in a different light or from a different perspective that adds to our understanding. Sometimes it challenges our beliefs. We integrate our experience and the data in new ways, and we develop new concepts that are useful to us. Our research findings will hopefully assist you in that process.

Our findings are not a matter of proof, though sometimes research is presented as 'proof' of a particular relationship. Statistics are meant to be persuasive not coercive. It is more a matter of progressively building up reliable information that leads to an understanding that becomes a more useful way of describing and predicting aspects of the area of interest. So, in looking at the evidence we present, constantly check it on the testbed of your own experience and judgment, and integrate it with your own insights. Our own experience in discussing our concepts with several hundred senior executives is that it makes sense of their experience, clarifies and deepens their understanding of corporate change and provides them with a framework for focused action.

Getting real, live data

From time to time you probably open your mail and find a request to fill in some sort of questionnaire. It's a pain in the neck even to contemplate filling it in, much less completing it! Unless you are a saint or a masochist you probably put it into the wastepaper basket. Or, of course, you might decide to delegate it to someone else, and the requestor, who wants your views, gets those of someone else without your experience.

To enable us to form reliable conclusions we needed many observations from executives who were *senior managers and who also had real experience of corporate change*. And we needed them to give us a lot of detail. That required them to fill in a long and complex form that took between one and two hours.

Fortunately for us, we were responsible for directing and teaching residential management programs for just such executives. So, as part of the *pre-program* work, executives were asked to complete a questionnaire providing the information we wanted. They did this before joining the program, and so their answers were not coloured by anything taught on the program. And we got *their* answers, not those of their assistants. Of course, the data we collected were used later as an important part of the executive program.

So our situation enabled us to collect information, on a scale and in a depth, from this strategically placed group of senior executives, which would otherwise simply not have been possible.[1] In total, we collected responses on 243 change cases in 141 private and public sector organisations in Australia and New Zealand.

Naturally the questions we asked in the survey were influenced by our own ideas of what were likely to be important factors to evaluate. Those views sprang from our own senior line management experience, our work as consultants and our academic work in interacting with many hundreds of senior executives in teaching executive programs about organisational performance and change. They were also influenced by some specific change cases which we studied in detail early in the project and which we describe in *Change Power*. Of course, like most research projects, if only we had known at the beginning what we now know at the end, we would have asked a few more or a few different questions!

A variety of change scenarios

When researchers conduct intensive case studies with organisations, it is far easier to get access to situations where the outcome was positive rather than those where it was negative. But for our purposes we needed cases with a wide range of success and failure in the outcomes. Our sample provided this. Almost half the organisations, as we mentioned in our Introduction, had two or more major setbacks in their attempted changes.

We also wanted to collect a great depth of information on many different types of change from many different kinds of organisation. This we also achieved.

Some of the changes described by our respondents were multiple and spread right across the organisation, affecting all its activities, its strategy, technology, culture, management and operations. Other executives described the introduction of a particular focused program across the organisation as a whole, or a major change in only one part of the organisation. Such programs included the introduction of multiskilling, benchmarking, workforce participation, total quality management, international standards accreditation, staff appraisal programs, new lending objectives, new budgeting methods, work redesign, and so on.

Other changes were driven by the introduction of new technology, such as computer technology, financial modelling processes, distribution and materials handling techniques, CAD systems, and many others.

Yet others came from organisations experiencing amalgamations, mergers, the combination of plants, divisions or regions, or their closure. And, lastly, there were government organisations, some of which were preparing for, or experiencing, privatisation in some form.

Many of the changes described had their origin in attempts to reduce costs, improve productivity, provide new or better products, change the organisation structure, alter the culture of the organisation (frequently to one more focused on the customer) and to meet intensifying competition, both local and international. Fifty per cent of the changes described took place over one to three years, a number took six months or less, while others exceeded five years.

So our range of changes and their outcomes, and our pool of organisations, listed in Appendix B represented a very wide spectrum of private and public sector organisations experiencing major changes of many differing kinds.

The nature of our enquiries

It is important to understand that *we did not ask our respondents to explain or give their reasons for the success or failure of what happened*. We selected the aspects of organisations and change that we thought might be relevant. We then asked our respondents to quantify the extent of each of these aspects in their particular situation. For example, respondents gave us their assessment of the scope of the change, the time it took, its focus, the extent to which people understood what was happening, or received training, the extent of staff reductions, the firm's profitability, its productivity, how effective operations were in the new framework, and so on. We described a number of competencies and asked respondents to assess the strength of them in their organisation at various stages of the change. There were over 300 items of specific information we collected, as well as a short narrative description of each attempted change.

We then looked for relationships between all these 300 aspects and two major outcomes:

- *Change Effectiveness*, which measured how effective the change was
- *Current Business Performance*, which measured how well the organisation was performing at the time of the change.

Drawing conclusions

To find such relationships, the sample needed to include cases that were high and cases that were low on each aspect, or item. For example, in the sample we needed a wide range of performance levels and a wide range of change effectiveness. In fact, our data include a wide range of values on all the aspects we set out to measure.

What we wanted to find out was *not* what people thought were the reasons for the success or failure of their change, but the *actual relationships across all the 243 situations* between the various aspects of organisations, management and change that we had included in the questionnaire. For example, 'What is the relationship between Change Effectiveness and a range of actions, such as consultation or monitoring? Or between Change Effectiveness and various competencies such as planning or marketing? Or between Current Business Performance and various organisational states, such as empowerment, conflict or esprit de corps?' The existence of a relationship between two factors does not, of course, necessarily imply one causes the other. It simply says they occur together. In the end we each have to use our own judgment about causality, but frequently the nature or timing of the relationship provides a strong basis for judgments about this.

Finding strong relationships

What we are, of course, seeking to discover are some relationships between the various factors, and to be able to measure the strength of particular relationships. We want to be able to say, for example, that there is, or is not, a particular relationship between Engagement capability and Change Effectiveness; or that the action of conveying a vision of the firm's future direction does, or does not, improve the effectiveness of the change; or that providing training does, or does not, increase Change Effectiveness and Current Business Performance. We do not want to link these factors simply based on some individual's personal beliefs. We want to be able to link them based on the relationships disclosed by the analysis of what happened across these 243 cases of change.

What might affect the findings?

As with all scientific research, there are a number of possible questions about the validity of our results. For example, does our collection method bias the sample? Does the presence of commercial and government organisations, or the mix of small and large organisations, lead to spurious results? How broadly applicable are the results? Are we simply reporting the models of change that people have in their minds? And so on.

In satisfying ourselves about the robustness of the results, we have had to consider all these and many other questions. Many of them have required additional tests and analysis to confirm that there was not a flaw in the conclusions.

As an example, we considered the possibility that having both government and commercial organisations in the sample might somehow produce erroneous results. So we separately analysed the sub-sample of only government organisations and the sub-sample of only commercial organisations. These showed essentially the same relationships, except for a couple of important distinguishing aspects. Marketing and Selling and Performance Management have greater relevance for the commercial organisations than the non-commercial ones. Otherwise the two separate sets of relationships are similar to those in the sample as a whole. The same is true when we split the sample based on organisation size. With minor variations, similar relationships are found for both small organisations and for large organisations.[2]

The end result of all the tests and analysis has left us very comfortable with the findings described in the following pages. *Nonetheless, in science there is never any absolute, irrefutable proof.* Instead there is an accumulation of evidence that supports the value and usefulness of a theory as a way of describing and predicting aspects of the world. We were looking for a persuasive level of consistency in the results. We are confident we have found it.

The two outcome measures

To establish relationships between the factors that would be useful to managers, we designed two outcome measures. The first was to measure the *Current Business Performance* of the organisation at the time of the change and the second was to measure *Change Effectiveness*.

Current Business Performance

For Current Business Performance, we collected survey respondents' assessments of the profitability, productivity, financial and competitive strength of the organisation at the beginning, middle and end of the change process. We combined these measures into an overall outcome measure, which we called Current Business Performance. This measure reports *how well or badly the business was doing at the time of the change.*

Change Effectiveness

The second measure we used—Change Effectiveness—*indicates the effectiveness of the change.* This examined the change process and how well the changes worked after they were completed. This measure combines a number of potentially positive and negative aspects of any change. It measures the appropriateness (with hindsight) of the direction of the attempted change, the loss or weakening of that direction, and whether the direction and form of the change were effectively controlled by some people to serve their own interests rather than the firm's. We collected assessments of the firm's capacity to cope with what it had taken on, and of the impact the change had on the credibility of senior management. Also included was the extent to which business was lost to competitors, and valuable people were lost along the way. Lastly, we gathered assessments of the effectiveness of the effort that was made to implement the change and the resulting effectiveness of the operations in the new framework. We combined all of these in an outcome measure called *Change Effectiveness*.

Change is different from performance

Tests on the two outcome measures show a weak correlation between them. That is, the data show that essentially they measure different things. For example, the fact that your organisation is currently show-ing good financial and market performance does not mean it will manage change well. Nor, because it is currently performing well, can you predict, on that basis, that it will manage change badly. A poorly performing organisation is a little more likely to deal badly with change than one with good current performance. Fifty-five per cent of better performing organisations are also above average in managing change effectively. But 45 per cent of poorer performing organisations are also above average in managing change. So while there is a difference, it is not strong. Other factors, which we will shortly describe, are far more important as contributors to effective change than current performance.

The sixteen competencies

To collect information that we could compare across a large number of organisations, we needed to use generic competencies that exist in most organisations at a fundamental level. Of course, no list can capture all the competencies found in organisations. The sixteen we chose comprise a wide range of the key competencies needed in the management and performance of a business.

Motivating and enthusing (getting people motivated about their work and the firm) is an example of a competence we described. Pathfinding (identifying, setting and spelling out new directions for the firm) is another. Resource application (obtaining and applying resources to best achieve the firm's aims) is another. Enaction (taking timely and effective action, not just planning and talking about things) is another. Other competencies that made up the sixteen were performance control, integration, communication, achieving commitment, developing resources, systems and practices development, environmental assess-ment, planning, marketing and selling, and financial, technical and operational competencies.

The description of each is given in Appendix A. As you will see each exists, in varying degrees, in your own organisation. While our choice of competencies is important, they were just the starting point of further work we then carried out to better understand and define what an organisation needs for effective change and performance.

We asked the respondents to assess the strength of these competencies in their organisation at various stages of a change they were describing. We also asked them to give us a great deal of other information about their organisation. Part of this information provided values for the two outcome measures we described earlier—namely, their current performance and the effectiveness of the change they were describing. In all they gave us over 300 bits of separate information about characteristics and aspects of their organisation.

We began to plot the data from the 243 respondents to show the relationships between the individual competencies they had assessed and our two outcome measures—Current Business Performance and Change Effectiveness. We expected to find that some of the sixteen competencies were more strongly associated with Change Effectiveness and others with achieving Current Business Performance. While this was true of individual competencies, much more importantly a pattern began to emerge in the way competencies grouped themselves into separate and distinctive groupings, or clusters, in relation to these output measures. These are shown in Figure 3.1.

The emergence of the five capabilities

Further statistical factor analysis revealed a pattern of underlying relationships between the sixteen competencies that enabled us to reduce and distil them into five factors. We called these five groupings 'capabilities'. We named them Engagement, Development, Performance Management, Biztech, and Marketing and Selling. In Chapter 2 we described what form each took in the story of the changes at Woolworths and we will explore them in more detail in following chapters. Each of the sixteen competencies proved to have a particularly strong

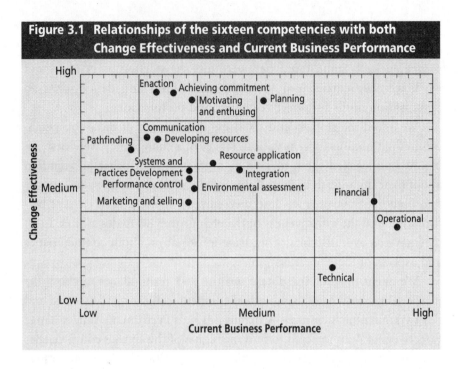

Figure 3.1 Relationships of the sixteen competencies with both Change Effectiveness and Current Business Performance

link with one or more of the five capabilities. The key linkages are shown in Figure 1.3, in the tables at the beginning of Chapters 5, 6, 7 and 9, and in Table A.1 in Appendix A.

The relationship between capabilities and the two outcomes

We plotted the five capabilities against the two outcome measures of Change Effectiveness and Current Business Performance. A very significant pattern of relationships emerged. We show these results graphically on the following pages and explain what each chart shows.

The charts show the relative impact that each of the five capabilities has on the two outcomes of Change Effectiveness and Current Business Performance. In particular, we want to show all of these relationships simultaneously, which we have done in Figure 3.4. But we need to build up to that by going through some intervening steps first.

The first step is Figure 3.2. It shows the actual relationship that Biztech—one of the five capabilities—has with *both* Change Effectiveness and Current Business Performance.

The single dot in the bottom right-hand corner of Figure 3.2 shows the *strength* of the relationships that Biztech has with the two different outcomes. It has high impact on Current Business Performance, which is indicated by its position being well to the right along the horizontal axis that measures Current Business Performance. It also has only low (that is, weak) impact on Change Effectiveness, which is measured by its position only a short distance up the vertical axis.

The strong relationship between Biztech and Current Business Performance should come as no surprise. Indeed we would have been astounded to find otherwise. However, the weak relationship between Biztech and Change Effectiveness is not so self-evident. While some people might have expected to find that result, others would have anticipated that Biztech capability would have a stronger impact on Change Effectiveness. After all, organisations with strong Biztech obviously

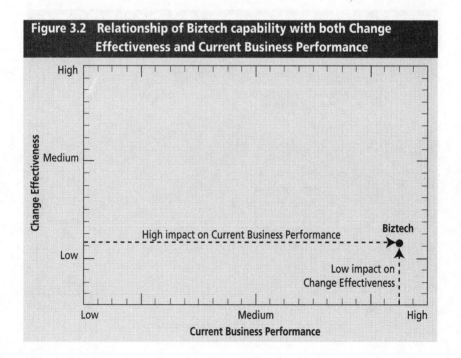

Figure 3.2   Relationship of Biztech capability with both Change Effectiveness and Current Business Performance

understand their business well. So it is not unreasonable to think that might give them a stronger grounding, or advantage, when making change.

In Figure 3.3, we have added another capability—Engagement—to the chart. It is immediately obvious that the relationships Engagement capability has with Change Effectiveness and Current Business Performance are totally different from those shown for Biztech. The dot for Engagement is high up the vertical axis, indicating it has a strong impact on Change Effectiveness. Conversely, it is only a short distance along the horizontal axis, and so its impact on Current Business Performance is quite weak, unlike Biztech which makes a powerful contribution to that outcome.

Finally, in Figure 3.4, we add dots for the other three capabilities to show their relationships with Change Effectiveness and Current Business Performance.

Well, you might think 'a chart's a chart. I've seen hundreds of them.' But we must tell you that when we first looked at Figure 3.4 we felt as though we had just climbed Mount Everest! We were exhausted, since

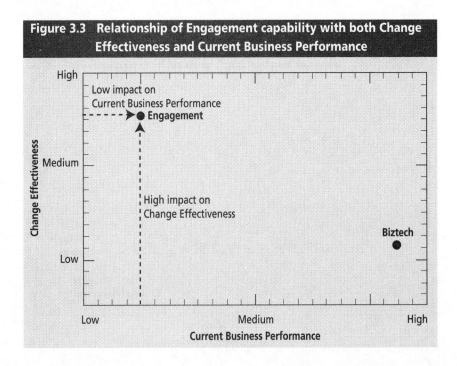

Figure 3.3   Relationship of Engagement capability with both Change Effectiveness and Current Business Performance

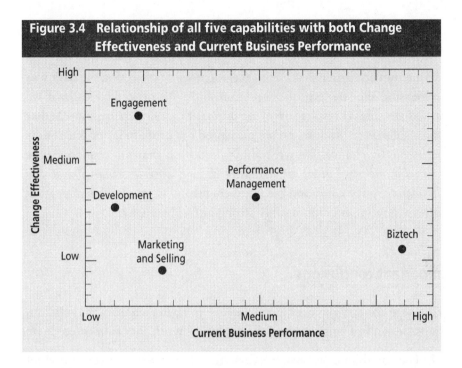

Figure 3.4 Relationship of all five capabilities with both Change Effectiveness and Current Business Performance

by then we had been collecting and analysing data for over three years, and we were not as fit as Sir Edmund Hillary. But we also felt a sense of real excitement, because we believed some new and important knowledge had emerged.

Because its axes are Current Business Performance (the present) and Change Effectiveness (the process of adapting for the future), the chart encapsulates the two foundation stones for sustained long-term performance—the ability to perform today and the ability to change for tomorrow. It also shows the nature of the contribution made by a small number of key corporate capabilities to these two necessary aspects of long-term performance.

What the positions of the five dots on Figure 3.4 told us was:

■ that the capabilities required to achieve Change Effectiveness are very different from the capabilities required for strong Current Business Performance

■ how strongly each capability was linked to Change Effectiveness and Current Business Performance.

We mentioned earlier that one of the purposes of collecting the data was to measure the strength of the relationships. We needed to know if we would get similar results surveying different cases of change or whether our results were random. So we measured the probability of our results occurring by chance. We were able to establish that *the chances of the key relationships having occurred by chance were less than one in ten thousand.* So the chart and the numbers behind it gave us this important information in an unmistakably strong and robust way.

Important conclusions

There are six very important conclusions to be drawn from the relationships shown in Figure 3.4 and the analytical work that supported them:

1 The capabilities to achieve Change Effectiveness are very different from those needed to achieve Current Business Performance.
2 Three capabilities are most important to Change Effectiveness— Engagement, Development and Performance Management. These are *reshaping* capabilities
3 Three capabilities are most important to achieving high Current Business Performance—Biztech, Performance Management and, to a lesser extent, Marketing and Selling. These are *operational* capabilities.
4 Both sets of capabilities are needed to achieve high long-term performance. One set is simply insufficient to achieve high Current Business Performance *and* Effective Change when needed.
5 Having one set of capabilities is not related to having the other. You can be good at managing current performance and good at making effective change, or good at managing current performance and bad at making effective change. Being good at running your business today has little relationship to your ability to change it, and vice versa.

6 One capability contributes to both Change Effectiveness and Current Business Performance—Performance Management. It is both a reshaping and an operational capability. If your organisation is strong in Performance Management it helps you both to perform today and enhances your ability to change.

These findings, which we explore in depth in the following chapters, are of fundamental importance to managers and stakeholders who are concerned with the long-term performance of their organisations. They apply in virtually every case of corporate change we studied. In Chapters 5 to 7 we explore each of the three reshaping capabilities in greater depth. In Chapter 8 we consolidate our findings and discuss their application in particular change scenarios. In Chapter 9 we explore the operational capabilities.

How organisational 'state' affects Change Effectiveness

In Chapter 1 we described how Susie Moroney became the first person to swim the 200-kilometre-wide Straits of Florida and how, in addition to her strong personal capabilities as a long distance swimmer, her ability to control her psychological, emotional and physical state played a vital part in her achievement. We suggested that an organisation's state might affect its performance, including its ability to change itself effectively. In the next chapter we explore this and present some strong data to you that identify particular corporate states that have a strong impact on achieving effective change. This is important for managers to appreciate because their actions to influence and alter their organisation's states can play a vital role in change success.

CHAPTER 4

The importance of organisational states

I N THE PREVIOUS CHAPTERS we have focused primarily on the relationship between capabilities and actions and their impact on Change Effectiveness. In this chapter we will explore the importance that the management of *organisational states* has on Change Effectiveness. In Figure 4.1, the thicker lines indicate the interaction between states and the other factors as part of the overall process. We will look at ways in which managers can influence the organisational states that help change success.

Managing personal states

In the run-up to the Atlanta Olympic Games, Kieren Perkins, the Australian 1500 metre swimming champion, just made the national team, while making a slow recovery from a weakening physical condition. He just qualified for the finals. In the final he won the Olympic gold, leaving the rest of the field way behind.

In responding to questions after the race about how they won, almost all Olympic champions describe their 'state'. They often talk of the confidence they felt from all the training, their commitment to perform at their best, or their desire to compete against others. They talk of

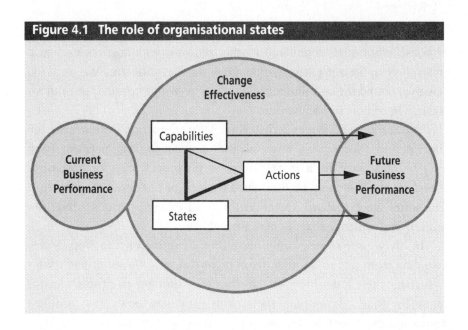

Figure 4.1 The role of organisational states

the resources they could draw on because they were in the peak of physical fitness and often how they psyched themselves up to perform, by visualising, or talking to themselves, or experiencing their winning before it took place. They have learned, by one method or another, to manage their state, and perform, when needed, often at their personal best. This is what Kieren did at Atlanta and what many other high performers do in the everyday walk of life, in every field of activity—sporting, artistic, or in the world of management.

While few of us compete in the Olympics, we have all had experiences of having to perform under pressure or over long periods of time. Perhaps we have put in some training or practice and developed a new skill and it works well when we use it. But on another occasion, our concentration may wander and our new skill seems to desert us and we begin to lose confidence. Other times, our performance may suffer because we are physically low so that when we need to draw on our resources we find it hard to find them.

For a whole number of reasons our performance varies because, for physical, emotional, cognitive or other reasons, we ourselves vary and this shows up in our performance. Our 'state' is different. We were fit, positive, confident and understood, last time we performed, but not so today. Or, of course, vice versa.

Often the states we experience are very transitory, lasting only for short periods. Sometimes, however, they can last for long periods. They may be buttressed by a strong sense of purpose, values or ambition. Alternatively, they may be weakened by lack of purpose and direction. The states we experience, whether for short or long periods, affect the level of performance that we actually achieve.

In life we see some people becoming a captive of transitory states swinging from one to another, from highs to lows. We see others trying to manage their states more effectively, maintaining their fitness, clarifying their goals, developing their skills, grasping new opportunities, increasing their confidence, and coping more successfully with the emotional, psychological and physical challenges of life. These people are trying to positively influence their performance, for whatever goals and in whatever ways may be important to them.

For many of us, our feelings of self-confidence and belief in our ability are particularly important at times of great change, when we may have to develop new skills, knowledge, values or behaviour. Managing our personal states, both in anticipation of change and in its implementation, is therefore likely to affect our performance and our ability to change.

Organisational states

Terms used quite often in the corporate world, by both managers and staff, as well as external commentators, refer to corporate states in much the same way as we, in day-to-day conversation, refer to personal states. Organisations are referred to as confident, cohesive, with high morale, committed, adaptable, resource rich, and, sometimes, as troubled, divided, defensive, rigid or weak.

In this way we can think of the 'state' of an organisation as a prevailing condition at any point of time. For example, we could refer to a state of *anxiety* during corporate change—that is, members individually and collectively are anxious about the change and its consequences. Or, we could talk about a state of *conflict* where the organisation is split and different people are pushing conflicting ideas. Alternatively, we might describe the state as one of *commitment*—that is, people are actively supporting the change and moving the organisation forward. If people understand what is happening to the organisation, and how the changes are expected to work, we might call that a state of *understanding*. Or, if people have the authority, resources and abilities to carry out the change, we could describe that as a state of *empowerment*. If people share strong confidence in the organisation's collective ability to succeed in what it is attempting to do and have mutual trust and commitment, we might describe that as a state of *esprit de corps*. Of course, these states would not be shared by all the organisation's people, and they could and would change over time.

Involving the many—not just the few

When managers take action to change an organisation's performance, the actual focus of their actions will vary. They may seek to change aspects of the firm's strategy or its structure or both. They may wish to introduce a new technology, or new ways of measuring performance. Or they may set out to build a new culture. But whatever is the initial focus of action, *any significant organisational change inevitably requires actions and changes on the part of many* before the change is embedded in people's beliefs, understandings and behaviours, and in the organisation's systems, practices and resource use.

While key individuals may play leading parts, effective change means change in the collective attitudes, behaviours and skills of the *many*. This is why the concept of organisational states is so important. States are pervasive. They are a shared, or widely shared, property of the firm. They affect our predisposition and willingness to act. They influence levels of energy available for action. They impact upon our collective resilience under pressure. Collective states help to provide the critical mass needed to move the organisation from inaction to action or from one action to another.

Nine organisational states

As part of our study, we collected information about organisational states. The executives were simply asked to rate the existence of a number of things in their organisation—for example, the level of trust in management, the strength of conflict within the organisation, the ability of people to adapt, and so on. Just as we built up five key capabilities from our respondents' assessments on competencies, we were able to identify nine generic corporate states. We then used an analytical process to link the existence, or absence, of these states in the 243 cases to the outcomes of Change Effectiveness and Current Business Performance for their organisation.

The nine organisational states identified by our research were:

1 **Understanding.** The people of the organisation understand what is happening and how any intended changes will work.
2 **Commitment.** People feel committed to the changes being attempted.
3 **Empowerment.** People have the skills and resources to carry out the changes, and the power and authority to do so.
4 **Esprit de corps.** People share confidence in the firm's abilities to succeed, with high levels of trust, openness and unity.
5 **Conflict.** There is conflict about proposed changes among the key members of the organisation.
6 **Resistance.** People are actively resisting the change.
7 **Anxiety.** People feel worried, anxious and threatened by the changes.

8 High workloads. People are putting a lot of effort into their work and have high workloads.

9 Systems and practices suitability. The organisation's systems and practices are suitable for the work being done.

As we did in Chapter 3 for capabilities, Figure 4.2 illustrates the impact that each of the nine organisational states has on the two outcomes of Change Effectiveness and Current Business Performance. For example, commitment is strongly linked to Change Effectiveness, and esprit de corps is strongly linked to Current Business Performance.

Figure 4.2 shows that some organisational states—those below the 'zero' horizontal line—have a negative impact on Change Effectiveness. The same three states—conflict, anxiety and resistance—are linked to poor Current Business Performance, and these are indicated by being to the left of the 'zero' vertical line.

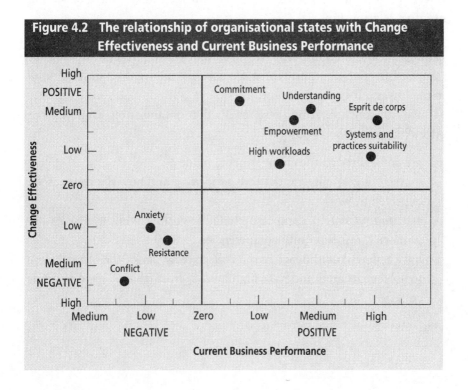

Figure 4.2 The relationship of organisational states with Change Effectiveness and Current Business Performance

Relationships between states and Change Effectiveness

Figure 4.2 shows that four states have a strong positive relationship with Change Effectiveness. These are:

- commitment
- understanding
- empowerment
- esprit de corps.

Two states have a lesser, but still positive, relationship. These are:

- systems and practices suitability
- high workloads.

One state—conflict—has a strong negative relationship with Change Effectiveness, and two states—anxiety and resistance—have lesser but negative relationships.

Positive or change-enhancing states are the six in the upper right-hand quadrant of Figure 4.2. The three states that detract or undermine Change Effectiveness, and which we describe as negative states, are all in the lower left-hand quadrant.

We can conclude from these results that organisations change more effectively when their people:

- are *committed* to the changes being made
- *understand* the changes that are happening and how the changes are expected to work
- are *empowered* to make the changes work, having the necessary authority, resources and competencies
- have a shared confidence in the collective ability of the organisation to achieve its aims and have high mutual trust (that is, have *esprit de corps*).

Relationships between states and Current Business Performance

As Figure 4.2 shows, two states are strongly linked to achieving Current Business Performance. These are:

- esprit de corps
- systems and practices suitability.

The same states that are linked to Change Effectiveness are also associated with Current Business Performance. However some states are more important to Change Effectiveness and others have a stronger relationship to Current Business Performance. Of course, there is not simply a one-way cause-and-effect relationship. When at a personal level we have high confidence we perform better, and when our performance is good it builds or sustains high confidence. So there is always likely to be an ongoing interaction between aspects of our performance and our state and vice versa. As managers we need to take actions to positively influence both states and performance.

The impact of organisational states on actual results

Some of the insights provided by Figure 4.2 are not new. Many of us would expect that some organisational states would be linked to Change Effectiveness. For example, most of us would expect that a greater *understanding* by people in the firm about what is happening and how the intended changes will work will help the change to be effective. *What the data show us is that this is actually what happens*. It makes a difference to the outcome. It's not just an ideal or a nice idea. It actually takes place. Similarly, when people have the authority, ability and resources to make change, a state we have called empowerment, the actual effectiveness of the change increases. The same is true for commitment and esprit de corps.

We say *many* people would expect such linkages to exist. But in fact not all do. Furthermore, and perhaps more importantly, some, perhaps many, managers, who may believe at a conceptual level that such linkages exist, simply do not act as though they believe it when they have responsibility for managing change in their organisations. Or perhaps in the haste and pressure of trying to achieve a particular change, they forget the importance of these states. In so doing they make their task so much harder. In these cases the actions these managers take do not actually lead to a state of understanding, or empowerment, or commitment, or of esprit de corps. Their actions, or often lack of action, end up instead with a corporate state of conflict, the most damaging state, or of resistance or anxiety, states that are negative in their measured impact on effective change.

Positive states and positive outcomes

Perhaps, not unsurprisingly, but nevertheless importantly, *all positive states are linked with positive outcomes and all negative states with negative outcomes*. While this might be what you would expect, such a belief is not shared by all managers. There are some who think that anxiety and threat leads to effective change, or that conflict is inevitable and may not matter all that much. The data show this is untrue. The outcomes were, of course, measured from other data not connected with the description or evaluation of the states, and so the linkage between states and outcomes is not simply in the minds of the respondents. It reflects actual performance differences of positive and negative states. It shows how they actually impacted on the success of the change.

In looking at Figure 4.2, it is important to realise that states affect what happens and what happens affects states, the not unfamiliar chicken and egg situation. Which comes first—the positive state or the related positive performance? The answer is that at a practical level they are both present and both affect one another. A manager should try to take action to achieve a positive organisational state that will be helpful, while recognising actions will be affected by the prevailing states. When you are positive, you perform better. When you perform better, you become more positive. Whenever progress is made with one, progress is likely to be made with the other. They reinforce one another. It is not an 'either or' situation. Good managers want and take action to get more of both.

Negative states and negative outcomes

Three states have a negative impact on change, with conflict having a stronger impact than resistance and anxiety. Conflict is particularly important because it can tear the organisation apart and stop action, which is the engine of change, from taking place. People often speak as though resistance is the biggest threat to successful change. Our research shows that this is not the case. Conflict is a more important threat. Conflict uses up enormous energy and separates one person from another in a way that anxiety does not, and which resistance does not to the same extent.

When resistance occurs managers have a real sense of knowing where to focus action and which actions might work best to lower or remove it. With anxiety, positive management action can often allay and diminish it. But conflict usually pits one part of the organisation against another, or one person, often a manager, against another. This is much more difficult to deal with and, as Figure 4.2 shows, much more destructive in its impact. It also requires much more skill and action to resolve. It often results in no change at all. We will discuss, later, an example of conflict in a Du Pont plant and the actions that management took to overcome it.

Our survey revealed that a number of the actions that take place in many corporate changes, particularly reducing staff, replacing people in key positions and bringing in new people, add to conflict rather than reduce it. Of course, such actions may be appropriate in some situations, but they often come at a cost which is better managed if foreseen. Action to clarify direction, and participation in the change process, make some contribution to conflict reduction, but communication, consultation and training lower conflict more effectively.

Conflict is almost the opposite of the unity that is a characteristic of esprit de corps, a state that contributes strongly to both Change Effectiveness and Current Business Performance.

Managers can strongly influence corporate states

Particular states do not occur because you hope they will. Something happens to cause them. Sometimes the cause is external or outside management control. But, whatever the origin, the way management acts and re-acts has an impact on the states that develop in the organisation.

Creating positive states and changing negative states is one way managers can influence the effectiveness of their change programs. In a moment we will see how that occurred at Woolworths. Furthermore, states can be changed and built more quickly than capabilities, so that influencing them positively can provide early momentum to the change process, and reinforcement as it continues. However while conscious formation of corporate states is never an easy task, some states are more quickly and easily influenced by action than others.

Creating an understanding of the change is largely a matter of competence and action to do it. Communication, participation and training, actions that help to engender it, can be taken relatively quickly and well by organisations that are motivated to do so, but this still requires a significant effort. Change commitment requires more sustained effort and action in conveying vision, setting priorities, monitoring events, and recognising and rewarding performance.

Achieving a state of empowerment, which relies most heavily on personal training and systems and practices development, is however likely to take longer. Empowerment not only means having the authority, power or freedom to act, it also means having the skills and resources to take action. Sometimes staff have the skills and resources to act but not the authority. In these cases empowerment is relatively easy. But where skills and resources need to be developed, simply empowering people to act without them has little meaning. The linkage between the states of

understanding and empowerment is also important. Without understanding the intent and direction of the change, empowerment can result
in mistaken and damaging initiatives by staff, which when they are over-
turned by more senior management can strip away empowerment and
undermine commitment and esprit de corps. So while states of understanding and commitment can be built relatively quickly, empowerment
in many cases will take longer. Nevertheless these three states can certainly be impacted by actions that can be taken by management if they
are motivated to do so.

However, while action has a relatively quick impact on some states,
esprit de corps is less easily influenced by short-term management
action. It is strongly affected by the existence of corporate capabilities,
whereas the other three key states are much less related to the possession of corporate capabilities. Our data show a strong relationship
between esprit de corps and the existence of all five corporate capabilities and in particular with Biztech.

This means that in the very short term, management actions that can
help to build change-enhancing states are best directed at building
understanding of and commitment to the change and the empowerment
of the members of the organisation to make it happen. This is where the
actions of the management at Woolworths were strongly focused.
As corporate capabilities were developed esprit de corps also grew. In
Woolworths' case strong leadership added to the change success.

Links between actions and states at Woolworths

In this section we will briefly revisit events at Woolworths to see the important links between the actions taken and the change-enhancing states that
were built to reinforce the change success. We will see that some actions
contributed to the creation or development of more than one state and
sometimes simultaneously to all four important change-enhancing states.
This helped to reinforce and integrate the change process.

The state of commitment to change

While there are many aspects to becoming committed to making change, our questionnaire identified three particular aspects that influenced the formation of commitment. These were:

- the extent to which people thought the firm ought to change
- the benefits they saw the changes would bring to them
- the incentive they had to make the changes work.

In Woolworths, the state of commitment to change was very strongly built up by the actions of management. One powerful way that Woolworths built commitment was the way it conveyed its vision to its people and used and involved them in the television commercials. Simply giving people a picture of a better future would have had some impact in itself, but the actions of providing training for new relevant skills in fresh food management and recognising performance with significant increases in bonuses and rewards substantially reinforced this.

As people develop new skills, they look for opportunities to use them. When they are rewarded for doing something their commitment is further stimulated.

The personal example of its leaders in communicating with its people was another way commitment was built. When the executive chairman and managing director came into a store after midnight to check that pallets were being loaded more efficiently, a problem the manager had struggled unsuccessfully with for a long time, it will have impacted on commitment. As the rest of the nearly one thousand managers, who also had suffered such unresolved problems, heard about it, the commitment of many would have been increased.

Commitment grows as people see relevant action. It does not grow by simply painting a future to excite people or involve them at a conceptual level. Reaching people's emotions can be important to building commitment. Stirring messages can produce emotional reactions that are strong, but they can also be quite transitory. Unless accompanied by real action by leaders that demonstrates their own commitment, focus and priorities, the emotional commitment will quickly fade and end in cynicism.

The monitoring action that Paul Simons carried out played an important part in developing commitment to action. Buyers and managers would have become more committed to appropriate action—for example, in pricing—on receiving a telephone call from the chairman. While their initial action may have been one of compliance, they soon developed commitment to further actions, particularly as they began to see how well they worked.

A psychological phenomenon, known as 'dissonance reduction', suggests that when we are induced to adopt a particular behaviour, we tend to adjust our thinking to rationalise and support the behaviour. Of course when the behaviours and practices begin to work well, the process is accelerated.

The state of understanding

Understanding what and why things are happening, and how the changes are expected to work, takes the organisation further along the journey towards effective change.

Harry Watts, Woolworths' managing director, frequently used a phrase that picks up an important aspect of understanding. 'People don't hear you the first time around.' Understanding often requires patience. Woolworths' change was not an explicitly planned or staged or rushed process. It proceeded bit by bit as the most urgent jobs were tackled. In the development of understanding, a crucial role was played by the actions of senior management.

An important aspect of developing a state of understanding was the willingness of the leaders to listen, and to question and consult. One manager said:[1]

'Harry Watts and Paul Simons came into my store together and asked, "How can we help you?" We talked together.'

When changes are being made, communication needs to be two way if understanding is to grow.

Many people's initial focus is, 'How will the change affect me?' When this is clear and they have accepted it, they will be more predisposed to take a positive interest in the organisation's future. This is often helped by growing communication and interaction across the organisation as well as up and down it. People are sometimes more open to meaningful communication with others at a similar level. As the fiefdoms began to break down in Woolworths, communication across the group became a significant feature in the development of understanding.

The requirement that all meetings should have an empty chair to represent the importance of the customer provides another example of getting people to understand what the change was about. While small in itself, it was very symbolic. People often understand more by these sorts of actions than by lengthy memoranda or speeches. The slogan, 'If you're not serving the customer, serve someone who is', reinforced that customer focus. Furthermore, it underlined that this was a responsibility at the top as well as for the front-line troops. Paul Simons' first meeting with his top team when he asked them to estimate prices for goods compared to their competitors' contributed to understanding what needed to be done.

The actions taken to use capital differently reinforced understanding of what the change was about. Money was spent on altering stores for their new purposes not, as previously, in continued store expansion. In fact, trading space was actually reduced in the early stages of the change.

When people see what is actually happening, and it is consistent with what is being espoused in relation to the future, understanding tends to grow.

While commitment is primarily about capturing hearts, understanding is primarily about informing minds. Of course, the two work to reinforce one another. The states of understanding change and commitment to change are similarly impacted by participation. However, understanding is more strongly associated with the actions of training, communication and consultation.

It is important to realise that it is not what you have done that should help people understand. It is what they actually understand as a result of your action.

The state of empowerment

The third state that enhances Change Effectiveness is empowerment. There are two important elements to empowerment. The first is whether people feel they have the resources and abilities to carry out the changes needed. The second is whether they have the power and authority to do so. While the first two important states, commitment and understanding, are more to do with emotional and conceptual attitudes to the change, empowerment is much more squarely focused on the issue of resources and the power and ability to act.

Our data show that training is the strongest of the actions that management can take to enhance this state. People feel empowered when they can do something about performing or changing. Training people in new skills, and then giving them the opportunity to use them, is what makes people feel more able to influence their situation. But the state of empowerment is also affected by action in the field of communication. Knowing what is going on increases the chance you will be able to use your skills and contribute meaningfully.

Woolworths followed a pattern of training and improved communication as the change progressed and the vision and direction had become clearer. But empowerment does not simply mean that power and ability to act is given to everyone. The price alteration powers that had previously been widely distributed to the stores were brought back to the centre because the power was not being used in the interests of the business. Empowerment needs some limits that are relevant to achievement of the new directions.

The action taken to develop systems and practices made a major contribution to developing a state of empowerment. People had new information to run the stores and to do the buying, and will have felt much more able to influence events. Change, in the final analysis, requires action. When people feel powerless, they do not act. Giving them skills, resources, good systems and a direction encourages action.

CHANGE POWER

The state of esprit de corps

The fourth state that enhances Change Effectiveness is esprit de corps. Esprit de corps is about shared confidence and mutual trust. It combines a sense of unity, a willingness of people to talk openly and express their views, a high level of trust in management and a shared confidence in the organisation's ability to succeed.

Woolworths is a prime example of the development of this state. As the changes progressed, it exuded everywhere in the organisation. It was buttressed by accelerating profit results, by growth, and visibly by a number of national awards—'The Top 500 Best Growth Strategy', 'The Businessman of the Year', 'The Most Improved Company in 1991', and so on. Watts and Simons' actions in taking along, not their top management, but representatives of their front-line troops—checkout operators, shelf fillers—is the sort of symbolic action that helps develop esprit de corps. It emphasises unity—that everyone counts and that teamwork is important. It helps to develop mutual trust. But, of course, it only works when it is genuine.

Unity is an important part of esprit de corps. Woolworths' action in using the Victorian operation, which had been acquired from Safeways and was not integrated into the national operation, as the basis for its new 'Fresh Food' training program helped in developing unity. As communication spread across the divisions and states, the old fiefdoms slowly disappeared. The business became more unified and national. As it developed its business competencies, and particularly its management and merchandise systems, people could take pride in its new standards of performance. Esprit de corps is strongly linked to the presence of a strong Biztech capability and Woolworths put major effort into this.

Esprit de corps would have been strongly affected by the fact that although Woolworths sold some of its older and smaller stores many staff were able to relocate to larger stores. It did not downsize its operation in any significant way. Its overall staff numbers did not fall; in fact they steadily grew. People knew it was worth acquiring skills because they would have an opportunity to use them. Woolworths did not recruit many from outside. Its revitalisation was accomplished overwhelmingly by insiders. At times when pressure was heavy on its top management, they still found time to visit the pensioners' Christmas parties. Woolworths had 'pride in its people', a requirement Harry Watts genuinely felt was important to success.

Links between states and Current Business Performance

Two states—esprit de corps and systems and practices suitability—are strongly related to Current Business Performance. These both reflect the ownership of capabilities.

In the field of personal performance, there is a growing amount of research evidence that shows that high levels of personal self-efficacy—a person's belief in his or her capability to perform a task—improve personal performance. In fields as diverse as selling insurance, academic research productivity, coping with difficult tasks, and adapting to the use of new technology, measures of self-efficacy correlate with performance. The corporate state of esprit de corps, which combines unity, confidence, openness and trust, though not identical with personal self-efficacy, has a number of parallel features. Our data show that esprit de corps aids both Change Effectiveness and Current Business Performance.

Esprit de corps reflects, however, more than just a belief in capabilities. In some cases organisations in the study with strong capabilities reported low esprit de corps and vice versa. Esprit de corps includes mutual trust and confidence in the firm's management. When these aspects are missing, belief in capabilities is not on its own enough to generate high esprit de corps. Conversely, exceptional leadership can achieve high esprit de corps despite weak capabilities. The generation or enhancement of a sense of esprit de corps is one way high leadership skills contribute to both Change Effectiveness and Current Business Performance. Woolworths combined both high quality leadership and a growing and demonstrated belief in its own corporate capabilities. This made a strong basis for the growth of high esprit de corps.

The state of systems and practices suitability reflects that the firm's systems, practices and procedures are suitable for the work to be done. It is, of course, very much focused on resources and competencies. It is a more powerful state for enhancing Current Business Performance than for Change Effectiveness. This is not only because it is more closely connected with capabilities, but also because it is primarily focused on task outcomes. While change is also about developing systems and business competencies, it is first about impacting upon the hearts and minds and development of the people who will do this. Systems and practices can, of course, be part of the change process and embody some of the change outcomes, but they are likely to have their major impact on actually achieving results.

Lastly, a factor that we were not expecting to figure much in the survey results was the impact of staff and managers' workloads. The survey shows that having high workloads is positively related to achieving high Current Business Performance, as one would expect, but it is also a positive factor for Change Effectiveness. This was, in fact, the anecdotal evidence we picked up from a number of discussions with executives during our preparation of the various cases, and it seems to operate widely across the change cases covered in the survey. It would suggest that high workloads are associated with high energy, effort, commitment and perhaps high participation, and that these and other characteristics operate, not only to improve Current Business Performance, but also to enhance Change Effectiveness. Obviously there are limits to this. Nevertheless the organisations in our sample that had higher workloads were somewhat more likely to be high performers and somewhat more likely to change effectively.

Summary

Organisational states affect collective behaviour, attitudes, energy and actions. They influence the many, not just the few. Their impact on Change Effectiveness is powerful, clear and measurable. Organisations that make change most effectively have high positive states, particularly commitment to change, understanding, empowerment and esprit de corps. Their staff carry relatively high workloads and believe their systems and practices are suited for their needs. Understanding by managers of the importance of the impact of corporate states and action by them to build change-enhancing states, or to reduce conflict, resistance and anxiety, play a crucial role in enabling organisations to make effective change.

The next three chapters

The next three chapters look at each of the three major capabilities needed for Change Effectiveness—Engagement, Development and Performance Management. We describe them in much more detail and give you examples that illustrate them in action. We start with Engagement, the capability most strongly associated with change success.

CHAPTER 5

Engagement

A tale of two CEOs

SOME TIME AGO, a company in the resources sector asked for help with its program of change. 'What seems to be the problem?' we asked the chief executive. 'Nothing is happening,' he said. 'Nothing seems to be changing. Everyone knows about the change and what we want to do, but it isn't getting off the ground.'

Some twelve months earlier, one of the world's top consulting groups had completed a review of the company's operations. We read the review. It seemed good. The recommendations were sensible and well grounded with impressive analysis and data about the organisation and its various markets. The consultants had suggested a focus on particular markets, which meant changes in priorities, in resource use and in the management structure.

The CEO had spent some time in thinking about the report and discussing it with the consultants and became satisfied that it was sound and made sense. He told his top team he agreed with the report and gave them all a copy. He decided to address all his middle and senior management and tell them why he felt the report pointed to the right way forward for the company.

The chief executive provided us with a copy of the speech he had made to his senior and middle management group. It was a good speech, as speeches go. It gave all the reasons for the changes. He sent all his executives a copy of what he had said. The CEO then passed over to his managers the job of getting on with it. Twelve months later nothing had happened. He said he could not understand why. His managers had agreed the report was good and the suggested actions right, but they were still arguing among themselves about how the report should be implemented.

We found it really hard to believe that the CEO had assumed that once people were told about the vision and directions for the future they would get on and do it. He had been CEO for quite some years, and, although his organisation now faced the need for change, he had managed it with average, if not impressive, results. As an engineer he had a strong focus on technical development and on high day-to-day performance standards. Yet the simple truth was that while he could conceptually see a need for change and what form and direction it could, or should, take he was *incapable* of engaging with his senior executives, let alone his organisation, about the proposed changes, and of dealing with the human and other issues involved. And, in the absence of action from him, no one else had taken action. But was this an isolated example?

During the course of writing this book, one of us visited a major manufacturer in heavy industry. The CEO opened discussion by saying that his recent attempt to change his organisation's performance by re-engineering part of the plant's operations had unfortunately failed. Did he know why? 'The simple truth is,' he said, 'and I'm embarrassed to tell you, is that we forgot about the people. We concentrated on getting the process right, but when we had solved the technical problems, I'm afraid the people involved didn't want to do it and, in spite of our efforts since to encourage them, it hasn't really worked.'

The CEO had been trained in a top-rated business school, had extensive corporate experience in a number of overseas operations for the company and had a good record in running existing operations. He may well have had the capabilities to engage the people, to motivate them and get their commitment to the new directions, but unfortunately he was just too busy, or interested in other matters, to do it, or to see that someone else did it. Retrospectively, of course, he knew he should have handled the situation differently. But the fact is, he didn't. Perhaps this is another isolated example?

The first CEO, in our examples, lacked some of the necessary personal capabilities, in particular those involved in effective Engagement, to reshape his organisation. The second one probably had the personal capabilities but had other priorities. What is just as important is that neither organisation had developed the corporate capabilities that might have made up for the lack of personal capabilities or actions in their chief executives. In neither case did the organisation, nor the relevant part of it, become 'engaged' in the change. Neither had ended up with a successful change.

Some managers may feel that such cases are untypical—that it wouldn't happen in their organisation. Our study shows that failures of this kind are, in fact, common. When we ask a group of executives if they have had similar kinds of experiences, typically a third to half the hands in the room go up.

A little later in this chapter we will describe how one of America's largest and most successful corporations had its own share of problems in engaging its people in change.

Other managers may feel that while engaging people in change may be needed for organisations in general, their particular organisation is different. Their organisation may, for example, be very strong in Performance Management, which our study shows is also an important reshaping capability, especially for commercial organisations. It doesn't need to engage its people to make successful change. Or, in some ways, its people are special or different from those in organisations in general.

Performance Management is a valuable capability to have. The more effectively it can be employed the better. But why managers should try to change their organisation without also having the contribution of Engagement, which is the capability most strongly linked to Change Effectiveness, is not at all clear. Why people, whose working world is being changed, would prefer not to be engaged in a process that may affect their lives is equally unclear.

The impact of Engagement

It is, of course, always possible that there are some unique situations or organisations where it is not necessary to engage people for the change to be successful. We tested the importance of Engagement in a variety of such subgroups in our study.

Our tests show that Engagement capability has a strong impact upon the success of change when:

- the organisation is small or large
- the organisation is commercial or not, and government owned or not
- the organisation faces an opportunity or a threat
- the organisational scope of the change is small or large
- the potential impact of the change is minor or major
- the change is swift or protracted
- the change occurs with little warning or not
- the business strategy being implemented is to contract the business, refine its operations, reorientate into new areas or introduce new developments
- the focus is on changing the corporate culture, or changing the top management.

The range therefore of organisations and circumstances where Engagement is strongly linked to Change Effectiveness is very wide. Organisations would need to be very unusual and in a unique situation not to need Engagement as an important part of their change success. Engagement is, thus, an important capability for managers to understand and learn to use.

While Engagement is a vital component of every change we tested, it is even more important in some kinds of change than others. Its impact is highest when the organisation is attempting to change its culture, a situation we explore in depth in Chapter 8. While still important, it has relatively less impact when organisations see the challenge of change as a threat rather than as an opportunity. This is particularly so when the source of the threat is external, such as governments, unions or the community, as compared to a threat from market-related sources, such as competitors. It is also somewhat less potent when contraction is being pursued as a strategy, and when the pace of the particular change is very quick. Its impact is higher when new development is the order of the day.

When culture is the focus of change, the need is to change the values, beliefs and behavioural norms of the way business is done. This requires a change in the way people think about the business, and does not occur unless a critical mass of the organisation becomes engaged—in their hearts, minds and action—in the change. So it is easy to understand the importance of Engagement in this situation. When change comes from external parties, the role of Engagement is less important. For example, when an organisation is contracting and downsizing, the nature and purpose of the change may be clear, if unwelcome, to many people, and Engagement is not so critical to achieving the intended results.

But what exactly is Engagement? What particular competencies or skills are involved? What actions typically foster its development? How does it help to form those change-enhancing states that make change effective?

In the rest of this chapter, we identify the competencies that contribute to Engagement, the states and actions that are linked to it, and the fundamental reasons why it is so important. We then discuss pathfinding, a competence that is central to direction setting for an organisation and forms part of Engagement capability. We highlight the extent to which Engagement capability depends upon both personal and corporate capabilities and the consequences of this. We illustrate some aspects of Engagement in three different corporate settings—at General Electric, Du Pont and at Robert's store. We then outline some actions and states that are typically linked with Engagement. We hope this will give you a sense, a picture and a feel for what Engagement is, to help you decide the actions you need to take in your organisation.

Competencies, states and actions

Table 5.1 lists some of the key competencies that combine to form Engagement, and the key states and actions that our study shows are linked to it. We are focusing here on the most important linkages. Many of the sixteen competencies have some linkage with all the capabilities. However, the linkage is very strong with one or two capabilities, but relatively weak with the others. In Table 5.1 'contributing competencies' are those competencies that have a very strong relationship with Engagement capability. Some of the other competencies may make some contribution to Engagement, but it is a lot less and those competencies are much more important contributors to other capabilities. Similarly we are focusing on the most strongly linked organisational states and actions, though they too often have some weaker linkages with other capabilities.

In looking at the competencies, states and actions we will be describing factors that will be familiar to you. Different writers, managers or mentors will have emphasised the merits of one, or some, of them as important to effective change.

What is new about what we have to say is that our data reveal that a number of what are normally seen as separate competencies, actions and states are part of a much more important comprehensive whole. Engagement is not just good communication. Engagement does not occur without an understanding of direction, which is why pathfinding is an integral competence, and effectively conveying a vision is an important action. People are not effectively engaged until they are committed and motivated. People normally need to be consulted and involved and need to understand. So although each aspect can be seen as important in itself, the whole is more than the sum of the parts. Together they

Table 5.1   Engagement: competencies, states and actions

Contributing competencies	Linked key states	Linked key actions
Communication	Esprit de corps	Conveying a vision
Achieving commitment	High workloads	Recognising contributors
Motivating and enthusing	Low conflict	Monitoring
Integration	Commitment	Training
Pathfinding	Understanding	Consulting people
Enaction		

constitute a capability that we have called Engagement. While critical to Change Effectiveness, Engagement alone is not enough. It is one of three reshaping capabilities needed to change and renew an organisation.

As Table 5.1 shows, Engagement is an amalgam of competencies, both personal and corporate. They are manifested in a range of actions. Our study will have picked up just a few of these and there will be many others. The actions impact on individuals and also help to build corporate states that enhance change success. The form particular actions take will vary with the circumstances and strategies of the firm.

Engagement is a unifying capability that is integral to change success. It needs to be planned, assessed, monitored and rewarded.

While individuals play an important role in Engagement, it can be built, in varying degrees, as a corporate capability. Yet, as we will see, it is often a badly managed activity, so often dependent, as in our two opening examples, on the variable skills of key individuals.

Influencing the hearts, minds and actions of the many

We called the capability Engagement because it is about engaging the people of the organisation—in mind, heart and action—in the business and its future direction. It requires the competencies to communicate, motivate and enthuse people, to identify and convey new directions for the organisation's future, and to achieve commitment and integrated action across the organisation.

Change usually involves many people in an organisation—sometimes everyone in it. Getting their commitment to the change is very important. That is not just our view. *Our study found that as Engagement capability rises, change success rises. Conversely as Engagement drops, change success drops.* In terms of enhancing Change Effectiveness, no other capability is a complete substitute for Engagement.

If you want to change your organisation effectively, you and many others will need to use or develop this capability. And if you can embed it, or aspects of it, in the processes, structures, values and practices of your organisation, you will increase further the possibility of effective change. Involving the many, which is what Engagement ultimately does, is not just an issue of values about sharing information, or about participation, though it may well include these. It's about influencing people to act. If change is to be effective it needs the support of a critical mass of the managers and people in the organisation.

Aiming for a critical mass

Nuclear Electric plc was formed in 1990 as part of the British government's nuclear privatisation program. To perform in its new corporate structure, it had to manage one of Europe's largest civil engineering projects, reduce its unit costs in 12 nuclear power stations to compete with intense competition in the electricity industry, and convince the government and the British public of the value and safety of nuclear energy after the Russian disaster at Chernobyl. Three years later the company published a report that reviewed the success of its major change program. The report stressed the importance of a 'critical mass' in the Engagement process—'to make things happen'. It stated:[1]

> 'Critical mass is a familiar concept in the nuclear industry: it's what you need to get a reaction. This is also true of the change process. When you introduce a major change initiative, you won't get everyone on your side straight away. In fact, attitudes in your organisation will probably follow a normal distribution. At one end will be those who support you and push vigorously to make change happen. At the other end will be the sceptics—people who may feel threatened by change and will try to stop it happening. In the middle are the majority, who tend to be passive and are open to influence by either group. To achieve a critical mass and make things happen enough people from the middle will need to join the supporters of change.
>
> 'The concept of critical mass applied to our managers as much as to anyone else. We couldn't win the support of all our managers straight away. What we could do was to identify those in key positions who were prepared to carry our change process forward and prevent it from becoming just another failed initiative. At the same time when we came

across managers who were effectively blocking the change process, we had to find ways of moving them aside. In this way the supporters of change could start to influence others and to build up a critical mass.'

Engagement is the capability that helps to form a critical mass. Communication is important to it and extensive ongoing communication was one of the outstanding features of change at Nuclear Electric, but strong supporting management action is needed to move the process forward. We will see this is a feature of many changes.

Engagement is a management responsibility

Engagement does not simply take place of its own accord. It does not normally occur spontaneously. It is a management responsibility and requires management action. Organisational change, to be effective in a competitive environment, should be managed like any other activity or area of the business to get performance and results.

Engagement is not a 'soft' process. Communication will often need to be very direct. Managerial power may be needed to shift attitudes or behaviour or remove opposition that will not accept persuasion. It needs energy, competence and action before enough of a 'critical mass' is behind the change to sustain it over time. People need not only to be engaged but often re-engaged, as the changes continue over long periods of time.

However, Engagement is not enough, on its own, to achieve change. It needs to be buttressed by actions that rest on the capabilities of Development and Performance Management. These are the other reshaping capabilities that more directly renew the operational capabilities through which the firm delivers value to its market. Carrying out the operational tasks are a part, sometimes quite a small part, of almost everyone's job in the firm, rather than a large part of the jobs of just a few. It is generally a collective effort and a collective knowledge that is involved and integrated in delivering value to a customer. That is why it is important to impact on the many rather than the few.

Engagement, which does impact on the many, supports this integration. It predisposes the many to learn new skills and methods of performance. When goals become clearer and motivations and commitment grow, learning becomes more focused and efficient. Engagement contributes to this aspect of renewal by winning the hearts and informing the minds of the many. It increases the motivation and commitment of those whose work delivers the corporate product and who can help to reshape, revitalise and renew the organisation. Leadership is critical to this and finds one of its expressions in Engagement.

The strong trend over the last few decades to computerisation and other forms of information technology, coupled with the development in most countries of the service sector, has created 'knowledge workers' at much lower levels and in much greater numbers in organisations. The commitment, understanding and involvement of these much larger numbers of informed people, many of whom have considerable discretion and freedom in the ways they work, is critical to effective change. Developments in technology can help reach these larger numbers of people, but reaching them is not enough. They need to become engaged. Anecdotal evidence suggests that in many cases, particularly where differences or conflict is involved, there is no effective substitute for personal interaction.

The importance of getting the commitment of a critical mass, which Engagement has the potential to do, is underlined in the case of changes that took place at General Electric under the leadership of Jack Welch.

Engagement at General Electric

Jack Welch was appointed CEO of GE, one of the biggest corporations in the world, in 1981. From his early days as CEO, Welch imposed his own vision on the corporation. The vision was that each business in the corporation had to become number one or number two in its industry or Welch would close or sell it. Welch focused on increasing earnings. In practice this was approached largely as a cost-cutting exercise. Much of the downsizing that characterised the next five years followed from this strategic intent. It was relentlessly pushed through by major personal efforts from Welch. When Welch began as CEO, GE had nearly 420,000 employees. Ten years later it had 285,000, even though its acquisitions exceeded its divestments. Tichy and Sherman in their book, *Control your Destiny or Someone Else Will*, which describes the story of Welch's management at GE, give a picture of the lack of commitment, resistance and low morale that accompanied the vision and this process.

Tichy, who had moved from a professorial post in academia to take up the full-time job of leading Crotonville, GE's major executive development centre, comments:[2]

> 'Welch had expected GE'ers to dislike his message. But he believed they'd see the obvious benefits of joining the revolution. He thought they'd understand. He thought they'd agree. He thought they'd help. He was wrong …
>
> 'Although a substantial core group of employees responded as Welch expected, the greater mass did not … The CEO couldn't understand their behaviour.'

Changes in management structure

Some five years into his appointment as CEO and after considerable downsizing, Welch made significant change in the senior management structure of the corporation. He removed the sector management, a substantial hierarchy of management that came between him and the thirteen CEOs that headed up the corporation's major groups. This enabled Welch to more directly interface and influence the major operations of the business. An 'office of the CEO', comprising Welch, Bossidy, Hood and Van Orden, became the central focus point of the corporation. With the powerful sectors out of the way, Welch set up a group of the thirty most senior managers in GE—the Corporate Executive Council (CEC)—who met with him for two 'intense' days each quarter to review all the businesses and discuss matters of general importance.

From the outset of his appointment in 1981, Welch's style was essentially to confront and challenge. He clearly felt this was the best way (and perhaps the only way for him) to create the revolution in GE he believed was needed. The CEC met in the 'cave'. Welch comments:[3]

'We tee up a subject and then they take each other on. We end up with a consensus.'

A similar approach existed at the meetings Welch regularly attended at Crotonville, GE's major management development centre. Here the meeting place was called the 'pit'. Welch took on all-comers attending senior executive programs. Comments Judy Quinn on a visit by Welch to Crotonville:[4]

'And as always this pugnacious hockey player is looking for a fight.'

In the late 1980s, although the focus of the changes was still on being number one or two in each business area, and there was still the same prime focus on increasing earnings, there was much more talk on the importance of particular values. Shared information, openness, candour and speed were talked of as important values. More focus was also placed on the globalisation of GE's operations, a policy aided by acquisition.

A new approach to change

In 1988, following one of his visits to the 'pit' at Crotonville, Welch realised in spite of seven years of considerable downsizing, structural and other changes, he was still hearing the same complaints from managers about poor work practices, outdated attitudes and lack of vision in their top management that he had heard when he joined GE. Welch recalls:[5]

'And so finally I said, "Jim, We've got to change this. We've got to get these issues dealt with. We've got to put the person who knows the answer to these frustrations in the front of the room. We've got to force leaders who aren't walking the talk to face up to their people."'

A new and different phase began at GE. A serious attempt, still ongoing and still developing, was made by Welch *to engage the people of GE in a major program of corporate change.* What he now did was new for GE and for Welch. The program was called 'Work-Out'.

Work-Out

Work-Out began with four major goals. These were to:

- build trust
- empower employees
- eliminate unnecessary work
- introduce a new paradigm for GE.

Trust meant people should feel free to speak candidly about GE without jeopardising their careers so that new ideas for business improvement would be generated. Empowerment meant giving workers close to the task more power, and asking them to take more responsibility. Elimination of unnecessary work was aimed at improving productivity and lowering stress. And a 'new paradigm' was aimed at Welch's goal of a 'boundaryless' organisation, which involved the removal of barriers and distinctions, and encouraging cooperation within the corporation and with the external environment.

To achieve these aims, Welch felt he needed to involve the whole organisation in the discussions and 'force the leaders' to deal with the continued high levels of dissatisfaction about the way the businesses were run.

The first stage of Work-Out involved groups of thirty to a hundred employees of a particular business spending three days at an offsite conference centre discussing their common problems and trying to develop concrete proposals for their solution. Casual clothes patterned the meetings after the style of New England Town Hall meetings. 'Bosses' were not allowed in the discussions but returned on the final day when they had to make instant decisions about each proposal in front of the meeting. About 80 per cent of these recommendations achieved instant yes/no decisions and those where further study was needed had to be decided in a month. Hundreds of Work-Outs took place all over GE. The process built strong momentum for change. Every session had to end with a list of actionable items. Many improvements occurred from the immediate actions taken.

Comments Carol Kennedy:[6]

'GE people reel off countless improvements and cost savings as off-shoots of Work-Out. Communication blockages have been cleared and many bureaucratic practices swept away. Simple issues can be resolved on the spot, building confidence in the process. In GE speak it is known as "picking the low hanging fruit".'

Work-Out was soon accompanied by GE's move into 'Best Practices'. This followed a visit by a ten-member team who had spent a year study-ing leading national and overseas companies to find the secrets of their success. Welch became committed to Best Practices and assigned to Work-Out teams the task of spreading Best Practices throughout GE. Set up as cross-functional project teams, they were empowered with new information and better tools, such as process mapping, to redesign workplace processes and practices. These teams had clearly defined problems to deal with, and mandates to solve them. Some major suppli-ers were also involved. Progress was shared across the organisation by intrabusiness training as advances were made within the corporation.

GE's vice-chairman Paolo Fresco comments:[7]

'Very seldom in the past have hourly workers been asked to suggest how they could improve their productivity, how they could simplify their work patterns and that's what Work-Out does. The traditional organi-sation asked maybe 5 per cent of its people to do 95 per cent of its thinking. What we have tried to do is to get 100 per cent of the people to do 100 per cent of the thinking. And what we are finding, which ought not to be a surprise, yet it is a novelty for many bureaucratic organisations, is that the creative ability and contributing ability at all levels is tremendous.'

A later phase of Work-Out began in 1992. Called the 'Change Accelerating Program', it used Work-Out to develop a new breed of manager able to manage the 'boundaryless' organisation, which, by now, had become part of Welch's extended vision for GE.

Lessons from GE

The major lesson from the attempted changes by Welch at GE is the importance of Engagement to the achievement of change. In spite of seven years of unrelenting effort, Welch had been unable to get the commitment of the organisation at large to his vision. This was now significantly hampering his efforts to get real productivity and performance improvement, particularly at the workplace level. The lack of commitment is not surprising, though it apparently surprised Welch. The form the implementation of change had taken was to force change by setting high earnings performance goals, which could only be met in the short term by savage cost cutting. It was not until he embarked on a major program of Engagement—Work-Out—that a change in the way people worked across the organisation was achieved.

Impact on the many

For a vision to be effective in helping to achieve change it must be credible and motivating for the many. Welch's original vision was not. For many, Welch's vision meant the end of their employment with GE. Welch's perspective, rightly or wrongly, was different from theirs. Welch was looking from a corporate perspective, with a strong focus on corporate earnings. Many others were not.

Engagement works and has higher impact when people believe there is a future of which they will be a part. That belief took quite a few years to come for the many at GE.

Much evidence is accumulating that often downsizing does not improve employee productivity or job satisfaction, and results in a 'survivor syndrome'. Initial improvements in stock values are often not maintained. Downsizing is repeated as the first efforts do not produce the expected results. Our own study shows that staff reductions in general are not linked to effective change. In GE's case downsizing continued for at least the first five years. Of course, control of costs is imperative to a business at any time, but downsizing, which may provide short-term profit improvement, does not on its own produce effective change in the way people work. Furthermore, Engagement has less impact on Change Effectiveness in these circumstances. Welch's early efforts were largely in the area of Performance Management, an area on which he focused and in which he had great strength. This is important but insufficient on its own to generate effective change. It needs support from Engagement. When Engagement did occur in the form of Work-Out it unleashed what Welch's vice-chairman described as 'contributing creative ability'.

Lack of support from senior management

While lack of commitment from the organisation at large is not surprising, Welch might have expected more support from senior management generally and those with whom he had regular contact. Welch's impact on his more immediate senior management may well have been influenced by his personal Engagement capabilities. He was comfortable with his strong confrontational communication style but clearly others were not.

Tichy ran GE's development centre at Crotonville and was close to the situation. He comments:[8]

'In my view Welch's own behaviour slowed the very process of organisational change that he was so urgently trying to accelerate.'

Engagement capability exists both as a personal and corporate capability. Whatever Welch's personal Engagement capabilities may be, he did not succeed in winning enough support from senior management to his vision, though his power as the CEO and his strength in Performance Management assured some compliance and action. Even in an organisation as large as GE, personal skills in key individuals can still be important and have substantial effects.

Reaching the many

Welch was very aware of the need to get through to the vast numbers of GE employees. In 1983, quite early in his tenure, he said:[9]

> 'Without everybody embracing what we want to do, we haven't got a prayer.'

Yet many of the key actions he took, until the introduction of Work-Out eight years into his tenure, had not led to many embracing his intended changes. His efforts to get big positive change—involving many—foundered on a vision that most people could not embrace, the lack of support from many intervening senior managers and his prime focus and reliance on Performance Management. Welch argues that it was necessary to make the early painful changes first before introducing programs like Work-Out, but this may not be so. Its genesis in 1988 seems more to have come from a realisation that what he was doing was not in fact changing the way the organisation was working, and he needed to do something different. When he embarked on Work-Out, he did so with the energy and commitment that characterised his work.

Embedding aspects of Engagement

When Welch finally established the Work-Out program, he had essentially moved from trying to engage those with whom he had personal contact to trying to build a corporate competence in Engagement. He had worked on establishing some corporate values that were very relevant to Engagement—for example, openness, candour, sharing information and 'walking the talk'. He established corporate-wide structures and processes for Work-Out that helped to ensure that these values were given a chance to operate. The 'Town Hall' meetings, which were held across the corporation, were part of this. The corporation required that the meetings took place and their structure and format was fixed. They were facilitated by outside consultants. They were designed to foster better communication, and involved virtually all members of the corporation, not just a few. Their progress was monitored and the program extended, and they became part of the established practice and way of running the business.

The particular form that Engagement took in the design and implementation of Work-Out is not important for our purpose. What is important is that to get effective change GE, personified in Welch, found that it was necessary to go beyond a prime focus on earnings growth, cost reduction, downsizing, acquisitions and restructuring, and to engage his people across the organisation in the program of change. Clearly his hope was that Work-Out would affect both the leaders and 'the led' to change their behaviour, and encourage them to buy in and become committed to the development and achievement of a more unifying vision. GE's impressive results suggest that this is happening.

Change is often two way

Interestingly, Tichy believes the program changed Welch himself:[10]

> 'The cranked up ferocity of the CEO's interactions with subordinates was giving way to a more wholesome attitude—an urge to respect and empower people that began to seem convincing and genuine.'

Tichy quotes Larry Bossidy who shared the office of the CEO with Welch and went on to head up AlliedSignal with impressive results:[11]

> 'I do think there was a change, vividly, from yelling and screaming for performance, to a much more motivational kind of approach. He became a lot more understanding, much more tolerant. "Hey if you get the job done even though your style is different from mine, that's fine." He wasn't that way in the beginning.'

Welch says that the program did not change him, but:[12]

> 'I try to adapt to the environment that I'm in.'

However, in an interview with Marshall Loeb in 1995, Welch commented:[13]

> 'Early in my career, and in many other careers, there was way too much focus on making the numbers, on delivering the goods. And a lot less on the softer values of building a team, sharing ideas, exciting others.'

It would be surprising if Welch had not developed and thus changed during the tremendous experience of trying to revitalise such a major corporation. It would seem from his comment to Loeb that significant change had occurred but that Welch did not see it compressed into the same time frame as others.

Engagement in a public sector organisation: the NSW State Library

Managing effective change in a hundred-year-old state library seems a far cry from managing change in the hurly burly of the competitive corporate world. However, our study shows that reshaping capabilities, and Engagement in particular, are just as important in the public and not-for-profit world.

When Alison Crook was appointed chief librarian of the NSW State Library she took over a public institution steeped in tradition, short of funds, and facing a major explosion in information technology that would challenge its focus on its book-based services. It would have to change from being a 'collection-based-you-come-to-us' mentality to one able to use and benefit from the accelerating communications technologies that were fast changing the dissemination of information. The library would need to develop new Biztech to survive.

Crook acted as the catalyst of change. She changed the structure by abolishing the post of deputy, and creating a team of four directors who reported directly to her. Welch acted similarly at GE when he removed the large intervening management structure that was between him and the CEOs of the major groups. Unlike Welch, she then moved immediately into a major Engagement process.

Crook started an extensive round of consultation to prepare a statement of basic philosophy, which would eventually reposition the library in the marketplace. The draft statement was created by the executive team and Library Council and then actively work-shopped throughout the 400 members of the organisation to get feedback from everyone. It had a positive feel based round the notion of action. As in the case of Woolworths' slogan about fresh food service, the final mission statement was printed everywhere:

'We are creating for the community a thriving dynamic organisation, leading the New South Wales library system so that it becomes one of the world's best in collecting, conserving and communicating information.'

The statement went on all library publications, including staff identification cards, so that everyone was continually reminded of it. All new staff on joining were also taken through the statement by senior managers.

But a consultative approach did not end with a mission statement. Ongoing pathfinding became a collective activity, based round the top team and the interactive processes. Consultation and communication were constant and ongoing features of Crook's management. The outcomes of weekly executive meetings were discussed at the next level of directors and branch heads meetings. Focus groups of supervisors provided the next level of consultation and met with Crook every six weeks. General meetings of all staff were held every six months.

Stace and Dunphy, in their account of the changes at the library, comment:[14]

'In our interviews staff frequently referred to involvement in formulating the mission and commented on how it is used to guide the library. A new supervisor comments, "When I came here from another organisation, I found it very refreshing to see documents like a mission statement and major corporate goals. I could go to my section and discuss what we could do within this overall framework." '

An Innovative Technology Group, an internal think-tank, was established to improve staff understanding of developing technologies and how these could be applied to the library's mission of information dissemination. The group drew in people using different information technologies from various areas in the library. Close consultation with staff took place to develop the job and work design process, which became a feature of the changes. The Director of Management Services commented:[15]

> 'It was a time consuming but worthwhile process because it ensured commitment from both sides to the changes.'

Stace and Dunphy, who have researched change in many organisations, comment:[16]

> 'The amount of communication and consultation about strategic directions is unique in our research to date.'

Along with a strong consultative process, considerable training for the new jobs took place. This did not only involve technical training, but also a program on 'Managing Personal Growth', the cost of which, in the absence of internal funds for it, was met by an outside sponsor of the library. All managers and supervisors were asked to attend off-site management development programs in an effort to build a critical mass across the organisation to provide momentum for the changes.

Job rotation became an important part of the strategy to develop multi-skilling, as did the formation of teams and semi-autonomous work groups, which negotiated their performance standards with top management.

Before Crook's appointment the more demanding and interesting research requests that required database searching were handled by a specialist group of highly trained competent librarians. The executive group decided that in the interests of the library and its customers research should be the function, not of an elite group, but of the general reference library as a whole. The benefits of this change were considerable, both to clients and the wider body of the staff—but several of the specialists left the library as a consequence.

A proposal to introduce a system of financial rewards for outstanding performance was so strongly opposed through the consultative process that a series of service recognition rewards was created instead. Clearly the culture of public service to the community was still strong and management responded to it.

A strong consultative approach to reshaping is entirely compatible with strong leadership, which Crook and her team provided. Stace and Dunphy comment:[17]

> 'The combination of decisiveness, direction, high standards for performance and commitment to people has characterised the leadership style of the executive team.'

Crook provided firm leadership aided, not limited, by the strength of the substantial Engagement action that took place.

It can be argued that it is easier to engage with members on a substantial scale with a relatively smaller organisation. Equally clearly there are many small organisations where Engagement does not take place at all. Equally clearly, as the experience of Work-Out at GE shows, when management is minded to do it, it can be done for an organisation with hundreds of thousands of people.

As at the library, change rarely occurs without some difficulties, and some losers as well as winners. Other public libraries have also questioned the entrepreneurial approach and the establishment of new technically based user-pay services.

Nevertheless, the impact of the actions was an increased esprit de corps in the organisation. One staff member commented:[18]

> '... the whole profile of the library is up and we all feel proud to be up.'

Our study shows that Engagement is as necessary to effective change in the public sector as in the commercial sector. It also shows, as we will discuss in more detail in Chapter 8, that all three corporate reshaping capabilities are usually significantly weaker in the public sector. This throws even more weight on the need for personal reshaping skills of public sector organisational leaders.

Stace and Dunphy conclude their review of the changes:[19]

> 'The State Library of New South Wales has become the acknowledged leader on the Australian scene and is held in high regard internationally.'

Engagement and pathfinding

Engagement is engagement about something. It's not just about being involved with the organisation, or about effective communication. In terms of change it's about being engaged with the organisation's future—with its future directions. *Pathfinding*, which is about the future directions for the business, is thus an integral part of Engagement.

Engagement capability helps to meet three broad requirements for effective change:

- the need for the organisation's management and members to become committed to action
- the identification of and commitment to the changes or new directions for the firm
- the integration of action and direction across the firm.

Our illustrations have picked up elements of all of these requirements.

The link between Engagement and the competence we have identified as pathfinding is an important one. This link is one of the integrative aspects of Engagement. When people talk about finding new directions, strategy or pathways for their organisation's future operations, they often describe it as a new vision. Other people use vision to describe the purpose of an organisation—the reason for its existence. It is helpful to separate some important aspects so that what we mean by pathfinding is clear.

Collins and Porras in their book, *Built to Last*,[20] suggest that really outstanding companies, which they call visionary companies, are empowered by two separate factors. The first is having 'a core ideology', which is stable, enduring and clear, and which is preserved at all costs. The second is 'a relentless drive for progress that impels change' and forward movement in all that is not part of the core ideology.

The core ideology consists of the organisation's purpose, plus its core values. The *purpose* is the organisation's fundamental reason for existence *beyond just making money*. The *core values* are a small set of essential and enduring beliefs or guiding principles not to be compromised for financial gain or short-term expediency.

Among the examples Collins and Porras give that differentiate between the unchanging corporate ideology and the changing strategies and practices are:[21]

- **Boeing**: "Being on the leading edge of aviation; being pioneers" is a permanent unchanging part of its core ideology; commitment to building jumbo jets is part of a non-core strategy that can change.
- **Merck**: "We are in the business of preserving and improving human life" is a permanent, unchanging part of its core ideology; its commitment to research targeted at specific diseases is part of a non-core strategy that can change.
- **3M**: "Respect for individual initiative" is a permanent unchanging part of its core ideology; the 15 per cent rule (where technical employees can spend 15 per cent of their time on projects of their own choosing) is a non-core practice that can change.'

When people talk about 'corporate vision' they often include the purpose, the values and key strategies of the corporation. Sometimes they only include purpose and sometimes they add core values. These things are of course very strongly linked. When organisations face the need to make change and start to look in depth at their operations, and what they might do, they often find themselves looking simultaneously at all three—purpose, values and strategies. The statement, or restatement, of these is often a part of the new vision. Sometimes the renewal process actually gives them a new purpose or values that are more enduring or more possible than those they had earlier. The outstanding companies explored by Collins and Porras did not start as outstanding companies. In some cases they developed a vision many decades after their founding.

Pathfinding competence

We use the term pathfinding to focus primarily on the notion *of developing, crystallising and articulating new directions or strategies to accomplish the purposes and values of the organisation*. This has two aspects: identifying a viable business path, and establishing a shared awareness and appreciation of that path. It is about what is often, but loosely, described as strategic choice or strategy. The competencies involved can be personal—possessed by only a few individuals in the organisation—or corporate—collectively owned and embedded in the fabric of the organisation.

Pathfinding takes place in a number of different ways with very differing levels of organisational involvement. There is no one right way for it to occur. Involvement levels often depend on the values of the organisation, but some aspects of pathfinding depend highly on individual competence. An analysis of the competence will make this clearer. In broad terms, pathfinding consists of five key elements. These are:

- information gathering
- conceptualising the business and its context
- insight and option creation and analysis
- integration and crystallisation
- articulation and conveying.

While we can conceptually distinguish the elements, they do not necessarily occur, in practice, sequentially. Nor do they necessarily occur separately. Often the process is simultaneous.

Information gathering

Information, in extreme cases, may be gathered by one person, often by the leader, and becomes the basis on which decisions are ultimately made. At the other extreme, information may be gathered by a rigorous corporate-wide planning process, and by highly developed systems and practices in which many members of the organisation are involved. In other words, information gathering can be both a personal and a corporate competence.

Conceptualising the business and its context

This is developing an understanding about the business, which is needed before the information gathered can be used. This understanding involves two levels. The first level is an understanding of the separate aspects that make up the business. The second level is understanding the totality of the business—that is, how it all fits together and why it works. For example, the second element would conceptually knit together the organisation's purpose, values, capabilities, markets and so on. Understanding the separate parts of the business is something to which numbers of people could contribute. On the other hand, the ability to synthesise the knowledge about parts of the business depends on those few people who have either the knowledge or the comprehension to do this. This synthesising aspect of pathfinding is, therefore, personal rather than corporate.

Insight and option creation and analysis

This is essentially relating the knowledge of the business to the market and other external environments that are changing and developing. Here, while analytical skills are valuable, so are those qualities of creative insight, and intuitive perception, which process information in a different way, beyond the realm of logic and analysis. Competence in this area will be personal, but it will not be the sole province of the organisation's leadership. Nor indeed may some, or any, of the leaders have this skill. It may come from anywhere in the organisation as managers and members grapple with problems and see possible solutions to them. It may come from the use of external consultants. While the creation of insights is a personal competence, the ability to collect such insights can be both personal and corporate.

Integration and crystallisation

This is essentially the integration of the knowledge and insight into a future path or paths for the organisation. It combines the skills of pattern recognition, the ability to deal with cognitive complexity and the emotional aspects of making decisions. This is essentially a personal competence. It takes place in one or a few minds, or in a very small group in which true dialogue takes place. It results in the crystallisation of future paths. In indicating that a competence is personal, we do not suggest that it can only be held by one person. But when matters of real cognitive complexity are involved, when the dynamics are in constant flux and the relationships highly interactive, the integrative and crystallising competencies necessary will be the property of individuals. They are very hard to share between many minds.

Articulation and conveying

This is the ability to convey the new path to the organisation at large—a competence that can be both personal and corporate.

Corporate and personal pathfinding elements

Table 5.2 summarises how pathfinding competencies tend to be distributed in organisations. The capacity to think strategically is relatively rare. Some organisations rotate their brightest and best to many different roles and parts of the organisation as part of their managerial development. This

Table 5.2 Elements of pathfinding		
Pathfinding element	**Ownership**	
	Corporate	**Personal**
An ability to gather information relevant to future directions	*	*
An understanding of the separate aspects that make up the business and its context	*	*
An understanding of the *totality* of the business—its purpose, core values, current core competencies, markets and strategies		*
Creative insights into ways core competencies, markets or environments might develop and change	*	*
The ability to analyse, recognise patterns, synthesise and integrate the above and to crystallise the path or paths to follow		*
The ability to convey or sell the new paths	*	*

significantly increases the chance that high competence in pathfinding is developed in key individuals. Sometimes the skills are not available within the organisation, or, if they are, top management may seek some challenge to, or validation of, their own views. In our opening example of the managing director of the company in the resources sector, external consultants had been used to generate some recommendations about new directions for the company. This approach relies on the presence of analytical skills and techniques, and accumulated knowledge and understanding, which specialist consulting firms, and individuals in them, have acquired through experience and exposure to these situations.

The difficult task, when the formulation of new strategy is carried out by outside organisations, is to get inside organisational understanding, ownership or commitment to the new strategy. When this is not achieved, Engagement, the strongest single requirement of effective change, is not achieved. This is a problem faced particularly by the management of many government organisations. Change is recommended, often in great detail by external bodies, public enquiries, commissions, parliamentary committees, and so on. The organisation has to respond to proposals in which it has often played little part. In these circumstances Engagement is difficult, if not impossible, to achieve.

Woolworths illustrates an approach where an inside team did some initial work to recommend a particular strand of a new path—the move into fresh food—but where many other elements of the change emerged as the leadership engaged the staff over time in the new directions. At GE, initial direction came more as a response to financial targets, focused on cost reductions. At the NSW State Library it was developed from a strong consultative process. At Du Pont, which we visit later in this chapter, it emerged in cooperation with a trade union.

Pathfinding and its dependence on individuals

Our own study shows that *pathfinding is the competence most dependent for its strength on individuals*. This means that for an organisation to be strong in pathfinding, it needs individuals in its leadership with these personal skills. Without these individuals, it will be dependent for pathfinding on external parties. Corporate pathfinding skills are valuable, but in themselves are not enough. But our analysis also demonstrates that parts of the pathfinding process can be substantially affected by the collective competencies and knowledge of the organisation. Pathfinding that does not use these corporate competencies, particularly for the collection of information, the development of options and the conveying of the new directions, will be generally inferior.

Pathfinding is only a part of Engagement capability. Of the five capabilities, Engagement is the one whose strength is typically most dependent on individuals. That is to say, when we observed the organisations in the survey, many of them tended to rely on a few individuals for achieving Engagement. Yet the data also show that *when Engagement is a corporate competence, it is usually stronger than when it depends on key individuals*. Organisations therefore benefit when they can build up a corporate capability in Engagement. But while they may develop some corporate competence in pathfinding, its strength will still depend on the presence of an individual, or a few individuals, who possess personal pathfinding competence.

Pathfinding, to become meaningful in its contribution to effective change, needs to be part of the Engagement process. To get real Engagement, there must be some real sense of future directions and some real acceptance of those directions. That acceptance may, or may not, have been influenced by the way those directions have been developed. Of course, in the end, in terms of change success, the most important fact will be whether the new directions are validated by performance.

Interestingly, across the study, the appropriateness of the chosen directions was thought, by the executives who were part of it, to be well conceived. Of course, there is usually not just one right future direction for each organisation. There are a number of viable possibilities. In fact, 88 per cent felt the chosen directions for their change were right. It was the inability of the firm to actually make the changes, to achieve those directions, which was the major impediment to success. Having a clear idea of future directions, though necessary, without the commitment, capabilities and action to achieve them, is not enough to achieve effective change.

Frequently pathfinding is not seen as a part of the Engagement process. It is split off as a separate activity. There is no reason not to have special groups or external input to strategy development or the change process. What is vital is that the organisation, or a critical mass of it, needs to be managed in a way that achieves commitment to the new directions. That offers opportunity for leadership and trust, for personal Engagement skills, or for actions like communication, consultation, involvement and participation. But if actions—for example, training—are not taken to turn the concepts about new direction into commitment, and action to achieve them, our evidence says the changes are unlikely to be successful.

Actions that help Engagement

Finding new pathways along which the firm may develop is one thing. Engaging the people of the firm so that action is taken to achieve them is another. Many actions contribute to Engagement, and our study clearly highlights only some key common ones. Some actions not only contribute to Engagement but also are linked closely with the other reshaping capabilities. Training is a good example of this for it contributes strongly to the development of all capabilities. Some of the actions that are important to Engagement are: conveying a vision; recognising contributors to change; monitoring people; and consulting people about the changes. Some other actions also important to Engagement are discussed later in the chapters on Development (Chapter 6) and Performance Management (Chapter 7).

Conveying a vision

Effectively conveying a vision of the organisation's future is the action most strongly linked with high Engagement. This must be done in a way that people will accept because they can understand it and find it credible. Without this, the commitment and enthusiasm, which is an important part of Engagement, will not be achieved. Management often finds difficulty in doing this. Many staff might, for example, believe the vision requires actions well beyond the organisation's capabilities. Or, it may be unappealing to them in terms of their values and self-image.

This is a problem many banks faced in the seventies and eighties in trying to project a vision of themselves as sales-oriented organisations. The mass of their staff had a sense of personal identity tied to professional skills other than sales. They valued their credit, procedural and service skills, and often the status of being in a position of power to grant loans. In their eyes, selling was a dubious and somewhat disreputable sort of profession. Additionally they generally lacked selling skills and potential role models with those skills. This vision was to them both unappealing and difficult to attain. The vision was in fact no more than a recognition of economic circumstances. Nonetheless, it took many banks a decade or more to make real progress towards this vision, and many still struggle with it today.

Recognising contributors to change

Recognising the efforts of those who contribute to change impacts upon the effectiveness of change. Supporting change not only involves effort, it also often involves risk. Those involved in change are attempting things in which they often have little skill and experience. The chance of failure or error is higher than with established activities. People who take risks to support change, particularly contentious change, need to be recognised and rewarded. Recognition also motivates and encourages others. This keeps up the energy level, which, as change absorbs considerable energy, is important to Change Effectiveness.

Although much is often made of the value of 'change champions', our study indicates that using them is typically less effective than recognising the efforts of contributors in general. Change champions are more valuable when the focus of change is on technology. Often in these cases, the champions have a technical role, which has a training element in it. However, when the focus is not on new technology, but, for example, on culture or structural change, champions have less impact.

Change does not usually take place as a discrete activity. It is fundamentally interwoven with the current operational activities. It is the staff who are currently producing and selling products and services, and serving customers, who must make changes in the way they work. They must make these changes as they continue to carry out their day-to-day activities. They sometimes need to make trade-offs between actions that enhance either Change Effectiveness or Current Business Performance. They are also in a position to identify actions that can help change without detracting from current performance. They can also, if minded, find ways to discredit good change ideas. Change champions do not often have this combination of operational and reshaping responsibilities. The contribution they can generally make is much less than that of the operational management and staff. Cases where change champions are successful are those where they are actually creating an operation separate from the current business operations.

Monitoring people and performance

Monitoring is important to Engagement because it enables feedback about how well the changes are understood and accepted, and about the impact of actions that are being taken to achieve it. The inclusion of monitoring as part of Engagement may surprise some. But Engagement is not just about communicating, or recognising contribution, or seeking people's advice on or involvement in change, though these are all valuable. It is also about action that pays off commercially. Our study shows the process has to be purposive. Pathfinding, plus monitoring, plus the other actions, helps to ensure it becomes focused on achieving outcomes.

Monitoring also identifies those individuals who are making a significant contribution to the change and is often a precondition to showing recognition of those individuals. Recognising contribution to the change is a feature of organisations with high Engagement capability. This was an outstanding feature of the changes in Woolworths. Equally, monitoring enables identification of those individuals who are not supporting the change. Dealing with these people is important because, aside from affecting their own Engagement with the change, such lack of supportive action by some undermines the motivation and work of others. In these circumstances, monitoring, with appropriate follow-up action, helps to maintain Engagement as at Nuclear Electric. Monitoring was clearly absent from the tale of the two CEOs with which we started this chapter.

Consulting people about the changes

Consulting people enables information flow and participation in shaping the change before final decisions are made. It means getting into the act before it happens and when it happens. It implies opportunity to make some contribution to developing the new directions for the firm and thus to pathfinding action. It exposes people to information and different options for action. It helps form opinion and judgment. It implies a sense of belonging and value. It offers the opportunity of ownership of outcomes. It has the potential to gain commitment and thus it can be crucial not only to short-term action but also to sustained action over time.

Consultation is essentially two way, whereas communication is sometimes, perhaps often, only one way. Consultation draws on the insights and knowledge of the people of the organisation and thus gives managers a rich base of additional experience and understanding. If managers depend only on their own insights and understandings, they are likely to limit their perspectives and narrow their options for action. Part of being an effective manager is about using resources other than your own. Consultation is one way of increasing resources, particularly the vital resource of information.

Widespread consultation is particularly important to effective change when the changes are across the organisation and a large number of people need or want to know, and have a contribution to make. While change is about changing organisations, it is also about changing people. Changing people is helped by shared experiences and views. Consultation facilitates this. Of course, consultation is not just about individual interaction. Much of the most valuable consultation takes place within teams and between groups when cross-fertilisation of ideas takes place on a wider scale. The ways in which such interactions take place, and the sharing, shaping and reshaping of knowledge, views and attitudes, will take different forms in different organisations.

Engagement and organisational states

In Chapter 4 we explored the impact that organisational states have on Change Effectiveness and described a number of states that enhance it. We said states are important because they are pervasive influences on large numbers in the organisation. States impact on the collective attitudes and behaviours across the organisation and also on performance.

When action takes place to engage the members of an organisation, it strengthens states that enhance change. Table 5.1 highlighted particular states that are strongly linked to Engagement. These are esprit de corps, high workloads, low conflict, commitment and understanding.

Engagement is strongly linked to esprit de corps. Aspects of esprit de corps include a sense of unity, a willingness of people to talk openly and the existence of trust. These were some of the explicit aims of GE's Work-Out program. They were central to the changes at the NSW State Library. Engagement implies trust; it benefits from openness; it helps to foster unity. It is not surprising that it fosters esprit de corps.

Firms strong in Engagement are characterised by high workloads. When people are willing to work hard it implies a commitment, a motivation and an energy level, which are understandably linked with being engaged.

Our study shows that Engagement action has a powerful effect in reducing the impact of negative states, in particular conflict, resistance and anxiety. Engagement action has strong impact on lowering conflict, the most powerful state for reducing Change Effectiveness. The actions of involving people and consulting with them also has an important bearing on reducing conflict. Pathfinding actions that identify new directions for the firm do the same. Conflict can arise not only because people do not want to go in a particular direction, but also often because they have no real idea what the change really means. Confusion and a feeling of being kept in the dark, which raises apprehensions easily, turns into opposition and conflict. While a great deal of conflict arises because of vested interests, a lot also occurs because people, who are equally well intentioned, have quite legitimately different views about which changes will be most valuable to the organisation. There may be no forum or opportunities to debate and resolve these conflicting views. Those with the most power may not necessarily be those with the best knowledge, insight or judgment. Real consultation provides the best chance of avoiding or lessening conflicts of this kind.

Lastly Engagement helps to produce the states of commitment and understanding—the two most powerful states that aid Change Effectiveness. All of the main actions we briefly noted earlier—conveying a vision, recognising contributors to change, monitoring people and consulting people about the changes—are directly focused on the creation of these important states.

Engagement in Robert's store

In Chapter 1 we met Robert. On his first morning in the store, he faced a number of differing viewpoints from his managers on the factors responsible for the store's poor performance. Robert soon realised that identifying, developing and crystallising what was the right direction for the store's future would be a major task. Until there was some shared agreement there would be little focus and energy for improvement.

Because of his own experience, Robert understood one of his group's major distinctive competencies was in its central buying activities, which it had spent decades developing. Another lay in the strength the group derived from the focus of the stores on selling and merchandising. These two major operational capabilities enabled the group to notch up continuous and substantial progress year after year. Both these competencies provided lower costs and better productivity through specialisation.

Robert's store, and a lot of its energy, had been focused on the differences between its own immediate local environment and that of the rest of the group—differences that clearly existed. However, the managers in the store, who had enthusiastically ventured into local buying to respond to the needs of a different set of customers, had no special skills, experience or purchasing power to do it well. Such skills would take some years to develop, if indeed that were possible, within the context of the group's overall operations and policies. Some welcomed the local buying, because it enlarged their potential skill basis and power. The energy some managers were putting into this new interest detracted from the time and energy they previously spent in managing their departments and looking after their established customers.

The store was now using a sizeable proportion of its total inventory for these new local customers, which meant that a reduced variety of stock was available for its established customers. But even so, it was also not providing a real choice for its new and less affluent customers compared with local competitors who specialised and had strength in that kind of business. The store's image had become fragmented and its customer appeal diffused. It had lost much of its attraction to its traditional customers who departed more quickly than new ones arrived.

Performance requires an alignment between the firm's positioning and its existing or developing competencies—a matching between what it is trying to do and its skills to do it. As markets and competencies change, it is easy for a mismatch to develop, as it had in Robert's case. The need for change therefore often arises as a need for realignment between positioning and competencies. Sometimes the realignment will require the firm to change its market. It is certainly likely to be easier to change an organisation's market than to change its competencies. But sometimes the firm will need to develop new competencies.

A good retail business can be built on central or local buying, or on poor or wealthy customers. There are major world players successfully using quite different buying methods and marketing approaches. But to compete effectively the firm's competencies must give it competitive advantages for its particular market/s. Robert's did not. They had become out of alignment. His store was trying to serve two different markets. In the process it was undermining and eroding its competencies for one market. But it did not have, and in practice would not get them, in the other.

After much discussion with his managers, Robert concluded that he would have to stop the local buying and go back to a fully centrally bought operation. As each day passed, he became more aware of this, but increasingly aware too that he would need the support of the people in the store to make effective change. He knew he could not achieve that alone.

Of course there was no certainty that such a course of action would be successful. A number of his staff preferred the local buying arrangements and would see such action as turning the clock back. As an ex-central buyer such action could be viewed as prejudiced and not supporting his own managers. How would he get their support? And Robert could not be sure that the market was there for the group's traditional standard and type of merchandise. After all the store had not been very successful before, and had developed some local buying because of that. So he would have to make the changes involved effectively and then run the store better than it had been run before. Robert was sure he had good reasons for what he wanted to do.

However, solving the problem intellectually and conceptually in his own mind was one thing. Getting people to understand, accept and implement it enthusiastically and effectively would be quite another.

Part of the reality with which Robert had to deal was that his store belonged to a much larger group, which had its own group competencies. Very many managers face such situations and need to change or revitalise their operations as part of a larger entity. This will narrow the field of possible action. If the group's competencies are strong, it may be the basis of real success. When the group's competencies are weak, however, change will be needed in the group as a whole. Sometimes an individual unit sets a new pattern for such a change. Sometimes a unit's special needs cannot be met, and a sale of the unit is the only solution. Such was an issue that helped Robert in confronting his store's reality.

Robert had to change the mindsets of his managers about how they could be more successful if the store reverted completely to central buying and they specialised in the job of managing their departments. He communicated with his managers openly, fully and passionately about his beliefs on the future direction of the store, and he listened to what they had to say. It took at least three months of daily communication and personal daily involvement before people really began to think through and believe his message. It surprised Robert that he had to repeat himself many, many times before managers and staff began to grasp the ideas and discuss them with him.

His message had two strands. The first was predicated on the success of the local buying, the second on its failure. The first said, if we are successful with our current local buying policy, our store will be sold. Why? The group's skills and its heavy investment are in the combination of its established and embedded central buying skills and its focused local selling operations. A big retail group will not keep one store out of many with a different policy that depends on local buying skills, which are essentially transient. The store will be sold off when a suitable offer materialises. The second message was, if we are unsuccessful with our local buying policy, we will also be sold. It's just that the price will be lower. The two messages combined to say, 'if we want to be sold, let's keep on doing what we are doing'.

As managers thought about it, they became increasingly aware of the enormous real benefits of staying in the powerful and respected group to which they belonged, rather than being sold to someone else. They had not realised before that the consequences of being successful in local buying might result in the sale of their store. They had in fact seen it as a way of safeguarding their future. They were in fact thinking at an operational level—not at the strategic level that was needed. People looking for solutions to strong and immediate pressures often fail to see the longer term consequences of their proposed actions.

The second point Robert made was that the group already carried the costs of its major central buying operation. As local buying had grown, managers had to give more time to it and less time and effort to specialising as managers of their departments. Some had appointed an additional section head under them as the manager gave more time to buying activities, some of which took place away from the store. In a few cases the section head did the buying. Robert felt that had lowered their selling management efficiency and increased its cost. He argued that specialising entirely as managers would enable them to manage wider groups of departments and earn more money since the costs of buying were already borne by the group. There was considerable doubt if not cynicism about this since they would appear to be returning to a situation that had not worked well before. Managers felt they would lose their buying and get nothing in return. Robert therefore provided an example.

The hardware manager had been one of the managers who had given early support to Robert's views. Robert merged some sections in this area, enlarged the manager's responsibilities, stopped the local buying in them and simultaneously significantly increased the manager's pay. The latter fact became quickly known round the store. Quite rapidly local buying lost some of its appeal and very soon some managers confided in Robert that they had never really liked it or thought it the right answer to the store's problems! Robert was also able to arrange the transfer of an outstanding young section head who had shown skill in buying women's fashions into the central buying group, a move that accelerated her career and went down well in the store.

What Robert was doing was helping to build a state of *understanding*, one of the most powerful states in achieving effective change. He was also sending a signal that contributors to the change process would benefit. His own personal communication style, which was predominantly two way, gave managers a sense of involvement and helped to lower anxiety.

Of course, Robert was backing his own judgment of what he thought was the right direction for the store. He was making an individual contribution as a pathfinder. He believed the group's competitive advantage lay in its combination of centralised buying and localised selling and his store had been moving down a track that would fail. He also knew that the store would have to be managed much better than before. In this he was, of course, backing himself. Managers who succeed do this. He could well have been wrong. Change is never risk free. But luckily his early moves were rewarded in increased sales, which increased managers' confidence that the changes would work and that they would benefit from them.

Other managers may have taken quite different actions. Robert's actions are simply one of the ways Engagement can be approached. He clearly based a significant part of his approach on the managers' self-interests, as a way of moving in the direction he felt was right for the firm. He used the leverage of personal interest, which in this case was positive to his policy. Motivating people, which is an important aspect of Engagement, has to deal with realities.

Robert did, of course, many other things to achieve Engagement. He was assisted by the embedded Engagement competencies that his store and group possessed, particularly in the area of communication, which we explore later in Chapter 10. He was also careful to communicate effectively with the central buying team who were more than anxious to provide special help to the store to bring them back 'into the fold'. He also often consulted with his boss at head office. Integration is an important part of Engagement capability. The new directions for Robert's store needed the active engagement of people outside the store, in particular, in central buying and central management. Robert took action to make sure he got it.

This was a case where the managers were reluctant to make a change and particular actions were taken to induce them to do so. Action, in this case by Robert, was critical to shifting opinion. Once over the hump, the managers found it worked and very soon became fully engaged and committed.

What of course works for GE, or Woolworths, or the NSW State Library, or Robert's store, to achieve Engagement with their particular type of staff, technologies, industry norms and specific situation may not necessarily be the action for you or your organisation. The approach at Du Pont to achieve Engagement, described below, illustrates a quite different but effective approach.

Robert's actions turned out to be successful. Perhaps he was just lucky. But with a clear store focus on the group's typical customers, the full support of the central buying organisation and his own store's efforts in selling and merchandising, the store was able to attract many more customers from the surrounding suburbs and significantly increase its business performance.

Engagement at Du Pont

The situation in Du Pont's plant at Girraween in Sydney was very different from that faced by Robert. The actions by its manager, Don Wirth, illustrate a different approach because the circumstances were different though the need for Engagement was the same. Wirth comments:[22]

> 'By 1989 I came to the realisation that I did not have a successful change process. It all depended on me. I was on every team and group. After a while I realised I was the champion in each team. When I was not there, the group collapsed. I think in the end I gave up. I saw it wasn't going to work. I needed something which was self-sustaining— something which did not just depend on me. Dick Warburton [then managing director of Du Pont Australia] allowed me and my top team the space to do it.'

Many managers have found themselves in situations like this when they felt everything depended on their own personal efforts and initiatives, and that their energy was beginning to wilt under the constant demands and pressure.

In 1986, Du Pont's photofilm conversion plant at Girraween in the western suburbs of Sydney was facing closure. When compared with other Du Pont plants elsewhere in the world, it was clearly inefficient. The cost of converting imported roll film into consumer and industrial film products was around twice that of other Du Pont plants. Protective tariffs in Australia were about to be dismantled. Such an inefficient organisation could not survive against Asian and Japanese competition.

Yet, by 1993, the operation had been transformed. Productivity had been dramatically increased and Girraween exported 70 per cent of its product into the fiercely competitive world of South East Asia. By 1993, the Du Pont world group had closed down its own Japanese plant at Shimozo and the Girraween plant in Sydney was supplying the Japanese market.

Without the introduction of new equipment, total film conversion costs were down to less than a third of 1986 costs and were actually lower than the target set by Du Pont under its 'world's best practice' program. Production output per person had risen throughout the period and in 1993 alone had doubled in some lines. Cycle time requirements showed the same pattern, dropping in some products to a quarter of the time required at the beginning of the period. Customer complaints had fallen even more steeply than the cycle times, and the plant was continually improving in every aspect of its operations with 360 individual improvements coming from the shop floor teams as well as from the management in that year.

It was not only the plant operations that had been reshaped. The attitudes of those who worked in the plant had been similarly changed. As one manager commented:[23]

'In 1986 there was a denial by the workers of the possibility of beating overseas competition.'

In 1993 a plant supervisor commented:[24]

'Now nothing seems impossible.'

At the time Wirth was appointed site manager of Girraween, the plant was not unlike a number of Australian manufacturing operations of that time. There was distrust and antagonism between workforce, management and unions. The legal system of industrial arbitration added to the polarisation of attitudes is reflected in these comments:[25-27]

'I had been trained in a system that saw management as basically giving orders and direction.'—supervisor

'If something could be done better, workers were not game to speak up.'—shop floor employee

'People didn't believe the company—there was a lack of trust.' —operator

Wirth was a chemical engineer by training who had a wide background in engineering consulting and two years' previous experience as a plant manager. His initial actions were to make some improvements in the plant operations, introduce some new shift arrangements and negotiate some personnel reductions on various machines, but he said:[28]

'I didn't do anything special in the first year or so.'

During this time Wirth absorbed some of the ideas emanating from Du Pont headquarters in the United States about leadership, teamwork and managing process based on the work of Charles Krone. His first action in this area was to establish a consultative committee consisting of union delegates and management. It met monthly with a formalised agenda and published minutes. He comments:[29]

'We put everything out in the open.'

He then embarked on establishing teams to tackle a number of operationally related issues:[30]

'I established a whole host of basically TQM style teams which included supervisors and operators and many people in the plant. We covered areas like just in time management; manufacturing process; safety; benchmarking; people development and so on. There was a lot of activity. The groups generally lasted for about nine months before they died. Only the safety and people development groups lived on.'

It was at this time that he realised that it all depended on him. He also realised that was not a basis for the future.

A vision for the future

As part of some national industrial negotiations concerned with restructuring the workforce's award system, Wirth invited the principal union, the Miscellaneous Workers' Union, to sit down with the consultative committee to discuss, 'How the people and the company could work together in the 21st century.'

Wirth chaired the meetings. The union provided a senior official and a research officer. There were five union delegates from the plant and two members of the management. The group met ten times over a four month period and each meeting lasted half a day. He comments:[31]

'I think the management had little to say; we basically listened. We discussed anything people felt would be important to our ongoing relationship. The union put down eight categories for discussion: increasing worker knowledge, improving employee responsibility, prosperity of the business, need for flexibility and others. Out of these discussions came the Joint Beliefs Statement of how Du Pont and the Miscellaneous Workers' Union would work together for the future.'

The Joint Beliefs Statement is a three page document with forty-two agreed points broken into eleven sections. They covered: work organisation; increases in skill and knowledge; growth; recognition and reward; flexible team make-up; contributions of individuals; greater knowledge of the plant; business and direction; more responsibility; and prosperity. The themes that run through the forty-two points are: team-work; the importance of the individual; skill development; equitable treatment of people; flexibility for both individuals and the company; enhanced workforce knowledge; and better communication of corporate purpose.

Engagement: a vision of working together at Girraween

In Du Pont's factory at Girraween, Engagement was substantially triggered by the development of a vision for the future to which the management, union and workforce had contributed, and which was credible for them. The vision was not about market direction or positioning, as it was with Woolworths and, to some extent, the NSW State Library. It was not about generating more profit, which was the early focus of change at GE. It was not about sticking to the basis of competitive advantage, as it was in Robert's store. It was about how they—the management, workforce and unions—could all work together. This vision, in fact, addressed their paramount need. Before they could achieve anything else, they had to alter their mindsets and their behaviour about their relationships. After that slowly altered, other things became poss-ible. Action and communication, from beginning to end, were constant features of the process, and though these did not manifest themselves in success in every case, the impact they had on the workforce was cumulative and finally successful.

The change at Du Pont was primarily focused on changing the culture of the plant. Changes focused on culture usually take longer than other types of change. Corporate culture is a shared property of the people of the business. It can only change through the combined actions of the people who make up the organisation. It cannot be successfully imposed by the leader, though leaders may have a strong influence on the shape it takes. Creating a vision and conveying it through action is vital to the success of cultural change. The joint understanding reached at Du Pont was such a vision. But cultural change calls heavily on all three reshaping capabilities. Unfortunately, many organisations facing the need for cultural change are weak in the capabilities they need most. That is why it calls on conscious action and sustained effort to change people's mindsets, beliefs and behaviours. In the next chapter we will follow further changes at Du Pont, which involved Performance Management and Development, the other two reshaping capabilities, but which built on the successful Engagement process we have briefly outlined.

Dependency on the skills of key individuals

Engagement capability as a whole is, in practice, more dependent upon key individuals than any other capability. As we discussed earlier, within that pattern of general dependency, pathfinding—a contributing competence to Engagement—is much more dependent upon individuals than the rest of the capability. The higher dependence of pathfinding on individuals simply stems from the nature of pathfinding. Organisations have to live with this situation. But when Engagement as a whole depends on key individuals it tends to be weaker and therefore not in the interests of the organisation. Organisations can take action to lessen this dependency. Our study shows the more Engagement becomes a corporate capability the stronger it becomes. Building corporate capability in Engagement therefore is an important management task in view of the crucial role that Engagement plays in the effective management of change. In Chapter 10 we discuss and illustrate how capabilities can be embedded in an organisation.

Summary

Engagement is the capability with the strongest link to achieving effective change. It is about engaging the people of the organisation in mind, heart and action in the business and its future. It is needed throughout the change process. It has to affect a critical mass of the organisation's managers and staff. Its prime focus is on people and the future. It stimulates hope, lowers conflict and anxiety, and increases esprit de corps and understanding. It involves people in the change and predisposes them to act. It resonates across organisations and helps to integrate them in vision and action. It is usually the weakest managed area of change and yet it is frequently the most important. In practice it typically depends more on individuals than the other capabilities, yet when it becomes embedded in the organisation it is strengthened.

Much has been written by many authors on the many separate competencies and different aspects of what we have called Engagement. Each particular aspect has been subject to exploration in depth in books and articles and used by countless managers. What has not been recognised is that each important aspect is, in fact, only a part of a greater capability, the sum of which is greater than the parts. It is the combination of the differing competencies that links the many aspects into a cohesive whole, and forms and encompasses a capability that we have called Engagement. It is action based on this capability that impacts on organisational states and strongly enhances the likelihood of achieving effective change.

CHAPTER 6

Development

Focus on the future

A JAPANESE ENGINEER was sent to Australia to fix a problem at an electricity generating plant. The electricity was being produced by twin 600 megawatt generators driven by the steam from massive coal-fired boilers. The two generators had been manufactured by the engineer's employer. One of them had developed a slight wobble, as sometimes occurs. As yet it was not a major problem, but unchecked it would become a disaster.

The engineer, who was highly experienced, spent the first day studying the problem. As it happened, it was not unique, and his company had a well-documented procedure for correcting it. So, assisted by several of the Australian engineers at the plant, he began the week-long procedure to fix the problem.

Mid-morning on the second day he mentioned to one of the Australian engineers that he thought there was a faster way to fix this particular problem than was documented in his company's manual. It could actually be done in two days instead of five.

'That's great,' said the Australian engineer. 'So we can get this baby back on line a few days earlier.'

'Not so,' the Japanese engineer advised him. 'The manual says there is a particular way to do it and we must follow the manual.'

Despite all the protests and pressure from the Australian engineers the Japanese engineer was adamant. They would follow the manual. That was in fact what they did, and they completed the repairs successfully in the scheduled time.

At the end of the assignment one of the Australian engineers drove his Japanese colleague to the airport. On the way, he asked him what he would be working on when he returned to Japan. To his surprise he said he would be revising the manual for fixing the problem on which they had just worked.

It turned out that the Japanese engineer was his company's top authority for these types of problem. When he returned, he would rewrite that section of the manual and thereafter the problem would always be fixed in two days instead of five.

While there are a number of varied and interesting aspects to this story, it demonstrates in a very concrete way the difference between operational and reshaping capabilities—between action to perform today and about changing things for future performance. The engineer was fundamentally concerned with reshaping capability, in this case Development. Creating something that would help the organisation in the future was actually more important than immediate performance. His learning would be embedded in the organisation's permanent procedures and systems and, in due course, these would be used by his colleagues, and the organisation's Biztech would be developed. The organisation would be able to provide better goods and services.

Development is unmistakably about the future. As Figure 3.4 in Chapter 3 showed, of the five capabilities, Development makes the least contribution to Current Business Performance. As many managers will have experienced, there is frequently a real clash between the use of resources for today's and future performance. This is seen, for example, in the choice between sending someone on a training program that will develop them for the future or keeping them on a current job needed for immediate performance. The difficulties internal trainers have in getting people released from work for training is matched by the number of cancellations external providers of management education experience because of 'the pressure of work' or because something 'important' has come up. But, of course, the choice between today and tomorrow,

between putting effort and resources into today's operational performance or building something for future use, extends over very many
aspects of a business.

Development capability

Development is the capability to develop all the resources—personal,
physical, technological, and systems and processes—needed to achieve
the firm's future directions. We start with an example of one aspect of
Development capability.

Motorola

Motorola is one of the world's leading providers of electronic communication systems, components and services for world-wide markets. Its stream
of successful products and its long-term growth and performance attests to
its Development capability. Motorola has among its core values:[1]

> 'Continuous self-renewal; tapping the "latent creative power within
> us"; and continual improvement in all the company does—in ideas, in
> quality, in customer satisfaction.'

Motorola has developed its own industrial university, which is larger
than many of the world's best-known academic institutions. With a
main campus at Illinois, Motorola University has fourteen delivery
centres and works in close collaboration with the business units scat-
tered across the world. Almost half Motorola's employees are outside
the United States and training is coordinated and integrated across the
company. Maintaining facilities and programs calls for substantial ongoing investment. The university acts not only in a training and educational role, but also as a change agent in Motorola:[2]

> 'It's the role of Motorola University to understand, design and develop
> learning interventions to drive critical business issues. We balance being

responsive to what our customers are asking for with the need to think about long-term learning interventions and initiatives that may be needed to deal successfully with market pressures 10 or 15 years down the road.'

Senior managers from the university's design and delivery centres work closely with key managers in the operating units in identifying critical business issues as part of an integrated business training planning process. This helps in envisioning the company's future requirements for training and in developing 'technology road maps' for the future.

Motorola sees training as a key competitive advantage. It has modelled the pay-offs from its employee training programs and concludes that some programs yield $33 for every dollar spent.

For an organisation with a culture that prizes development, not only is the content of what is taught continuously developed but the means of delivery gets the same development focus:[3]

'About 25 per cent of our training courses are ready to go on the web or our intranet via satellite delivery, CBT [computer-based training], or e-mail and CD ROM. We also have advanced teaching manufacturing laboratories and a virtual reality lab.'

Of course, Motorola believes in lower costs and high market penetration, like its competitors, but its predominant behaviour is to develop those competencies that underlie its business technologies and deliver value to its customers, rather than pursuing direct cost reductions and downsizing based mainly on financially driven strategies.

We are not suggesting an organisation needs its own university in order to have a strong Development capability. But we are sure that Development capability is needed if an organisation is to change effectively and grow. This requires commitment to long-term goals, competencies and action.

Table 6.1 lists the key contributing competencies that our study found were linked to Development capability, and also the corporate states and some actions that are typically linked with this capability.

Table 6.1 Development: competencies, states and actions		
Contributing competencies	Linked key states	Linked key actions
Systems and practices development	Esprit de corps	Training
	Empowerment	Consulting
Developing resources	Systems and	Not replacing people
Resource application	practices suitability	Introducing technology
Pathfinding	Commitment	and systems
Planning		

Contributing competencies to Development capability fall into two related groups. The first group—systems and practices development and developing resources—consists of the abilities to develop the resources that will be needed for the organisation's future, and the systems and practices to underpin them. It is to do with the 'what' of Development— what the firm needs to build in the way of competencies and new resources. This aspect of Development is primarily focused on the improvement or creation of new operational capabilities, which enable the firm to deliver value to its customers. Development builds the resources—the people, the skills and the systems—that will be needed to form new capabilities.

The second group—resource application, pathfinding and planning— is more concerned with the direction that Development takes—the 'where and how' of Development. Development is not usually an end in itself. It is a means to the end of enabling the company to perform more effectively. So the Development needs to be the 'right' Development to be of real value to the organisation. Getting it right therefore calls heavily on pathfinding, planning and resource application so that the Development is in alignment with the organisation's direction, strategy and commercial needs.

It is the integration of these two groups of competencies that forms the capability. Development is not effective unless and until it is fused with the directions the company wishes to follow. And the direction will not be achieved unless the organisation's resources, systems and practices are built to support it.

Development and Change Effectiveness

Development has a very positive impact on Change Effectiveness. Like Engagement, it affects the success of a wide variety of changes, but, understandably, particularly those changes focused on new developments. Some organisations put great weight on Development, invest significantly in it, and succeed in building capabilities in this area. Motorola is a good example and there are many others. But they are substantially outnumbered by those that do not, and whose need to make effective change is hampered by its absence.

While Engagement, in a sense, stimulates and motivates the organisation to the prospects of change, Development empowers people in the organisation to be able to do something about it. This of course also motivates them, but at a deeper level and in a way that leads to the sustaining of motivation. We will see this in the continued story of Du Pont a little later.

Development capability lays the foundation for the improvement, development and creation of the firm's future Biztech. It is also manifested in action to institute systems, processes and procedures that result in efficient and effective work, and which develop the firm's resources for its future. But, although its focus is on the operational future of the business, it can also contribute to the building and maintenance of the firm's reshaping capabilities.

Investment in resources for future performance is much easier to make when the return can be estimated and measured and is reasonably certain. This is often relatively easy to do for investment in plant and equipment, or even for new systems, but it is often difficult to do for less tangible investments. For example, investing in management development, which in turn develops the firm's future, or in Engagement competencies such as better communication, is much more difficult to quantify in financial terms. Without a commitment to the long-term success of the organisation, investments in developments that are hard to quantify on normal commercial criteria, but are often very important to effective change, are hard to justify. When the organisation has a short-term focus, developments of this sort are often simply not made.

Development capability can be both personal and corporate. As a corporate capability, it will be found in systems and practices that foster Development. For example, planning systems that highlight gaps in capabilities, systems of human resource development and practices of investment evaluation all illustrate how Development can become a corporate capability as well an individual one.

Development capability is typically weak

Responsibility and accountability for Development capability is often diffused across the organisation. Furthermore, the normal management processes of goal setting and review and reward, which help to maintain the effort behind the application of operational capabilities, rarely apply to Development. Bottom line performance is relatively easily measured. Developing skills in people, or new processes, or improved systems, while recognisable, are much harder to measure and often occur over long time spans not catered for in the normal appraisal processes. The difficulty of measurement, the diffusion of responsibility, the lack of accountability, and the infrequency of audit and related rewards undermine the strength of Development. This together with the real clash between the needs of today and tomorrow, at the coalface, as well as at the top of the organisation, goes some way in explaining why Development capability is typically weak.

Motivation needed to build Development capability

Strong motivation and a long-term perspective are needed to build Development capability. While motivation may come from many sources, some organisations are motivated to take Development action in response to new opportunities or threats, which results in a new strategic direction. This was the case at Woolworths. It needed to develop not only individual skills in buying and selling fresh foods, but a whole host of associated corporate competencies in inventory management and distribution as well as dedicated resources and systems. Pressure to move into new information technology at the NSW State Library provided both an opportunity and a threat, and required Development action. Later in this chapter we will see how StorageTek's decision to alter its strategy and enter new markets required it to develop new competencies, values, roles and structures.

There are many well-known organisations that have Development as part of their core ideology and vision. This provides a constant motivation. Motorola, which we mentioned earlier in this chapter, is one well-known example. Other examples include: 3M, Hewlett Packard and Boeing in the United States; Sainsburys, British Airways, and Marks and Spencer in the United Kingdom; and Lend Lease, the Department of Defence and Macquarie Bank in Australia. These, and many others, value Development or continuous self-improvement and renewal. This focuses them on Development, not just in response to specific opportunity but more as a way of corporate life. This acts to motivate the organisation into a continual drive for Development and renewal. In the process a culture supporting Development is built up and this helps to sustain the capability. 3M and Sony illustrate different aspects of this.

Development at 3M

3M like any company, including the best in the world, is not immune to troubles and difficulty, but it is buttressed by its purpose and values to develop itself and new products. It has consistently produced new products that have fuelled its growth. Development is encapsulated in some of its strategic intents, one of which is to get 30 per cent of sales from products that are less than four years old—a goal it has consistently achieved. Development practices have grown up to support such goals. For example, staff can spend up to 15 per cent of their time working on something of their own choosing, which is not part of their primary work. Additionally, a scientist who has an idea not connected with his or her normal work can apply for a Genesis Grant. This is not dealt with by management in the normal way, but by a panel of fellow scientists.

3M is very patient in waiting for results when many companies would have closed projects down. Some of its striking successes have slowly materialised over time. Thomas Stewart traces its current success with microreplication over a more than thirty year history of development, from its beginning in the treatment of a lens for overhead projectors, to its impact on film, illumination, reflective materials, abrasives, adhesives, materials and electronics products.[4]

One of the important aspects of Development is that it requires real collaboration, not just communication, internally, between departments, or externally, with suppliers, customers or research institutions. When a firm has Development as one of its core values, this collaboration is expected and supported by the culture and is much more likely to take place. A feature of many firms with strong Development capability is the networks, shared undertakings and joint ventures they build with other organisations.

Development at Sony

Sony's corporate mission is written substantially around the notion of Development, with a strong technological focus. Its vision was driven from the outset by what has been called 'The Sony Spirit', even though it started life in the bombed-out corner of a department store in Tokyo, and in its first more permanent premises had roofs that were so leaky that experiments had to be run under umbrellas.[5] Its statement of incorporation included not only its purpose and values about developing its own people and products, but also placed these in the context of developing its nation and its culture. Sony's original aims included:[6]

'... to establish a place of work where engineers can feel the joy of technological innovation; be aware of their mission to society; and work to their hearts' content.'

'... to pursue dynamic activities in technology and production for the reconstruction of Japan and the elevation of the nation's culture.'

'... to apply advanced technology to the life of the general public.'

Of course, vision statements on paper do not necessarily accord to the reality of life in a corporation, but when they do they provide a motivating energy to develop its future. In practice not all development is successful. What the organisation does when it is not successful is also important in maintaining Development capability.

The treatment of failure

The treatment of failure is an important part of building a Development capability. One cannot only develop successes. The story is told, it is possibly apocryphal, of IBM's founder, Thomas Watson, calling into his office a young executive who had been responsible for losing $10 million dollars (when dollars were much more valuable!) on a risky project. The young man began the discussion by volunteering his resignation. Watson responded, 'You can't be serious. We have just spent $10 million educating you.'[7] True or not, it makes an important point that some developmental activities will fail and the way such failures are seen and treated is important. Lopping heads off, unless actions have been irresponsible, will deter Development in the future. Furthermore some developmental activities may not in fact fail, but are not taken up by a company simply because better ones are available. The way the organisation deals with failures and non-preferred options is important to people's ongoing commitment to take the risks involved in all Development. In the *Intelligent Enterprise*, Quinn gives a picture of some aspects of the way this is handled at Sony:[8]

> 'Mr Morita and Mr Ibuka [Sony's leaders] proved their commitment to innovation and high principles in their handling of people. Key to inculcating these values in the organisation were their unflagging support of innovation, active participation in the innovation process, sacrifices to encourage the intellectual growth of their engineers, inspirational visits to technical laboratories, and willingness to take complete blame for losses and down-turns at Sony—while maintaining full employment for their workers.'

While there are many companies that do not have Development so strongly in the forefront of their vision, many build this capability in response to a change in strategic direction. Such a new focus makes clear the need for Development and energises, explains and justifies the investment and action. Woolworths invested heavily in Development—in training, introducing new systems and practices, and substantial reallocation of its resources as part of its repositioning into fresh food. When such a clear direction is established both the action and its justification need less explanation. StorageTek took firm action in developing itself for a new strategic direction and in the process successfully changed and grew its Biztech and its operations.

In the rest of this chapter we illustrate different aspects of Development in StorageTek, Du Pont and professional service firms and end by describing some actions and states associated with Development.

Development at StorageTek

StorageTek provides information storage and retrieval solutions to mainframe, midrange and large network computer users. It provides systems that enable users and organisations to manage their data more effectively, efficiently and economically. With StorageTek systems (and those of its competitors), data can be moved into 'libraries' where it is stored in cartridges and then accessed efficiently when and by whom it is needed. One of its automated cartridge systems holds the equivalent of 400 million pages of typed text, which, if stacked on top of each other, would reach over the height of four Eiffel towers! Combinations of software and storage systems enable customers to design storage capabilities suited to managing their growing quantities of data. With headquarters in Louisville, Colorado, StorageTek operates in many countries in the world and has total sales of approximately one and a half billion dollars. The subsidiary in Australia employs 140 people, has sales in excess of $50 million and is a growing and profitable business.

A changing marketplace

Like many other companies serving the computer market, StorageTek in Australia faced massive changes in the marketplace in the mid-1980s as IBM's dominance in the industry started to erode and customers began to demand an open-systems approach to computing. Computer users generally began to shift from almost total reliance on centralised mainframe computing to a combination of distributed and centralised computing with emphasis on distributed computing capability throughout the organisation.

The development of workstations and networks, and the growth of desktop computing, added a new dimension to data generation and stimulated new requirements for data storage systems. Industry forecasts in the early 1980s indicated that the amount of data generated by desktop systems was expected to grow at a rate of 35 per cent annually over the rest of the decade. As processing capability in all computer configurations grew exponentially, users everywhere produced more and more data, increasing the requirements for data storage and retrieval. Spending on information technology began to shift from buying computing power to investing in storage capacity and management.

The growth in data output presented StorageTek with a massively burgeoning market, but also with a threat. Something in excess of 80 per cent of its business was generated in the mainframe environment which, while still likely to remain a substantial market, was now under looming threat from the growth in distributed systems.

Furthermore, almost all of StorageTek's business was based on IBM's hardware or related operating systems and software. While IBM had achieved an almost unbelievable 60 per cent share of the world's market for computers, in the early years of the decade it began to decline rapidly. By the end of the decade it had dropped to 17 per cent. Computer users wanted to be able to move to open systems, to use a range of appropriate hardware, software and operating systems, and to do so with whatever combinations of mainframe or distributed computing suited their needs.

Jeff Hodgins, managing director of the Australian operation, became involved in many discussions at world headquarters in Louisville and in a series of corporate planning meetings with his executive team in Sydney in the mid-1980s. The need to be able to offer a much wider and different range of solutions to the changing market became pressingly more apparent. In 1988, the decision was made to develop new products for this much wider and expanded marketplace, which would enable StorageTek's products to connect to a multiplicity of other platforms and systems.

Broadly, all StorageTek skills in Australia in 1989 related to IBM systems, with 100 per cent of the company's revenue coming from IBM/MVS systems. There was little knowledge of other systems or languages. While the parent company in the United States began to develop new products, which they were confident would enable StorageTek worldwide 'to leap ahead of the competition', Hodgins and his people in Australia began to prepare to enter a new segment of the market of which they were largely ignorant and for which they had no products. This would entail the acquisition of new knowledge and the creation of new business technologies.

Development of knowledge and skill

The first step in 1990 was to recruit a marketing manager who had no IBM mainframe bias, but was very experienced in open systems software and services. One of his major tasks was internal education. As Hodgins commented:[9]

'We did not know at management levels what skills we actually needed.'

The next step was to recruit people with technical skills in non-IBM systems. The new marketing manager was involved with all these appointments. These newcomers were placed into the technical pre-sales area to develop people's knowledge within the company about non-IBM systems, in particular Unix. This role was important not only in developing new technical knowledge in StorageTek's people, but also vital in building their confidence in the changing strategy and their commitment to it. Since virtually all StorageTek's people had been focused entirely on

IBM/MVS products and applications, the company's new directions could easily be seen by some as a threat to the investment in skills and knowledge they had already made.

Before the new appointments were made, no one in StorageTek Australia understood, for example, the Unix system, an operating system of which they would need to have an expert understanding to operate effectively in the new market. The new technical recruits also began a process of building technical support in the marketplace for the emerging strategy by talking to customers about their growing needs for different products and services.

For these key posts, StorageTek recruited not only people with specialised knowledge of particular products or platforms, but looked for people with some experience and skills in passing on their knowledge to others. StorageTek then ran a development program to improve the training skills of these technically focused recruits. This was followed by a substantial training program, conducted by the newcomers, focused initially on technical people with national responsibilities. It was then extended to anyone in the company who would need to be able to, for example, 'speak Unix'.

After training, key sales and technical people from the company joined the Australian Unix users' group and began to build relationships with Unix users. Information about StorageTek's new and emerging products was fed through every possible conduit. This was particularly important to try to prevent existing customers from changing to competitors' products and systems, which would make it difficult for StorageTek to regain the account later. It was also important for StorageTek to reposition itself in the marketplace generally as a provider of a much wider range of solutions than those associated with mainframes and with IBM only. It had to promote itself as offering products and services to meet customers' needs for an enterprise-wide strategy for managing, sharing and storing data.

StorageTek had defined the key market segments it wished to enter —for example, Unix, Supercomputers, Unisys and Bull. Each area was assigned to a key executive to oversee and develop, in addition to his or her existing responsibilities. This helped the integration process. After this structure had been in place for about a year, full-time technically qualified 'product drivers' were appointed to develop each chosen market segment. These posts were cross-functional and the executive concerned could take action in any area to speed the growth of StorageTek's knowledge and position in the particular segment.

As the process of change continued, the Australian management became concerned, in retrospect, at its previous reliance upon the personal expertise of a few key individuals when it had been focused on the IBM-related market. Hodgins was determined to spread knowledge of the new market segments and technologies widely across his staff to lessen such dependence in future. About half of the 140 staff were given a detailed understanding of the new developments. He comments:[10]

> 'In previous times we simply had not given ourselves enough options in markets or people.'

The considerable jolt to the company caused by its realisation of its precarious position in the marketplace triggered or accelerated many other changes in management activity. While StorageTek Australia had always been a direct selling operation, it now began to develop new distribution channels through the use of resellers. It was able to do this because of the new technical support it had already put in place early in the change process.

Internally the company improved its strategic planning process and involved a wider number of executives in the process. The Performance Management process was overhauled with key result areas being more clearly defined in terms of individual outcomes with negotiated and agreed targets. Each employee was given a training program on writing job goals, and individual training needs were identified for each specific skill needed to reach these goals.

Need for new personal competencies

The change in strategic direction did not clash with any of the strongly held values the company had espoused and practised during the previous two decades. It did, however, confront people with the need to develop new personal skills. It also challenged the company to ensure these skills became corporate. Its heavy investment in people and in their training for products not yet available were underpinned by the parent company's stated policy of being willing to sacrifice short-term gain for reliability and excellence. In terms of its commitment to its employees, the program reinforced its long-held policies and values. As the new knowledge and methods became embedded in processes, practices and systems, the company achieved certification for many of its operations under the relevant Australian Standards.

The changes also started to alter the way the company recognised performance. Previously, recognition was focused on people who had ever more deep and finely honed skills around a particular product or application. Gurus with in-depth, focused knowledge were the heroes. Now the focus was switched to those who could maintain their current technical knowledge *and* could step over the boundaries into new technical areas needed by the wider product and applications strategy. In research and development, some software engineers who were excellent in an MVS world could acquire these new skills and make this progression, but others could not.

More emphasis was increasingly put on innovation and change, and this in turn required improvement in management skills. It also required changes, some quite subtle, in corporate culture. Most of StorageTek's senior management had come to their positions through a technical or sales route. They now found they had to give more time to develop new competencies in process management, people management and interpersonal skills.

The reshaping of the Australian operation required considerable investment in recruitment and training long before there were new sales or products available to give a return on the investment. Personal leadership at the top, strong commitment from the team, and planning and performance management were necessary to keep profit moving forward, which it did, during the time it was consciously developing the new business technologies needed to meet its customers' changing needs.

Developing new capabilities to align with a new strategy

This short cameo on StorageTek Australia illustrates the utilisation of the five contributing competencies, listed in Table 6.1 earlier in this chapter, which combine to form Development capability. It describes a case where a choice about future market positioning depended for its realisation on the building of quite new operational capabilities. Had StorageTek chosen to stay with its previous strategy, which locked them in with IBM, they would not have needed to develop any new capabilities. But they could not reposition themselves without developing new Biztech, Marketing and Selling, and Performance Management capabilities. The Development involved new systems and practices not only in the field of technology, but also in management. It required Development of people, including the establishment of new posts, and it required a change in the way StorageTek applied its resources to meet its new strategic direction. It also required a great deal of planning. It is easy to look back and see in retrospect the drop in a decade of IBM's world market share from 60 per cent to 17 per cent, but few, certainly not IBM itself or those who invested in it, saw it in prospect.

The conscious process StorageTek's top management planned and followed, particularly the strong use of middle managers and technical people in the communication and Development process, underlines not only the potentially strong position of top management to influence outcomes, but also the key role of middle management in the effective management of change. This was also important to an effective diffusion of the new Biztech. The process of changing the tacit knowledge of the newcomers into explicit and codified knowledge, in which others could be trained, was an important aspect of developing and embedding competence.

The actions that were taken also built those states that enhance Change Effectiveness. Clearly much of the action was taken to empower people in the company and to build systems and practices in which they could feel confident. Commitment grew over time as Development proceeded. A state of anxiety is not, in general, positive to the overall change process, but when it is combined with a clear sense of new directions, as it was in the case of StorageTek, it can act as a stimulant to Development, which otherwise might not take place. This was the situation in StorageTek where concern about the changing marketplace and its dependence, particularly in Australia, on IBM helped motivation and action to develop new competencies.

StorageTek's actions were focused on training, widespread consultation and making the fullest use of its current people as well recruiting people with new skills. These are actions found consistently in organisations with Development capability.

Since its change in strategic direction, which it began to implement in 1989, StorageTek's total trade in Australia has continued to grow significantly. From 100 per cent income from IBM/MVS products, by 1995 it generated 40 per cent of an increased business from non-IBM related systems—a major shift in the pattern of its business in a relatively short time.

Development at Du Pont

Development at StorageTek was very clearly focused on the vision of building a new market. Development at Du Pont was focused on the vision of building a new relationship. Du Pont's vision arose out of a different agenda, 'How the people and the company could work together in the 21st century.'

One feature of the Joint Beliefs Statement agreed with the union and workforce was a leaning to 'volunteerism'. This became a major feature of manager Don Wirth's Development initiatives. A sound relationship cannot be forced. It needs time and room to grow. Sometimes people need to grow themselves before they can develop and sustain relationships.

Personal development and skills development

The personal development program that was offered to the workforce on a voluntary basis was not a sophisticated, state-of-the-art training program, but something really quite simple. But it had a considerable impact on the effectiveness of the change, because it was directly relevant to the change that had to take place. Interestingly a personal development program was also one of the features of the changes at the NSW State Library.

Core Process Mark 1 was a training program in personal development, offered to shop floor employees only, *on the basis of their volunteering to take part.* Supervisors were excluded. The program was designed by Wirth, his recently appointed assistant site manager, Phuong Tram, a head office executive, and an external consultant, who also presented the program. The training program ran seven times, covering about half the workforce.

There was a strong shared agreement between managers and workforce that it was a significant milestone in the development of the vision that managers, workforce and unions should try to work more effectively together. It affected the attitude that employees had to their jobs and the way they thought about the management and the company. As such, it was a factor in the change of the culture of the plant. Employees' comments included:[11–13]

> 'I think Core Process has changed the way people think about their job.'—operator

> 'I think it was the first time they [the workforce] could see they could improve themselves in the work environment.'—manager

> 'What happened in Core Process 1 was that a group of people came back from the first program and formed an energy-sustaining team and sold it to the plant.'—supervisor

Of course, in a plant still moving very, very slowly towards greater trust, there were many cynics:[14]

> 'Some of them thought the training was all bullshit.'—supervisor

Core Process 1 was followed by Core Process 2 and, in time, by 3. This Development process moved towards the building of operational capabilities. It covered six critical processes: safety, people development, supply chain management, quality management, facilities planning and metrics, the last being Du Pont's term for measurements. The programs were voluntary, had an ethos of standing for important values of personal development, and were seen by many as a key aspect of the improved relationship between management, unions and workforce. As one person commented:[15]

> 'I suppose when the Core Process programs started the "non-believers" were about 90 per cent of the plant. Now they are down to about 10 per cent.'—operator

The process of volunteering for programs, and the restriction of them to the operator level, created undoubted problems for the first level of management, the supervisors. The supervisors were being asked to see their roles in a completely new light—as empowerers, supporters and coaches, rather than as instructors, controllers and enforcers. Progress towards dealing with this issue was slower, but it was part of the focus of the work of Phuong Tram, who became site manager on Wirth's promotion. During the early 1990s there was a substantial investment in supervisor training.

As the training program continued, a number of cross-functional small teams were established in areas such as productivity, machine output, communication, training and work skills. As in the initial phase of the change, results from these teams varied. But alongside the seemingly ad-hoc arrangements for 'teams of volunteers', the plant began to build up its methods and systems to become accredited under the International Standards (ISO) registration scheme.

Systems and practices: moving towards embedding

Du Pont used its task team structure to develop the processes, activities and systems needed as part of its ISO accreditation. It was headed by a man who in earlier years was a union delegate in the plant and a member of the original group of seventeen employees who volunteered for the first Core Program in personal development.

Over time a transition took place that turned the personal skills and ideas of individuals into corporate competencies. The first phase was the development of individual skills and practices. These became to some extent collectivised by team working. Then the generation of ideas and improved practices of the teams became systematised, formalised and documented into standard processes, systems and practices. These ways of doing things now were owned by the organisation and part of the way the organisation performed. As such they existed independently of particular individuals.

Impact on organisational states

Enormous and persistent effort was put into giving the workforce power and responsibility to do things. This fostered the growth of the state of empowerment, which is important both to Development and overall to Change Effectiveness. Confidence in systems and practices grew and esprit de corps, which earlier had been absent, was developed—'now nothing is impossible'.[16]

Although there was a threat to the future of the plant from South East Asian competition and cost reduction was important, it was not used by management to drive action. Wirth commented:[17]

'We never talked about cost reduction.'

However, as a consequence of improved working together, and the increase in ideas that flowed from this, together with rising output, costs were substantially reduced.

At Du Pont the first and continued major Development effort was put into the development of people and the changing of its culture. It was not until long into the change process, 1993, by which time significant improvement had been achieved, that new technology was brought on stream. As a senior manager commented:[18]

'... technology has not changed—the people have changed.'

Development in professional services firms

Managing accumulated knowledge and experience, and bringing it to bear on improving service to its clients, is one of the major developmental issues that faces all professional services organisations. For consulting companies, their major competitive asset is usually the intellectual capital of their people, particularly that of their most experienced partners.

Andersen Consulting is one of the largest and most successful firms specialising in systems consulting and the management of change. But just as its clients need to develop their resources and systems to make successful change, Andersen Consulting needed to do the same for itself. Andersen's clients clearly would all like the services of its most experienced partners, but there are not enough of these to go around. Says Charles Paulk of Andersen Consulting:[19]

> 'When one of our consultants shows up, the client should get the best of the firm not just the best of that consultant.'

The Development issue Andersen's faced was how to gain access to the accumulated wisdom of senior people and transfer it to its considerable number of very bright, but inexperienced, new consultants. Its 50,000 staff deal with an enormous diversity of clients and industries. Ronald Henkoff quotes Andersen's managing partner for Europe:[20]

> 'The bigger we get, the more difficult it is to deliver experts. The harder it gets to figure out who knows what.'

To enable the newer consultants to give better client service, and to apply techniques and accumulated wisdom much greater than their own, Andersen's developed its 'methodology'. The methodology sets out guidelines:[21]

> '... for analysing a client's problems, proposing and designing a solution, building a prototype, and putting the solution into practice.'

The building of this methodology required great Development capability. More important from the perspective of change management is that:[22]

> 'Andersen's updates the methodology every six to twelve months, incorporating actual experiences from people in the field.'

It also relies on its own consultants rather than using professional trainers. Andersen's connects all professionals to its Knowledge Exchange, a series of interactive databases that track client engagements, consultants' experience and general market information for each of Andersen's major industry practices.

Andersen's first task was to turn the tacit knowledge that a relative few of its people had gained over the years into explicit knowledge that could be structured and taught to others. In doing so, it developed a corporate asset available to many. This enabled it to expand relatively quickly through the recruitment of young consultants who, through training, interaction and access to its corporate methodology, could offer more to clients than their own skills and knowledge.

Like many large companies around the world, Andersen's has its own international training centre and it invests substantially in its educational activities. But Development meant that its training had to garner, structure and formalise much of the firm's own intellectual capital to make that training relevant to its growth needs. This highlights again the link between resource development and the application of these new resources to strategic aims. Andersen's illustrates one example where the collection of existing knowledge and skill creates the basis for a new technology that gives it a distinctive competitive advantage. This enables it to use relatively inexperienced people to deliver a very sophisticated and advanced service at a lower cost. It also opens the gateway to faster expansion since new young untrained people are more numerous and cheaper than experienced ones.

Arthur Andersen, a separate but related company to Andersen Consulting, has a focus on leveraging knowledge as part of its strategy. Quinn quotes Robert Elmore, its managing director of Business Systems Consulting:[23]

> 'Our business strategy says we will leverage the intellectual capital of our people, the intellectual capital of our firm, and the intellectual capital of the business world at large.'

Its Group Talk interactive computer system enables people on the system to network with six thousand other minds to ask questions and get answers to consulting problems they face. He comments:[24]

> 'We are going after the brand new employees and getting them trained in the habit of use. You can no longer think about just the technology.

You have to think about the process that goes along with it, the attitudes, values, processes and people involvement you can use to get a better answer. Most of the investment in our type of company is not in the software but in the training.'

Of course Andersen's is not alone in this quest. Coopers & Lybrand used to operate more than 100 physical libraries around its operations, which contained the organisation's collective knowledge about strategic technology and business areas. Collected on its own intranet it contains not only external data but:[25]

'... the organisation's accumulated expertise on specific issues, industry-specific best practices and client information, including key contacts.'

Facing the same need to develop themselves by embedding personal knowledge for the use of the organisation at large, Booz Allen & Hamilton, Ernst & Young, Price Waterhouse and very many other professional services firms have created similarly embedded knowledge which can be readily accessed by authorised staff around the world at any time.

To create such embedded knowledge, individuals who initially create such knowledge and often then feel they own it must be, or become, willing to share it. That sharing can be encouraged by a supporting culture. But many professional services firms do not typically have such a culture and need to take specific action to develop one. Quinn describes some actions taken that address this need in Arthur Andersen:[26]

'... a conscious effort is made to de-emphasise localised profit centres and the performance measures that do not contribute to sharing information. Partners share in total firm profits instead. People seeking promotion to partner are evaluated in part on the number of "case solutions" they have submitted to the system for sharing. The frequency with which a person is sought for a team or to solve a complex problem and how well that person cooperates in team endeavours are also important components in performance evaluations ... The entire culture is managed to develop and share new information and solutions.'

In Chapter 10 we will illustrate further the linkage between culture and building and maintaining corporate capabilities.

Actions that help Development

We mentioned earlier that some actions contribute to more than one capability or state. For example, action to consult and involve people, which contributes strongly to Engagement, also makes substantial contribution to Development capability. An important aspect of development is that adults want a say in their own development. It is likely to be more effective when it is freely entered into, as was the case at Du Pont. Consulting and involving people in their own development helps to form motivation to learn. Learning is an important aspect of creating Development capability.

Training

Not unexpectedly training is strongly linked to the existence of Development capability. It is also strongly linked to the existence of all five capabilities. It is the single action that contributes *strongly* to both Change Effectiveness and Current Business Performance—to the present and the future of an organisation. It is particularly beneficial when the challenge of change is in technology for this requires the development of new knowledge and skills. Where training is relatively strong in an organisation, capabilities tend to be relatively strong.

Training, of course, means far more than the provision of programs and courses. Much of the best training is on the job and it stimulates interest and action in further development. Investment in the development of individuals often takes place as a result of the planning process. The role of top-line management seems often to be more one of agreement and authorisation rather than shaping or driving. This makes it all the more important for human resource managers, who usually carry this responsibility, to be fully involved in and alive to their organisation's strategy so that decisions taken about the development of individuals have the firm's strategic needs in mind.

Training managers is a significant feature and expenditure of most organisations that seek excellence in Development. Some companies have built their own corporate competence in developing their managers to the point where it becomes a part of their competitive advantage.

Formal training of individuals may be important to the development of individual managers but to make real impact on an organisation's Development, training needs to cover a significant proportion of the organisation's management. This is particularly true when change is sought in the organisation's culture. Cultural change needs to involve many people to be effective and requires both a sense of new direction as well as behavioural change. This is one reason why a great deal of management training has moved 'in company' where considerable numbers of managers can be trained together and the training is simultaneously focused on the particular needs of the organisation. Crotonville in GE and Motorola University are examples of the major effort that many companies put into this aspect of Development.

Training was a significant activity in the development of new skills and attitudes at StorageTek, Woolworths and Du Pont. However, it is not a significant activity for very many companies. Many leading companies spend 3–5 per cent of payroll costs on training while a few spend substantially more. Others set minimum prescribed days per employee to be spent in training. Yet many spend little and some nothing at all. Training is a key activity strongly related to Development capability. It separates those that will develop their people and their organisations from those that are unlikely to do so.

Introducing technology, systems and practices

While there is, in practice, some reluctance on the part of some employers to heavily invest in the training of individuals who may leave and take their skills with them, investing in technology, systems and practices leverages the skills of many and gives ownership to the organisation of new advances. Embedding the skills and knowledge of individuals and groups in systems and practices opens up possibilities of new and better ways of doing things.

System and process development was a key feature in all the cases we have so far discussed. It was a central feature of StorageTek's change. Du Pont over time improved and redesigned almost all of its systems and practices as it moved into accreditation. Woolworths' action in developing a range of competencies in fresh food depended initially on training, but was followed by comprehensive redesign of work flows, job structures and systems. At the NSW State Library a major effort in consultative practices accompanied changes in skill and system development. Changes at Andersen's had a strong focus on introducing technology and new systems and practices. And many of the new developments in training itself depend upon new technology and newly designed systems of workforce and management education.

Reduce, replace or retrain?

Our study shows that when Development capability is high, the replacement of people in key positions, and reduction of staff, is low. When firms have high capability in Development they tend to train and retrain their people rather than retrench them. This is because their people are trained, often multiskilled, and can therefore be used in different situations. Of course this does not mean that retrenchment is not sometimes necessary, but our study does show that across a large sample of firms, when replacement and staff reduction are high, Development and Change Effectiveness tend to be low. The data suggest that higher investment in training and retraining would, in many cases, result in more effective change than staff reductions and replacements.

Should Development capability be outsourced?

It is quite common for organisations to outsource some Development activities. The use of external training programs and the use of consultants to develop IT systems and business processes are major examples. This poses some important questions. If Development activities can be bought in the marketplace whenever they are needed, why do firms need to have Development capability as an important part of achieving effective change? Is Development capability something that can be purchased in the marketplace? If we wish to outsource some of our Development activities are there some internal related competencies we need to have and retain in order to achieve the particular development that we want and yet retain our Development capability?

We want to look at these questions by considering what is involved in the development of a computer system in an organisation, a situation faced by almost every firm in greater or larger measure. We use this example as a basis of developing some guidelines for managers facing developmental opportunities that involve choices about outsourcing aspects of their Development capability.

A lot of computer software is simply purchased on a standard basis. Most firms do not develop it for themselves. Examples include operating systems, such as Windows and Unix and applications software, such as word processing, database, spreadsheet, Internet browser and accounting packages. These are all so generalised and adaptable that one package can serve thousands or even millions of organisations. So the continuous development of that software is done by the small number of specialist companies that offer the software as products. It is certainly not something firms would be able to do well for themselves.

However, computer systems used by many organisations are actually closely integrated with the firm's complex business processes. For example, an insurance company's underwriting and claims assessment software forms an essential element of the business processes for selling insurance, evaluating risks, and assessing and determining payouts on claims. The software doesn't work alone. It is integrated with the actions of staff involved in various roles, all of whom need to follow consistent practices. It is not possible to change the software without impacting on the way people work and on the way they ultimately interact with customers.

The same is true for the specialised software used by a tax office or customs department, or by a manufacturer in process and materials control, or by a hospital for managing patient care, facilities and medical technology. All of these IT systems need to be developed, or at least tailored, as an integral part of the business processes for each organisation. These business processes are also often undergoing change.

In order to develop the computer systems in the business, someone has to understand the various ways that the software system will affect the work of people directly using it, and those indirectly influenced by it. It is also necessary to understand the implications of changing work patterns and how people—both staff and customers—will respond to particular changes. The skills of the staff, the facilities available, and the impact of the system on operational controls within the business, also need to be understood. This understanding and knowledge influences decisions about the priorities and trade-offs involved in developing and introducing the new system. These decisions need to be taken in the light of the individual organisation's strategies, culture and resources—not with those of a competitor or with those of a firm in a different industry about which an external provider might be knowledgeable.

It is not possible to make these decisions in a responsible or meaningful way unless the decision makers understand and appreciate the position and linkages of the full range of factors and relationships that will be affected by the new computer system.

Making sound decisions about the development of a computer system needs an understanding of the options available to the firm, their possible impact on one another, the way they will affect, link and integrate with other aspects of the business, and the likely costs and benefits for the firm. Outsourcing all this really means outsourcing responsibility for a vital element of the future shape of the business to someone who, by definition, is simply not in a position to judge what is appropriate for the business, nor really can be primarily motivated or accountable for its future in the same way that insiders would be. The same is true of outsourcing pathfinding, or the planning that links together the breadth of change activities across an organisation.

But while a firm cannot responsibly outsource its computer development capability, it can use external expertise provided the internal competencies exist to apply the external expertise. There must be some familiarity, within the firm, with the external specialist technical expertise. To effectively make use of external expertise in such a case, a firm must:

- be able to recognise the need to undertake appropriate computer systems development
- have a good idea of the systems options available
- understand the way each option would interact with the firm's staff, other resources and, in some cases, customers
- understand the options that exist for developing staff and other resources

- be able to assess which options can be costed accurately, including their impact on the organisation's strategies
- be able to integrate the systems development into the organisation's operations, including dovetailing it with any concurrent developments.

These requirements have some important implications for the action that firms should take when outsourcing any Development activity.

Choosing a Development capability strategy

Figure 6.1 uses two factors to determine the most appropriate strategy needed to achieve and retain Development capability. The two factors are:

- the extent of the integration needed between the proposed Development activity and other business processes—called 'Integration with business processes' (horizontal axis)
- the relative costs, diseconomies and efficiency aspects of the firm providing the competence itself—called 'Relatively costly to provide oneself' (vertical axis).

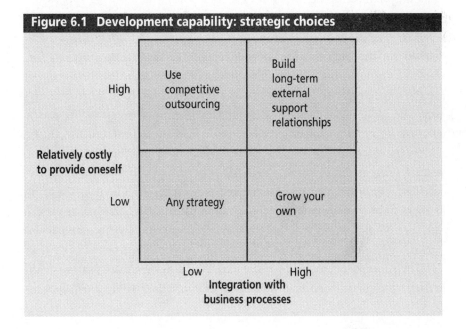

Figure 6.1 Development capability: strategic choices

There are four possible Development capability strategies that are appropriate depending on the relative importance of these two factors. The first three strategies are:

- *competitive outsourcing* of Development capability (top left-hand box)
- *growing your own* Development capability (bottom right-hand box)
- *building long-term external support relationships* with external providers of Development capability (top right-hand box).

The fourth strategy—bottom left-hand box—is where any of the above three strategies would be appropriate. We will now take a closer look at each strategy.

Competitive outsourcing

Every organisation has some comparative advantage or disadvantage in developing and maintaining particular Development expertise within the business. This is true whether the expertise relates to the example we used of computer systems development, or of accounting systems development, the development of sales practices or manufacturing processes, and so on.

The relative cost of maintaining the expertise at a high level will depend on the organisation's size (it tends to be less economical for smaller organisations) and on how frequently the organisation needs to use the expertise. For example, a large retailer is likely to be frequently adjusting its logistics processes, a bank or insurance company its product systems, and a consumer electronics firm its manufacturing flows and production processes. In these cases there are opportunities to efficiently create and maintain internal expertise to support these regular changes. This expertise is consistently renewed through its use. Yet even in these cases there are likely to be some technical skills that are used only occasionally and are therefore more economically obtained from outside specialists.

The other key dimension is the extent of a system's integration with broader business processes. When a system is relatively independent of most of the organisation's business processes—for example, a payroll system—changes can be made without attention to the broader and more fundamental business processes. It does not matter whether those involved in determining and carrying out development of that system understand many of the other business processes in the organisation.

Therefore, when it is relatively uneconomic for a firm to sustain the particular Development expertise *and* the system involved needs little integration with other business processes, it is optimum for a firm to outsource the Development to specialists. It can do so without harm to its own Development capability—and it can do so on a competitive tendering basis. This is the situation when the firm occupies the top left-hand box in Figure 6.1.

Growing your own

Conversely, when the firm uses particular expertise so much that it can be sustained economically *and* the systems to be developed are closely integrated with the broader business processes, then outsourcing is damaging. It is far better to organically grow and sustain the expertise internally. By doing so, the firm ensures that the personnel who possess the particular expertise are also in a position to be familiar with the broader business processes with which the system is integrated. Consequently, they can apply knowledge of both (that is, the system and other processes) in their work. Additionally, they help educate and advise the decision makers who have overall Development responsibility, so that the latter are able to make comprehensive and informed judgments on Development options. This is the situation when the firm occupies the bottom right-hand box in Figure 6.1.

Building long-term external support relationships

As Figure 6.1 illustrates, there are two intermediate situations. The first is when it is not economical for the firm to provide its own Developmental activity, but the proposed activity needs to be integrated with the firm's other business processes (top right-hand corner of Figure 6.1). Internal maintenance of the expertise is too expensive and/or ineffective—but it is important that personnel outside the firm who have the expertise are familiar with the firm's broader business processes. This is best satisfied by an external specialist who provides a long-term support relationship and who has the opportunity to gain familiarity with the business processes.

In this case the firm's Development capability depends on how it maintains and draws on its relationship with the external specialist, and on the specialist's skills and ability to comprehend and relate to the firm's broader business processes, culture and strategies. Many firms have long-term relationships with external providers who really understand how the firm works and provide specialised expertise to help it change and perform.

Any strategy would be appropriate

The final situation—the bottom left-hand box in Figure 6.1—is where it is not uneconomic to provide the Development activity and the activity is not integrated to any real extent with other business processes. In this situation there is much more latitude about the appropriate access to expertise and no strong benefit in a particular course of action. Competitive outsourcing, building long-term external support relationships, and growing and maintaining the capability internally are all practical strategies. In practice, action is probably determined by tradition, the costs of change and other management priorities.

Applying the Development capability decision structure

The decision structure we have discussed is not only appropriate for the development of a computer system, it is also valid for all other aspects of Development capability. For example, it could be applied to training within the organisation, which is a very different form of Development from developing a computer system.

Some training is not closely integrated with business processes. External specialists can provide this training far more economically than most firms can for themselves. Basic accounting and business finance (which apply community standards), engineering, marketing theory, medicine and management practice are all examples. Organisations typically rely on external sources for this training and do so without prejudice to their Development capability, providing, of course, they can judge the most appropriate external sources and the extent to which they need this training for staff.

But in all of those disciplines, there is also often firm-specific expertise that cannot be acquired through general external training. In these cases firms develop internal training programs (like Motorola's University, GE's Crotonville and Woolworths' training system) and tailored internal staff development schemes. Of course, very few organisations can afford to develop their own university, and so in those cases they often consciously establish long-term relationships with external trainers who acquire knowledge of the business and its processes and adapt their training accordingly.

Thus we see the same pattern of factors and actions whether the Development concerns computer systems, training personal skills, or developing business processes.

In many cases, strong Development capability depends on using some external resources. It is important to find the optimum balance of external and internal resources, taking account of the different economics for particular expertise and the extent to which the expertise needs to be applied to integrated business processes. Even when external resources are important to the firm's Development, all of the relevant decisions cannot be outsourced. An ability to select, guide and integrate external resources needs to reside within the organisation.

Summary

Whereas Engagement is more about finding future directions and motivating and building commitment to action to achieve them, Development requires courage, faith and discipline to make investments in the future.

Development capability helps organisations achieve Change Effectiveness. It assists in the development of new operational capabilities. It has a strong orientation to the future, and makes little contribution to Current Business Performance.

Development capability combines two groups of competencies—one concerned with resource and system development and the other with the planning and application of those resources in line with the organisation's strategic direction. It is the integration of these competencies that forms the capability.

Using external expertise in Development activities can be valuable in some situations, but decisions about outsourcing have substantial implications for the organisation's future Development capability.

Organisations with high Development capability have relatively good systems and relatively low rates of replacing key people and staff generally. They rely more on what they can do internally to develop their people than on replacement. They have high levels of involvement and empowerment of staff to make changes. Strong Development capability is linked to training and the ability to introduce new technology and institute systems and practices.

The creation of Development capability is motivated and sustained in some firms by the purpose and values of the organisation, as it is in others by strategic and operational needs. Development is more likely to be strong when top management has a long-term commitment to the firm.

CHAPTER 7

Performance Management

An unrelenting focus on safety

THE AIRCRAFT began to descend slowly through the clouds towards the airport. Its pilot, Hank, approached the airport from the south as he had done many times before. He knew the hilly terrain well. His airline's standard operating procedures for approaching airports surrounded by difficult terrain use Distance Measuring Equipment (DME) steps. These enable the pilot to make a stable, gradual, measured descent to the runway, but always to keep at a safe height over difficult terrain. DME tells the pilot how far the plane is from the airport and, when used with other equipment, enables the plane to fly on a line accurately towards the runway. Hank carefully consulted his approach chart. There were three descent steps to be taken to approach the runway. He started his 'Step one' descent, and then 'Step two'. The cloud cover was light but obscured the ground. At 'Step three' he looked up at the altimeter. It registered 6000 feet. It should have read 7000. Hank was a thousand feet lower than he should have been. He carefully corrected the situation and landed the aircraft without incident. The plane was never in any danger as the 'steps' are very conservative. He had, however, somehow got the aircraft one step out in its descent.

According to his company's performance standards an inadvertent breach of the procedures had occurred. Hank was a very experienced pilot. He knew that all the highly technical equipment that records much of an aircraft's flight would not have picked up such a minor departure from the rules. He knew no one could ever know.

Dwight turned his Boeing B747 onto the runway having completed preparation for take off. His company's fleet of aircraft included a large number of B747 aircraft and a few special performance aircraft B747SPs. On this occasion Dwight was in command of one of the special B747SPs. The preparation completed, Dwight eased back into his seat and the plane began its take-off run.

Boeings have two flap settings for take off. Flap 10 setting causes the aircraft to take a longer ground run, but allows for better climb performance. Flap 20 gives a shorter ground run, but not as good a climb performance. Flap 20 is usually the preferred flap setting and it was so for this particular take off. As the speed of the plane increased along the runway, Dwight became aware the plane was not lifting off as early as he expected for a flap 20 setting. He immediately looked up at the gauge and realised he had selected the wrong flap number. There was, however, sufficient runway available for Dwight to continue the take off, and so he continued and the plane became safely airborne. Dwight's Boeing aircraft had been in no danger, but a standard operating procedure had been breached. As in Hank's case there was no way of anyone knowing, other than Dwight, that this had taken place. No one need ever know.

But both their airlines soon knew. Immediately on returning to base, Hank had reported his breach to his chief pilot and Dwight had seen his director of flight operations. Dwight was an extremely experienced pilot. He was not sure exactly why he had selected the wrong flap setting. 'If it can happen to me,' he said to his general manager, 'it can happen to anyone.' Hank had landed at that airport many times. He had never got the step descent wrong before.

It is not normal behaviour for people to report their own mistakes, especially those no one else could ever know. Pilots are very proud people about their own level of flying skills. But the airlines that employed Hank and Dwight needed to make sure, if they could, as part of their performance management of safety, that their pilots would report every breach that occurred. Many things happen when planes are in the air. A safety-focused airline wants to know *anything* that ever goes wrong so that it can eradicate or minimise it. It wants to know anything its pilots ever do that is the slightest variation from the strictest possible safety procedures that it has developed. Such a departure is an opportunity to learn and increase the safety standard of the whole airline. This particularly applies to events experienced by its most skilled and senior pilots, which they alone could know had happened.

Electronic tracking and advanced recording technology pick up many acts that occur in the air that could jeopardise customer safety. Both Hank's and Dwight's airlines use these latest technologies to the full. Both airlines invest heavily in the training of pilots and ground staff, and are certain training is a factor in their good safety record. Both airlines have the highest engineering standards and are confident that these standards are an important factor in their good safety records.

But both airlines also believe there is another important factor that contributes to their high safety records. They have developed a policy of not taking penalty action against pilots who report their own breaches of standard operating procedures and who commit what the industry calls an 'unsafe act'. Such a 'no penalty' or 'no blame' or 'no retribution' policy helps to keep their airlines among the safest in the world. Of course such acts are thoroughly investigated, as in our two examples, and corrective action taken. When breaches of safety are detected that are not self-reported, appropriate disciplinary action, including dismissal, takes place.

Close expert examination of the chart that Hank used, which showed the DME steps for descent to the airport, revealed that it was in fact possible to misread some of it. This possible error had never been noticed before. It was brought to the attention of the international authority that approves these charts and the situation was rectified. In Dwight's case, the aircraft cockpit of the special B747SP that he was flying was similar to the layout of the other B747s in the fleet with the exception of the flap position indicators. Flap 10 position on the special performance B747SP was in the position of flap 20 on all the other B747s. Dwight had looked up at the indication needle on the gauge without realising the position of the gauge itself was different. The airline had discussions with Boeing and the gauges were altered on the B747SPs so that the mistake could not re-occur.

So the actions of individuals, the development of a supporting culture, in this case safety, and the correction and improvement of the current system and its results, all flowed from the impact of a specific performance management system and policy. Because safety is so central to airline performance, many regional and international airlines have their own variants of a 'no blame' system. They find it works. Similarly, other businesses, where safety is central—for example, railways and car ferries—can build their own cultures of safety. When these fail so does safety. The enquiries into the major rail crash at Clapham Junction in London and into the Herald Free Enterprise Ferry capsize at Zeebrugge emphasised a poor safety culture as a factor in the disasters.

Just as change in a performance management system of incentives, rewards and punishment may be needed to change the mindsets and actions of pilots, it may also be valuable in changing the mindsets and normal behaviours of observers. Staff in other aviation areas who may become aware of hazards outside their own areas of responsibility are encouraged to report safety hazards, if necessarily anonymously, and are often provided with security to safeguard their anonymity. It is often easier to look the other way when hazards may be outside your area of direct responsibility, particularly if retribution is likely, and so mechanisms are needed to change typical behaviour. In these instances establishing an effective confidential safety reporting system that safeguards anonymity is part of an effective performance management system. The importance of providing processes and mechanisms to get maximum information about possible safety hazards before they result in an accident is one way regulatory bodies try to build the systems of safety for members of the travelling public.

The contribution of Performance Management

Performance Management is the capability to proactively manage the factors that drive the organisation's performance—to ensure it consistently and effectively achieves what is intended. As Figure 3.4 showed, it is the only capability that contributes significantly to *both* Current Business Performance and Change Effectiveness. It is a capability to make things work well and better.

The link with Current Business Performance, which it achieves largely by increasing operational efficiency, is a bedrock of the approach of many managers to improving performance. In our airline illustration both pilots were able to take immediate corrective action to deal with the events. Secondly, Performance Management contributes to incremental change by improving relevant Biztech. In our example changes were made to operating instructions via changes in the charts and to cockpit layout via the manufacturer. Performance Management detected a systemic flaw, which was then eliminated. So these incremental changes became embedded in the organisations and their technology, and became available to leverage the skills of all pilots in those kinds of situations.

To achieve major changes, particularly those involving cultural change, frequently means changing behaviour and mindsets. The introduction of various forms of 'no penalty' policies was only one part of the airlines' approach to safety management, but it supported the development of a mindset in pilots and changed important aspects in some of their behaviour. They reported mistakes they made that no one else could know. As a consequence, both airlines and the industry in general have built up, over time, safety-related information, skills and practices that has made flying continuously safer. Such major programs to introduce change often take on the characteristics of a major project, or series of projects, before they become incorporated into the normal way the business is managed for performance. This is typically the way some changes are introduced. When this is the case Performance Management capability makes a major contribution to Change Effectiveness in keeping the project on target and taking action to ensure this happens.

So Performance Management is not just about improving task performance, though it certainly includes that aspect. It is also about altering people's behaviour so that they see things differently and learn to do different things. Performance Management thus impacts on the existing organisation and helps create the future organisation.

In the rest of this chapter we discuss significant aspects of this capability. We explore the important contribution key individuals make and how Performance Management becomes embedded in the organisation's systems and practices. We discuss its contribution to cultural change and to organisational integration. We lastly look at its linkage with actions and states.

A many-faceted capability

To be good at Performance Management you and your organisation need to be good at a number of things. While Engagement is primarily a people-focused set of skills, Performance Management deals substantially with people, tasks and processes. It calls on both a wide skill base and a wide knowledge base. It also needs knowledge of the critical factors that actually affect performance. While 'business' knowledge is useful to Engagement, it is absolutely central and essential for Performance Management. It is about knowing how the business, or part of it, works and helping and influencing it to work better.

Operational competence is an important part of Performance Management capability, and so are financial and planning competencies. While the latter are more generic in their base, operational competence requires specific business knowledge. Many of the systems, processes and measures used for Performance Management need to be specifically developed for the particular industry and company. For example, loan delinquency rate, a very important performance measure in banking, is not important to most other industries. Conversely, measures of raw material yield, or of product return rates, important to some industries, are irrelevant to banking. Business-specific knowledge is important not just to performance measures. It is essential in order to make realistic judgments about the ease or difficulty of targets. It is also important when evaluating business and personal performance, which requires an appropriate allowance for the impact of external factors on performance.

Performance Management performs several functions. It guides and invigorates change efforts, playing a key role in setting expectations and changing behaviours. It stimulates and provides evidence for resource reallocation. It identifies systemic flaws in the business and directs attention to the need to rectify them—thus giving impetus to change as well as guiding change. It results in action being taken—and there is no change without action. And, lastly, and very importantly, the same competencies contribute to, guide and motivate Current Business Performance.

Table 7.1 lists the competencies that combine to form this important capability, and the states and actions that, our study shows, are linked to it.

Table 7.1 Performance Management: competencies, states and actions		
Contributing competencies	**Linked key states**	**Linked key actions**
Performance control	Esprit de corps	Training
Resource application	Systems and practices	Introducing technology
Enaction	suitability	and systems
Financial	High workloads	Monitoring
Planning	Commitment	Recognising contributors
Operational		Setting priorities
Integration		

Performance control

The competence most strongly linked with Performance Management capability, which we call *performance control*, is essentially a performance process control. It is about setting goals, monitoring what happens, and taking action to keep performance on target. We could sum up its elements, at a very broad level, by saying it consists of:

- setting goals
- supporting these goals with resources
- evaluating performance
- rewarding performance.

What is done in each of these specific areas of action will vary with the situation, but it is the linking of all four aspects that most strongly influences successful performance. On its own, without the reinforcement of the others, each aspect contributes relatively little to performance. However, the integration of all four, especially the linking of goals and support, and goals and evaluation, has a marked effect on results.

This approach to process control can apply to any individual task—aimed at improving Current Business Performance—and to many aspects of managing organisational changes. This is another reason why Performance Management capability contributes to both Current Business Performance and Change Effectiveness. Some of the key management actions associated generally with effective change, such as monitoring and setting priorities, are linked with this competence.

Performance Management, action and key individuals

Performance Management capability is strongly linked to taking action, rather than talking about taking action. It exists to improve action. It is focused on action, often as it happens. It sets goals for action, supports action, gives feedback on action and rewards action. We saw in Chapter 5 how Engagement capability stimulates early action in relation to corporate change. Performance Management continues and reinforces that process, and improves the quality of the action that takes place.

Nowhere is that more visible than in the actions of chief executives who have strong personal capability in Performance Management. As part of our study, we were able to measure the degree to which each competence depended for its strength on a key individual or a very few. To our initial surprise, performance control, the competence that is most strongly related to the capability, has a high level of dependency on the skills of key individuals in the organisation. Pathfinding has the highest level of dependency on key individuals and we discussed the reasons for this in Chapter 5. Performance control has the second highest.

There is a tendency to see Performance Management as the application of systems and practices that are embedded in the organisation's control and influence processes and routines. This is an important aspect of performance control, the more so because much of it continues automatically and is less affected by the absence of individuals. Because of this it is easy to overlook the key shaping role that an individual often plays. Perhaps the most important aspect, which individuals influence, is the level or standard of performance they expect, or in many cases demand. This has to be coupled with the shape of those expectations—that is, the particular aspects of performance they value, which is also frequently determined by the focus and interest of top management.

Welch's Performance Management at GE

Many of the aspects of change at GE illustrate this. Jack Welch has outstanding capability in Performance Management. His approach from the beginning was to use financial measures to drive the change process. Welch comments:[1]

> 'The starting point was always lousy financial returns. It would become obvious that cutting costs was the only solution.'

Strategic goals for the businesses, to be number one or two in their industries, were also clear.

Intense personal evaluation of progress, whether in a general interactive way in the 'cave' with his top management, or in the 'pit' with other managers, was one way he continually confronted reality. The rewards for achievement at a general level were also clear. If you couldn't achieve the goals, your business would be closed or sold. No doubt if you made it, the rewards were equally concrete, certain and appropriate. A major focus of Welch's efforts, certainly until seven years after his appointment, when he started Work-Out, was on Performance Management.

It was through actions based on this capability that he made his significant impact on the business in the first long phase of his tenure. Since Performance Management impacts on both Current Business Performance and Change Effectiveness, Welch's individual capability affected both. When later he realised that change was not taking place sufficiently at the business level, he moved into Engagement and Development as key aspects of generating and sustaining long-term performance. What, however, for our present discussion is important, is the impact that a key individual made on a business with over a quarter of million people. Our study shows that this is most often done through pathfinding and Performance Management and, in his own style, Welch was strong in both of these.

Simons' Performance Management at Woolworths

Paul Simons at Woolworths had enormous strength in both Performance Management and Engagement. He started displaying this at the first meeting of his top team. The meeting did not start with a survey of company strategy or a discussion about the future, but with a bag of their products, which top management were asked to price in relation to a chief competitor. Price competitiveness was the chief focus of Paul Simons' Performance Management action. He phoned the central buyers directly when he found uncompetitive prices. He intervened at the level at which those decisions were taking place. Simons' actions to improve the performance of pallet loadings was similarly direct. He and his managing director checked things personally at midnight, when pallet deliveries were taking place. He approached improving customer service in the same way.

Woolworths is a big company with over a thousand stores throughout Australia. Some people would argue that Simons should not have spent time in these direct intervening actions. But his personal Performance Management capability expressed in his actions had a major impact on people's behaviour throughout the organisation. He found it a better way, for him, to get change moving—to dynamite the logjam. Other CEOs would, of course, have done it differently. Their different actions may have also been effective. The underlying capability is what is important.

What is also important is that Woolworths built on the personal competence of Paul Simons by developing capabilities, systems and practices that embedded these improvements in the business. For example, pricing practice was changed. The logistics involving the distribution of goods were upgraded and systematised. Computer-based inventory management impacted on customer service. New processes and new related positions were introduced to improve store performance, and so on. When he retired a few years later they were, broadly, in place.

GE consists of businesses in many industries. Woolworths is almost wholly in mass retailing and Paul Simons had expert knowledge of it. Jack Welch would not have had the expert knowledge of his many businesses to intervene in the way that Simons did, and it may not have been his preferred way. But both leaders used their own personal capabilities with marked effect. They set standards for what they expected and took action to ensure others knew and responded. They are good, but not untypical, examples of the ways in which key individuals can contribute to the effectiveness of change through personal capability in Performance Management.

Setting standards at Robert's store

Robert had a first-hand experience of the impact on his own behaviour of the Performance Management competence of the group's chief executive. He had just finished a major refitting and relaying of the big department store to which he was promoted. The job had taken place over twenty-six successive weekends when the store was closed. This meant that Robert had worked without a real break for six months. The group's chief executive delegated the job of managing the department store group to the store's director and his own personal visits to the department stores were relatively few. Robert was therefore surprised to get a telephone call to say the CEO would be visiting the store to see the results of the refit.

It was rather like a visit from God. The CEO was not a man who exuded personal warmth, though there was no shadow of a doubt about his commitment to performance or his personal competence. Robert walked the CEO through the newly refitted eight floors. He was clearly impressed and took great interest in the new fixtures and displays. It took quite a time from the morning start, and lunchtime, which was not scheduled, began to loom.

'Robert,' said the CEO, 'why don't we have lunch together in the restaurant?'

Robert, who had not lunched alone with the group's CEO before, quickly arranged a table for two in the store's restaurant. He hoped the meal would be of a good standard, as the CEO was known for his interest in food. The meal was fine. Robert was beginning to feel quite good, even good about the CEO, who had always been a somewhat distant, aloof and cold figure. Towards the end of the meal, the CEO found it necessary to visit the men's toilet. Robert watched him returning to the table. He sensed something was wrong.

'Have you seen the condition of that toilet?' the CEO asked as he sat down.

Robert paused. 'No. Is there something wrong?'

'You had better go and see for yourself.'

Robert, feeling like a chastened child, rose and walked to the toilet wondering what disaster waited for him. The toilet looked completely normal. Robert looked in each cubicle expecting a shock. They were all in good condition. The pull-down towelling had not run out. The floor was clean. He looked around carefully. Something must be wrong. On the small table was a glass ashtray on a white tablecloth. Robert moved the ashtray. Completely hidden beneath the ashtray, the tablecloth had a small ragged hole, its edges coloured by a faded cigarette stain. Robert thought of the acres of floors they had walked through about which the CEO had been so complimentary and he felt a surge of anger. Nevertheless he took a deep breath and kept an exterior calm. He returned to the CEO.

'I assume you are referring to the tablecloth,' Robert began, but the CEO cut him short.

'Who is responsible for that toilet?'

'I am,' said Robert.

'I know that,' replied the CEO testily, 'but which manager is responsible to you for that toilet?'

Robert paused, feeling anything but calm. 'Well it comes under the restaurant manager, but you have to remember, Sir, that manager has been working for the last twenty-six weekends feeding those of us who have been relaying the store. He's probably tired and I expect he overlooked it.' By now Robert was feeling more in control and he spoke quite firmly.

The CEO looked at him unblinking. 'Robert,' he began, 'you are responsible for the standards in this store. Everyone else will set their standards by yours. If you accept low standards, if you overlook table-cloths like that, standards will become low in your store everywhere. If you do not do it, no one else will. It is your responsibility.'

Robert took a longer pause. 'I'll talk to the manager,' he said. He did. He made the same points, but differently.

Robert passed that toilet hundreds of times in the following few years, but he never went in it without thinking of the CEO's comment. He nearly always looked at the tablecloth and also the tablecloths in the other toilets. His behaviour had in fact changed. He did not like what had happened and the way the CEO had dealt with him. But he knew in his heart of hearts, and found in his own experience, that what the CEO had said about standards, and expectations of performance being set at the top, was true.

Robert's CEO was also consistent. He increased Robert's salary by 50 per cent at the end of Robert's first year in his first store. He believed and practised high standards, set high performance expectations and gave appropriate rewards. In his own style, he had high personal Performance Management capability.

Reliance on corporate saviours

While key individuals can make a major impact on Change Effective-ness, particularly in the area of Performance Management, dependence on these individuals can be dangerous and become self-perpetuating.

There are frequent stories in management magazines of the appoint-ment of a new CEO to turn round the performance of a troubled com-pany. This effort is typically led by chief executives who are described in terms of outstanding drive, relentless purpose, energy, tough, challeng-ing, confrontational, and so on. The immediate improvement, in some cases in quite large corporations, is seen to be the result of the new indi-vidual's skills and effort. There is often a substantial reduction in the organisation's operations. Large parts are sold and investment in some areas is lowered to improve returns. A focus is then placed on the organisation's limited better performing areas for which high expectations and goals are set. This is accompanied by the introduction of new performance benchmarks and measurements, and further efforts to cut waste and reduce costs.

Poor performing organisations may well have no option but to depend upon a saviour, but, unless the organisation begins to build its collective management strengths and its corporate capabilities, it is essentially still in a weak situation with little influence over its own destiny. When the new leader's energy flags or fails, or when an irresistible financial offer replete with high rewards for rapid improvement in share price arrives, and it impels a move to the next flagging firm, the organisation is forced to look for another energetic and charismatic replacement to rescue it. The pattern of failure and rescue will be repeated until the organisation has begun to develop its own capabilities.

This does not suggest that a great contribution from top management is not wanted or needed, far from it. It is dependence upon it that is dangerous.

Collins and Porras, in their research into outstanding companies with long-term high performance, found that high performing companies essentially grow their own top management. The eighteen companies they put into this category had been in existence for a combined total of seventeen hundred years but, in that very long time:[2]

> '... we found only four individual cases of an outsider coming directly into the role of chief executive.'

What these companies have undoubtedly done, and very many good companies do it, is to develop a corporate competence in management development. Such companies can not only fill their top role from inside but also frequently have a wide and difficult choice to make among several qualified candidates. Welch's own appointment in GE was an example of this.

This does not mean that outside appointments cannot be successful. Very many are. It does mean, however, that long-term success requires the development of collective and embedded capabilities if the organisation is to lessen its dependence on temporary leadership.

Resource application

Resource application is another area of Performance Management where individuals at the top of the organisation are well placed to make a significant contribution. Here the link with pathfinding is important. Setting priorities for new directions is a key action for Change Effectiveness and competence in resource application enables priorities to be met. Top managers have an overall perspective and knowledge of the business and its future. This enables them to decide between competing requests for resources knowing the constraints of the business and the time pressures in the marketplace. Some of the opportunities the business faces may be for a limited window of time. Some of the demands will be for particularly limited resources—for example, computing resources—or for people with special skills that cannot be rapidly expanded within the firm. So setting priorities, which is important to Performance Management, is often best done at the highest levels if the best use is to be made of resources, and if change is to be steered and pushed in the right direction.

A good deal of the thrust of Jack Welch's work at GE was about the way GE should allocate and apply its resources. Welch wanted to concentrate resources in businesses that could dominate their industries, compete on a global scale and return high earnings on the resources. There was a program of divestment and acquisition to hasten that. At Woolworths, there was an initial reduction in the number of stores and a concentration of resources into stores in the supermarket division, which would be in the vanguard of the new fresh food policy. At the NSW State Library resources were transferred from a small group of information search specialists to a more widely distributed group to improve service. At StorageTek, resource application took the form of resources being applied to the recruitment of people with the specific skills needed to implement its new strategy. None of these businesses was facing failure. In fact the businesses were all successful—even Woolworths, whose significant profit drop was the first in sixty-two years. But every business took firm action to apply some of their resources differently to achieve the changes they sought.

Systems and practices

While the personal skills of key individuals are important to effective Performance Management, many competencies that combine to form this capability become part of the organisation's embedded systems and practices.

The advent of computerisation and the capturing of processes, of all forms, in software, has hastened the flow of information on which actions need to be based. The stronger application of statistical techniques, often at factory floor level, and the development of financial, production and other forms of measurement generally have upgraded the knowledge base of performance control competence. While professional judgment, or gut feel, will always be an important component of decision making, developments in information gathering and processing have improved the knowledge and skill basis for much Performance Management.

Operational skills tend to be more compartmentalised and are usually measured in terms of particular functions. For example, production departments will measure output, work in progress, capacity utilisation, labour costs, aspects of speed of manufacture, and so on. Marketing will collect results of market share, penetration of geographical areas, the cost of selling, advertising response, and so on. So change action in these areas often impacts only a part of the organisation.

Financial competencies, however, while employed within functions, are used more often to measure cross-functional or organisational results, such as revenues, margins, profit, debt or cost of capital. Their influence can therefore be more widespread and pervasive, and influence mindsets and behaviours on a much wider scale across the organisation.

Performance Management draws heavily on financial and planning skills. The importance of this in aiding effective change is becoming more widely recognised in practices involved, for example, in the 'balanced scorecard' approach to performance and change.

A great deal of Performance Management capability is also embedded in the practices of the business. Woolworths, for example, built practices, in store reviews, which were the specific responsibilities of its managers. Their requirement to ensure a vacant chair was placed at every meeting to represent the customer was an attempt to improve performance and embed the practice across the organisation. Du Pont embedded many of the practices of Performance Management into their accreditation programs.

Bernard Fournier, as chief executive of Rank Xerox, in outlining some of the firm's actions which led to its receiving the European Quality Award in 1993, comments about the impact of embedded practices on the Performance Management, in this case, of aspects of customer satisfaction:[3]

> 'What Leadership through Quality did was to focus our energies, planning and ways of working on the goal of 100 per cent customer satisfaction. We came to regard customer satisfaction as the route to sustained business success, since it has a direct impact on their likelihood to repurchase.'

Jerry Bowles, in illustrating Rank Xerox's approach, describes three formal mechanisms for listening to customers:[4]

> 'First there is a post-installation questionnaire that is sent 90 days after an installation to determine how the company performed throughout the ordering and delivery period. Second, an annual customer satisfaction survey seeks comments on the company's general performance. The survey is continuously updated to reflect those issues that are most relevant to customers. Finally an anonymous survey is conducted each year to determine who customers believe is the number one supplier in Rank Xerox's target markets.
>
> ' "Above all," comments Fournier, "we tie our employees' rewards to the results".'

What we see in this description is a linking of goals, evaluation and reward. The particular actions, techniques or systems used are simply the manifestation, in action, of the underlying competence. Performance Management is a major way in which firms make incremental change and improvement. It therefore links current performance with a continuing process of improvement, which over time achieves effective change.

It might be thought that high capability in Performance Management could be associated with high or undue pressure on staff and consequent loss of staff to the organisation. Our study shows that this is not generally the case. Organisations reporting high Performance Management capability do not reduce their staff, or change their staff, or introduce new people on a different scale than organisations with low Performance Management capability. They do, however, introduce more new practices and technology just as they are more active in training. Thus strong Performance Management capability actually drives change. By identifying systemic flaws it focuses effort on changes that will clearly improve the business. In so doing it improves existing assets, both people and systems, raises their value to the business, and reduces any incentive to replace them with external resources.

Performance Management and cultural change

Our study shows that Performance Management capability is strongly linked to success in cultural change. Part of the process of cultural change is to get people to alter the way they see and do things, and to adapt to new ideas, strategies and methods. Goals play some part in this but it is feedback on performance—a critical part of Performance Management capability—that assists people to make these adjustments. Feedback helps people understand how they are functioning in the changing environment. Monitoring enhances the prospect of effective feedback and thus aids successful adaptation.

We could contrast the strong impact that Performance Management has on cultural change with the impact on change focusing on reorganisation. Reorganisation involves changes to the management and reporting structures of the business. Reorganisation can be achieved and established by management action and authority. It is at a visible and rational level. So there is much less need for changing behaviour than there is with cultural change. Even so, though less important to reorganisation, Performance Management still affects the success of reorganisation.

A lot of people treat achieving quality management as about engendering the 'right' attitude and spirit to the process. Indeed in some cases it almost develops a religious flavour. They forget that central to Japanese quality management, following the gospel of Deming and Juran, was measurement, the use of benchmarks and action to deal with measured results that fell outside the benchmarks. Performance control was vital to the process. The latter stages of changes at Du Pont exemplify this.

Du Pont's reshaping involved a major change in workplace culture. It took place against a background of long-standing poor industrial relations. The creation of some level of trust was necessary before any real sustained progress could be made. This was provided substantially through Engagement and Development capability. Performance Management, however, played a key role in influencing behaviour over longer periods of time. The establishment of project teams at the non-managerial level focused discussion on performance improvement and on ways to measure it. The cross-disciplinary nature of the teams aided the integration process, which is an important part of Performance Management capability. Many of the changes began to surface as collective ideas from the small teams. Monitoring performance and reporting on progress was an important part of the new emerging culture. As the changes became embedded in the benchmarking and accreditation process, and in other practices, they played an important part both in Current Business Performance and Change Effectiveness.

Performance Management and integration

For very many managers, dealing with operational issues is relatively straightforward. They are trained to do it and their staff have been similarly focused on delivering current performance. Frequently such issues yield to analysis, have a solid factual basis, can be relatively easily measured, and managers can be held accountable for the results.

But change is frequently less clearly defined. There is less certainty about what should be done. Indeed, in the absence of solid data, what needs to be changed and the action to take is often hotly disputed. Both relevant knowledge and appropriate action may only emerge as the changes progress. The ramifications of the changes often go far across the organisation and integration then becomes a major challenge. As one chief executive put it:[5]

> 'It's like the company is undergoing four medical procedures at the same time. One person's in charge of the root canal job, someone else is setting the broken foot, another person is working on the displaced shoulder and still another is getting rid of the gallstones. Each operation is a success but the patient dies of shock.'

One of the biggest challenges of change lies in the integration of effort—the knitting together of what is going on across the organisation as change widens in its impact. This takes place across a number of dimensions. First, it is necessary to integrate the new directions with the actions needed to achieve them. Performance Management processes are important to this in setting goals, supporting action and giving feedback and reward. This helps to link new strategies with relevant action and assists in behavioural change.

Second, it is necessary to integrate the current with the future. Some of this linking takes place through the improvement and development of the organisation's current business technologies into future technologies. In some cases linking of the current with the future is also encouraged by Performance Management systems, processes and actions that result in incremental change. Changes arising in this way become more easily and efficiently embedded in the processes and systems of the business, and incorporated into its regular behaviours. However, when major or transformational change is needed pathfinding plays a key role in integrating the current with the future by identifying what must be changed in the current organisation to lay a base and enable a bridge to be built to the envisioned future.

Third, it is necessary to integrate all parts of the organisation in the change. Engagement enables different parts of the organisation to take their own integrating action as a result of a shared vision, improved communication and information flow. But Performance Management makes a number of important contributions and mechanisms. Performance review systems help to integrate the person and the task with the organisational goals for change. Steering committees can provide an overall perspective and influence on the performance of the change process. Cross-boundary task forces, or work groups, can help to integrate across divisions or units or functions. They influence individuals as well as groups. In some situations new roles, such as change program director, or specialised liaison roles, may help to integrate complex activities and processes.

Actions that help Performance Management

Some of the actions that are particularly linked with Performance Management are also associated with the other two reshaping capabilities, Engagement and Development. These include training, monitoring, introducing new technology and systems, and recognising contributions to change. We have commented on these earlier and their relevance to Performance Management capability is relatively clear.

Setting priorities

Setting priorities is important at the beginning of any change attempt, but reviewing and sometimes resetting them as change develops may be just as vital. Setting priorities is linked to Performance Management and it has a strong role in Change Effectiveness. Change is a dynamic and often continuous process. Setting priorities early in the change process also helps generate the involvement of others. It helps to change focus and behaviour. It is often the first visible step that signals to the many, on whom effective change depends, that top management really means business—that top management is moving to action and others need to get on board. Setting priorities usually involves allocation of responsibility so that other managers and the workforce are asked to take responsibility.

One of the criticisms of some approaches to Performance Management is that it sets up too many goals and measures too many things. People become overwhelmed with information, confused and end up by not taking action. The recent development of 'plans on a page' is not only a reaction to the plethora of measurements and aims of some performance improvement programs, but an extremely effective and practical way of setting priorities, often right down the line. When these are effectively linked to corporate goals, they can be an important element in the impact that Performance Management has on Change Effectiveness.

Performance Management and organisational states

It is little surprise that high esprit de corps exists where Performance Management is high. High Performance Management goes with high performance and results in confidence. High Performance Management is associated with successful firms, not with failing firms.

Having suitable systems and practices for the work that is needed is also an understandable result of having high Performance Management capability and vice versa. And by now we are used to seeing high workloads associated with high capabilities. Capabilities do not grow on trees. They are developed by hard work and talent over time and maintained by them. Heavy workloads imply high energy and high interest, and these are also needed for managing performance improvement. They also usually go hand in hand with high commitment.

Summary

Performance Management plays a key integrative role in change and performance. It is important to both Current Business Performance and Change Effectiveness. It calls on a wide skill and knowledge base. It affects task performance and has a major influence on behaviour change. When it is strong, the level of action in the business is high. Individuals can have high impact on change through their skills in this capability. It is of particular importance in cultural change because of its impact on how people see their work and responsibilities. While much of it is embedded in systems, processes and practices, its efficacy can be improved when it is reinforced by shared values and culture.

Firms strong in Performance Management capability tend to have relatively strong systems and practices and are skilled in developing them. They are good at monitoring, generally strong in training and have high workloads. Their staff turnover is similar to organisations with low Performance Management capability, but their processes and technology change faster. As with other capabilities, when Performance Management capability is strong, esprit de corps is high.

CHAPTER 8

Reshaping capabilities: a consolidation

THE MANAGING DIRECTOR wanted to introduce a new set of performance indicators. He had been persuaded by the human resources manager to have a workshop with a few senior managers to help identify the areas to be targeted and the form the measures might take. We were to facilitate the workshop. The managing director was very clear about what he wanted to do and what the meeting should achieve. We asked: 'Suppose the meeting comes to some different conclusions?' 'Well, of course, I would have to think about it,' was his not too enthusiastic reply.

The workshop made good progress. The managing director contributed positively to it. There were some differences, which had been largely resolved. The chosen indicators included those on which the managing director was focused, and a few others not high on his agenda. The meeting, which had been losing momentum as it grappled with differences in view, turned with a new-found energy and drive to thoughts of implementation and action.

Let's 'roll it out' as quickly as possible was the managing director's view. He said, 'We know what we want, and we need it in the shortest possible time.' The thought of bold, firm, decisive, mandated action clearly caught the small group's attention. 'Roll it out', frequently repeated, seemed to bring the group to life and dates for immediate action and early dates for 'completion' were suggested.

We suggested the meeting should think about the substantial number of managers who would be involved in developing and implementing the system, and who would be judged by it. They, unlike the few managers in the workshop, had not been exposed to the process, ideas and requirements that had helped to fashion the final outcome. Perhaps there was some need to get them positively engaged. There was a distinct chill in the warmth that the thought of action had engendered in the meeting. Having made their own minds up most, though not all, of the senior managers wanted to institute the changes involved without delay. The view was that 'we can say something in the memo about that, but we want to get on with it without too much time and talk. We're running a business, not a debating shop.'

'Could you tell us,' we asked, 'what was the last new change intervention you instituted?' There was a pause. 'It was the new performance appraisal system.'

'How is it working?' There was a longer pause. 'Not at all well,' said the human resources manager. When asked why, he said, 'Well I'm afraid we didn't really explain it very well. People thought there was some hidden agenda, though there wasn't. The managers who had to do the appraising, in some cases, didn't have the skills. And we didn't set up a system to monitor it in the particular region we introduced it. I think it's more or less run into the ground. We will have to put it back on track.'

On another occasion we were interacting with a chief executive who had been appointed to her position a year or two earlier. She had high managerial and interpersonal skills. In her first few months, she had made some changes in which she had engaged her people. They had been successful. She had become more knowledgeable about her organisation and more confident about what needed to be done to improve its performance. She was now thinking of further changes. 'What I realised is that I was just about to make a significant change and because I knew what I wanted I was going to skip what you call Engagement. It takes such time and energy and I just wanted to get on with it. I realised, in thinking about why the previous changes had worked, that the people involved really did become engaged and committed. I realised, in time, Engagement was not an option, it was a necessity.'

Many of the actions that managers want to take have the potential to make significant improvement and change in their organisation's performance. Besides specific action arising directly from their own analysis and experience, a range of particular forms of intervention has offered opportunity to apply measures or approaches that have worked in other organisations. Change intervention approaches or tools have emerged in increasing numbers during the last few decades. Many are potentially valuable. For example, outsourcing, re-engineering, the balanced score card and EVA (economic value-added) join earlier versions of specific approaches such as TQM, MBO, JIT, Kaizen, ISO accreditation, matrix management, job redesign, and so on. On a broader canvas, downsizing, reduction to core competencies, concentration rather than diversification, and market dominance by acquisition, are examples of recommended change interventions that spread more broadly into the strategic realm.

Some of these particular approaches may well be relevant for your situation. However, what our data show is that unless your organisation is managed in approaching these changes in a way that achieves Engagement, the Development of the skills and resources involved, and the Performance Management of the process, they are unlikely to succeed. The failure rate of all these interventions is high, yet the substance of many of the ideas they represent may well be sound. Hammer who pioneered the ideas of 're-engineering' is quoted as saying that:[1]

> '... two-thirds of re-engineering efforts ... have crashed in flames, shot down by people's reluctance to go along and by management's— especially top management's—own ineptitude and fear.'

The 'Kiss of Yes'

The development of a new set of performance indicators may well be an important aspect of improving performance or changing the culture of an organisation, as was the case in our first example. However, the process was about to be managed in a way that was likely to fail to achieve the Engagement of a number of relevant people or to address vital aspects of their needed Development. The preceding approach of intro-ducing a new method of performance appraisal as part of change was in fact failing in terms of Engagement, Development and Performance Management, and yet the organisation was about to repeat the mistake. In the case of performance indicators there was an attempt to engage those at a senior level and this was valuable. But it was not going to go to a deep enough level to engage a critical mass of those directly affected who needed to be engaged if it was to work. They would simply have to comply as they had also been expected to comply with the failing performance appraisal system. Hammer calls this the 'Kiss of Yes'.[2]

Engagement, of course, takes time, effort and skill. Even those who may believe in it, and can achieve it, are tempted, as in our second example, to give it, or Development or Performance Management, a miss for a variety of real pressures, only two of which are time and effort.

The framework of the three reshaping capabilities—Engagement, Development and Performance Management— provides a basis for action that is needed to achieve effective change, whether we are looking at 'popular' forms of change interventions, like those mentioned above, or action to more generally change the structure, culture or important aspects of the way in which the organisation works. The fundamental thing is not so much that the particular ideas or concepts being intro-duced have themselves to work, but rather that the organisation has to work, using and integrating the new concepts, or different ones if these do not fit the need.

Action in the three reshaping areas helps initiatives to work to move the organisation from its present position and its current results, to its new position and its future results. It also shapes the key questions that managers need to ask: Are our people engaged in this change? What action can we take to improve Engagement? Are we developing the resources, skills, systems and processes we will need for our new direc-tions? What further action is needed? Are we managing the processes of change effectively? What more can we do to ensure we achieve our intended aims?

The framework also provides a fundamental test against which any proposed action can be measured: Will the proposed action help Engage-ment, or Development or Performance Management?

As the framework distils the essence of what needs to happen, it is useful for any manager responsible for change, but it is particularly important for those at the top of an organisation. Top management should never lose sight of the main game—the key things they need to achieve. A lot is happening when an organisation is undergoing substantial change. It is all too easy to be distracted by the myriad issues that clamour for attention. While undoubtedly many top managers can play a key role in problem solving and technical matters, making sure the fundamental needs of change success are met is more important.

The particular actions that any manager takes in these three key areas need to be relevant to the organisation, its history, positioning, culture, competition, and the changes it is trying to make. The examples we have described—including Woolworths, Du Pont, GE, StorageTek and others—illustrate what managers did in their particular circumstances. This helps to develop a sense of the part each capability plays in the process of change and establishes a base of understanding to which you will add your own insights and perspectives.

Can one framework really apply to all change situations?

When we think of the enormous range and variety of changes that organisations face, it seems hard to accept that one framework can provide a sound basis for action in all of them. Some changes are minor, while others are massive. Some changes take place to exploit a market opportunity, while others introduce a new technology or a change in business culture. And so on. While we may believe that action in Engagement, Development and Performance Management may apply in some situations we should ask ourselves: Can one framework really apply to all situations of change? Does action in Engagement, Development and Performance Management always influence the effectiveness of change in all situations? Surely they are not relevant in some circumstances.

In answering these important questions, the first and vital point to make is that *every change is different*. In no situation can the capabilities framework be unthinkingly applied. In some respects, perhaps in many, your organisation and circumstances are unique. For example, your organisation will be stronger in some capabilities than others. The states of your organisation will reflect your situation—no one else's. Even though there may be some things in common with other organisations, your particular changes will be different in many others. Some of your actions will have more impact than others. So your particular actions in Engagement, Development and Performance Management will need to be relevant to your situation and changes, and they will have a particular impact in that context.

We mentioned earlier that we carried out many tests to check the reliability of our data. We also checked the validity of our data in many different situations and contexts. For example, we looked at whether the impact of the three reshaping capabilities on effective change was different for small organisations compared to large, or for those that had, or had not, experienced previous change, or for those in the public or private sectors. We examined their impact on organisations following different strategies—for example, in contraction, or development, or reorienting into new markets, or continuing but constantly refining a current strategy. We looked to see if there were differences in the importance of the capabilities in situations where change was seen as an opportunity or a threat. We explored the impact of the three reshaping capabilities where the focus of change was principally on cost reduction, or on organisational restructuring, or changing culture or values. And we also looked to see if there were differences when the focus was on market factors, customers and competitors, or on introducing new technology. We tested whether it made any difference if the change occurred over a short or long time, whether the pace was gradual or fast, or the changes were major or minor.

In all these differing situations our data show that capability in the three areas of Engagement, Development and Performance Management is always linked with the achievement of effective change.

It is against this background of the general universality of the framework that we want, in this chapter, to consider the applicability of particular capabilities to effective change—first in *cultural change*, secondly in *change in public sector organisations*, and thirdly in *change that results from mergers and acquisitions*.

Cultural change

A threat or opportunity creates a challenge for an organisation. The resulting change often has a particular focus. It might be a focus on top management, corporate culture, reorganisation, operating practices, staff numbers, technology, market scope, and so on. So while the purpose of the change is to improve the performance of the business, it often tends to be focused on a particular factor that is felt to be the prime cause of current weakness. Approximately half our sample believed changing culture was a primary focus of their change. Of course culture was not the only aspect they were trying to change.

Changing culture was central to the changes at Du Pont where the purpose was to change the fundamental relationship between managers and workforce—to get them to work together as a precursor and enabler of other changes. Cultural change may well be combined with entering new markets, as it was at StorageTek, to a lesser extent at Woolworths in its focus on fresh food, and at the NSW State Library in its entrepreneurial seeking of new commercial markets. A change in culture is where 'the way we do business here'—the values, beliefs and behavioural norms of the business—are the focus of change.

What our research shows

Figure 8.1 shows the *impact* each capability has on Change Effectiveness and the *average strength* of each capability for organisations attempting cultural change. The left-hand bars show the impact of the capabilities on Change Effectiveness in two situations:

- when cultural change is the primary focus of the change (the black bars)
- when cultural change is not the primary focus of the change (the white bars).

The longer the bar the more the capability impacts on the success of the change. The right-hand bars show the average strengths of the capabilities that organisations typically have at the time when change is

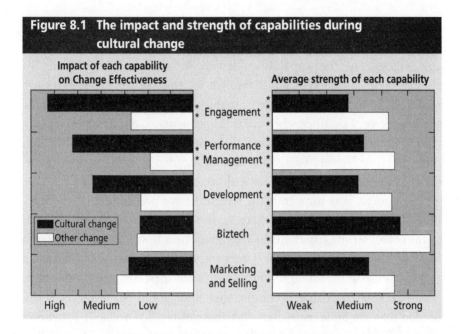

Figure 8.1 The impact and strength of capabilities during cultural change

attempted. The black bars show the strength of the capabilities for organisations attempting cultural change and the white bars for those attempting other changes.

We indicate whether the difference between two bars is significant by placing some asterisks at the base of the pair of bars. The more asterisks there are, the more significant the finding and the more certain the difference. If there are no asterisks present, then the difference is not statistically significant. It may nonetheless still be important. It is simply that we do not have enough cases in the subsample to say definitely one way or another. These instances are ones where you particularly need to take account of your own experience and observations.

Capabilities typically weak, when strength is needed

If we look first at the impact of each capability on Change Effectiveness (the left-hand section of Figure 8.1), you can see Engagement and Performance Management have a significantly stronger impact on the success of cultural change. The impact of Development is also stronger but not significantly so. If we look at the right-hand section, at the average strength of the capabilities which organisations attempting to change their culture typically have, we see that all the capabilities are significantly weaker and the two capabilities most important for change success are very significantly weaker. So, in general, organisations facing cultural change need to be especially strong in the capabilities in which they are typically very weak. So the tools needed to reshape the organisation, in particular to change its culture, are in poor condition.

Of course, it is important to remember we are talking of averages here. The data do not mean there are no organisations facing cultural change with strong capabilities. There will be a few. But very many will have very weak capabilities. It is very important for managers to have a realistic sense of the strength of capabilities in their organisations—both personal and corporate. Without this understanding, what is really needed may be underestimated and changes tackled without providing for the effort, resources and skills necessary for success.

One reason why capabilities are low may be that the pre-existing culture put little emphasis on performance or professionalism, or developing new skills, overlooked inadequate performance and failed to reward good performance. When capabilities became less valued by the culture of the firm, they weakened. So the low level of capability was a reflection of a culture of the firm, and thus an important factor requiring the firm to try to change the culture. Another reason is that the situation of the firm is now changed and the pre-existing capabilities, which were built on the pre-existing values and beliefs, are no longer relevant and therefore are diminished and weak for the job that must now be done. Members of the firm are now asked to change not only some of their skills and actions but also the beliefs and values on which they are based. The change now involves substantial 'unlearning' to change the culture and develop new relevant capabilities.

So cultural change is about changing ways in which people think about the business, the things they value and the behaviours they typically show—'the way we do things around here'. Some of these aspects are illustrated in Gavin's story.

Gavin's story

'I started with the company as a trainee, working in one of the depots. It's an industrial equipment hire firm. We hire out compressors and rollers, generators, lifting equipment, sheds, trades gear—all the equipment that construction companies and industrial operators need from time to time.

'I'd worked my way up to a managerial level a few years back. Then the board appointed a new chief executive—Jack. This was just at the start of the recession. The board was looking for sustained high performance, and apparently didn't think we'd been doing well enough up to then—though all the management had been pretty happy with how we were going.

'Jack was from outside. He obviously impressed the board, since they appointed him. However, the rest of us weren't that taken with him. He'd been around a bit, worked in several industries, but not ours—not the hire business. He didn't come at a good time. The hire business dropped off quickly at the start of the recession.

'Jack spent some months getting to know the organisation and its key executives. Then he talked some of the regional managers into leaving. They were probably happy to go. They had been with the company a long time. They were getting close to retirement. They got a good payout to take an extended vacation and they didn't have to cope with the recession.

'And it wasn't so bad for some of us younger ones. We got to step up. That was when I became a regional manager. Jack filled most of the positions with insiders, though he did bring in a new chief finance officer from outside.

'About five or six months after he started, Jack held a planning conference of the regional managers and their finance managers to establish plans and promote the message he was trying to get across about a profit-oriented culture.

'The conference started quietly. But there was already a lot of repressed heat. The company had owned the franchise rights to sell a very popular brand of trades tool. The depots used to act as sales outlets for these tools, as well as hiring out gear. The tool sales were a sideline, but a good revenue generator, and they brought customers in the door. Jack had sold the franchise rights to someone else. We didn't have it anymore and some of the guys felt pretty snaky about that. They'd put a lot of effort into building up that sideline.

'Jack explained to the conference what he was expecting in terms of profit results and the fact that all of us would need to make some tough choices. Given the way the recession was going, we were really expecting that. However, then he began telling us we would need to change how far we went to satisfy customers—that we were doing too much for not enough return.

'The meeting got pretty heated after that. Some of the regional managers reckoned the business could not survive that way. I might have been one of them. Our feeling of outrage about the loss of the trades tools franchise came out too. It had brought in good, steady income that helped to cushion downturns in hire income. We needed that now and we no longer had it.

'We were also pretty unhappy about the new constraints on capital expenditure. We were used to a pretty free spending approach to get the gear our customers were asking for. That had been our approach. Look after the customers and the revenue would roll in. Get the revenue and you would be profitable enough.

'That wasn't Jack's message. He said we needed to get our assets working harder and focus more on the clients who were most valuable. We had to pay attention to things like better credit control. The tools franchise was gone forever. The company needed the cash from it for the base business. He also wanted our people focused on being good hire operators, not mini-merchants. He stood up for himself and took the flak.

'None of us would admit it at the time but we knew there was a grain of truth in what he was saying. Some of our customers were real rogues and lurk merchants. Even if they paid us, often it did not match the damage they had done to the equipment. But others were great. We just needed more of them.

'Jack and the new chief finance officer introduced a revised reporting system showing profit of units and sub-units. It provided much faster information than the previous monthly reports. Jack didn't make any major structural changes, but he kept leaning on each of us regional managers to come up with changes to support clear line management profit responsibility and accountability.

'He kept the focus on profit through the reporting system and his contact with his managers. You couldn't accuse him of sitting comfortably in head office. He was always on the go. He'd spend two or three days a week out with the regions. Sometimes you'd wish he was more attached to head office.

'He expected us to come up with the changes necessary to achieve real profit focus up and down the line, without damaging service to important customer segments. He made a lot of suggestions, but he was willing to give us our heads a bit. We could try out our own ideas, as long as they seemed generally consistent with the culture he wanted and we were prepared to argue they would improve profit.

'Jack started a series of training programs for managers at all levels. This was teaching them how to take profit responsibility and reminding them they were expected to. We were taught to manage our inventory levels better, how to develop and use information about margin and volume control, and how to evaluate the results of the money we spent on promotions. The company hadn't had this sort of training before.

'Also, it was soon clear that the regions getting most of the new gear were the ones who were earning most and whose capital expenditure proposals were built around a good profit forecast for the gear. We grumbled a bit, but that got us all paying attention to what profit we could earn with any new equipment.

'At the regional level we brought in some new people and moved others around to give more authority to individuals who were profit oriented. The culture did shift. Not everything we tried along the way worked. We went up a few blind alleys; so did Jack. But he was willing to back out and he didn't hold it against us. Just so long as we were clearly trying to get profit better managed.

'We still think about revenue and about how to satisfy customers. But we also think about costs, and about asset utilisation, and about which customers really matter to us. It has really changed the way we now think about the business. And all the time we are thinking about profitability. In fact to be honest I think I almost dream about it.'

Organisational states and cultural change

Organisations attempting cultural change tend not only to have weak capabilities, both reshaping and operational, but typically are low in states that are positive to change and high in states that are negative to change. Understanding the change, commitment to the change, esprit de corps and empowerment are lower, while anxiety, conflict within the organisation and resistance to the change are higher. So typically organisation members do not understand what the change means, why it is necessary and whether they can do what the new culture will ask of them. They feel threatened by it, resist it and often become embroiled in conflict. Many of the people in the organisation will have developed the existing culture. Attempts to change it challenge their values, implicitly criticise their past behaviour and disturb their work patterns. Frequently there is low motivation on the part of many to change. So not only are the capabilities frequently low, but they are also reinforced by the existence of low levels of positive organisational states and high levels of negative states. Jack, in Gavin's story, faced this sort of situation.

Changing minds and behaviour

Culture not only encompasses values and norms of behaviour, but also beliefs about things, shared mental models of the world and how it operates, symbols and the meaning they have, and even the meaning of words and behaviours. So changing culture means changing minds and changing behaviour. If a culture is to change, it has to be through the actions and interactions of members of the culture. It is reinvented through the interactive experiences and interpretations of the culture's members. We could contrast this situation with what is involved in, say, *reorganisation*, or *refining* an existing strategy through incremental change.

Reorganisation changes reporting structures, roles, and resourcing and integration mechanisms. These are relatively objective, visible aspects of an organisation. A single mind can invent and promulgate an organisation structure. A single mind cannot invent and propagate a culture, since a culture is the shared property of minds, each with its own unique embellishments and interpretations that make the culture real and meaningful to each person.

Reorganisation is a rational design activity, which can, and should, be conducted as a largely centralised activity. By contrast, corporate culture is a complex shared mental property, which can only be reinvented through the dispersed actions and interactions of the bulk of the organisation's members. It cannot be redesigned centrally and imposed— though powerful actors within the organisation can provide inputs that encourage evolution in preferred directions.

Changes to restructure an organisation should be in the hands of a small, unified group who understand how and why the organisation currently works, and how and why it needs to change. In the case of cultural change you have no choice but to involve the bulk of the organisation. They have to live the change for it to occur.

Organisations following a change strategy of 'refinement', where the business keeps its current direction but seeks continual incremental improvement, typically start from a position where all their capabilities are relatively strong and all the states that enhance Change Effectiveness are also strong. Change in beliefs is likely to be relatively small, the mechanisms to monitor and consolidate continuous change are likely to be in place, many of the changes can be embedded in the organisation's ongoing current systems and processes, and people are generally empowered to take action and expect support and agreement. None of these advantages is usually available to organisations trying to change culture.

Implications for managers facing cultural change

Actions based on all three reshaping capabilities are needed if cultural change is to be achieved, with Engagement and Performance Management playing the most powerful roles. Pathfinding competence, which is part of Engagement capability, gives a clear sense of direction so that people can see the need for changed behaviours and values. This can help people to recognise problems and start altering their mindsets to see the situation and their role and responsibilities differently. This usually takes time but can be assisted by reiterating a common theme over time and continuously returning to its relevance.

Du Pont's common theme was 'working together', and this pervaded all the actions Wirth took over a long period of time. Woolworths went to considerable lengths to engage its staff in increasing its culture of service and is still using its main slogan more than ten years down the track: 'If you're not serving the customer, serve someone who is.' The two key actors, Simons and Watts, spent a great deal of time and effort in achieving this. As Watts put it, in what turned out to be a substantial understatement, 'people don't hear you the first time around'. In Gavin's story Jack was always continuously pushing the focus of profit. Gavin now not only thinks about it all the time, but also 'almost dreams about it'! At GE when Welch finally turned to the Work-Out program, the first two aims of which were to develop trust and empower employees, he was using Engagement to try and achieve some real change in the culture of the business.

While being very definite about the core values in the new culture and critical performance measures, CEOs should not try to define everything. Managers and the workforce need room to develop themselves and to elaborate and build the culture. Wirth's approach at Du Pont—emphasising 'volunteerism'—gave the workforce room to move and time to do it. Above all, senior managers have to continually demonstrate their commitment to the new culture, by consistent personal behaviour that models it. 'Do as I say and not as I do' will get nowhere. For a new culture to emerge managers must be, or become, true believers. This can be very hard if they have been part of the old culture. But without their personal commitment success is impossible.

Introducing new people can have a very positive impact but they need to have certain characteristics. They need to be 'carriers' of attitudes and behaviours compatible with the intended culture, and they must be able to influence existing members of the organisation. If they lack either of these characteristics, their contribution will be slight. The right new people can provide a model of the new values and skills, which helps existing members see that the new attitudes, behaviours and skills actually work.

However, while individuals can play a positive role and the example of top management is important, our data show the extent of workforce influence makes a big difference to the success of cultural change. That is not the case with most other change situations. Culture develops through action and interaction. The workforce must be actively doing things through which the culture emerges. They need to be actively involved—not passive spectators receiving direction from on high. Genuine consultation, two-way communication and appropriate involvement in pathfinding enable people to understand what is going on and what is expected from them. This is one of the characteristics of GE's Work-Out program. The 'Town Hall' meetings symbolised this in an important way. Often the people being asked to change are those who built the culture. This was obviously the situation at Du Pont where the union had been a major builder of the culture. Involving the union in the solution became a vital part of changing from one culture to another. It is highly unlikely that the culture would have changed without that involvement.

But explaining the reasons why culture should be changed can be like trying to explain to coffee drinkers why they should prefer the taste of tea. They need not only good reasons to think about changing, but also substantial motivating, reinforcing and sometimes compelling action over time. At some stage they have to start drinking tea and persist in doing so until they have acquired a taste for it.

Performance Management is very important to reward or reform, as appropriate, and to focus resources on supporting appropriate new behaviours. If culture is changing, new behaviours will emerge, but some old behaviours will persist. This will require some changes in the control and motivation systems. The airlines described in the previous chapter introduced 'no penalty policy' to alter the behaviour of their pilots; real attention to the signals that current controls and rewards send is important. At Sony the way the company accepted failure was vital to the maintenance of its innovative and entrepreneurial character. In Gavin's story, Jack retired some of the managers who were deeply immersed in the old culture. He introduced new reporting systems to give managers the information to do their job differently and he kept monitoring them with these new data and pressuring them when profit was not improving.

Development, and the organisation's practices and systems, are important because they illustrate, constrain and support behaviour consistent with the intended culture. If you want people to behave differently they will need to see benefits in so doing, and will need positive and salutary reinforcement. At Du Pont the workers were offered programs in personal development, which were needed to give them the confidence to play their new roles.

However, cognitive change is not enough. Performance Management capability also makes a strong contribution to cultural change through setting new kinds of targets, monitoring their achievement, providing meaningful feedback, and shifting resources and authority towards those staff who demonstrate an appreciation of and commitment to the intended culture. It involves rewarding and punishing those actions that are respectively consistent or inconsistent with the intended culture, setting targets that attract actions consistent with that intent, and reallocating resources to support the intended change. This is aided by the psychological phenomenon of dissonance reduction. When we are somehow induced to adopt and maintain a particular behaviour, we tend to adjust our thinking to rationalise and support the behaviour. This is what happened to the pilots at the airlines. It happens when people actually drink tea and acquire a habit and liking for it.

If you are trying to achieve cultural change you need to look very deeply at whether the control and motivation systems do, in fact, encourage the behaviours you want to build. If they do not, change them to ones that do.

CEOs trying to achieve cultural change—for example, moving from a focus on sales volume to a focus on profit, as in Gavin's case—need to give their managers new performance management tools, and work to help them learn how to use those tools. So development of new resources and skills is often critical to achieving cultural change. University deans trying to introduce a culture that values teaching as well as research need to introduce new measurements of how academics spend their time, and help researchers learn teaching program design skills and effective ways of program delivery. Very importantly they need to reward teaching performance through its inclusion in promotional criteria and salary rewards. Putting emphasis on new targets, monitoring them and rewarding results are typically part of the process of culture change. As we will see in Chapter 10, changing a culture, in particular introducing a new culture, can unintentionally displace or undermine other valuable cultures and can sometimes incur very heavy costs. Some banks discovered this in the 1980s when, in trying to introduce a selling culture into the loan business, they undermined effective credit management with disastrous consequences for their overall performance.

Leaders trying to change a culture can provide stimuli that contribute to and influence the reshaping. But they cannot control all the actions that occur, nor the way they, and the responses evoked, ricochet through the organisation. So they cannot fully determine the culture that emerges. This creates an enormous constraint on changing corporate culture.

Without action and interaction of the organisation's members you cannot shift culture. But you cannot control all the interactions, and so the cultural change you get may not be the one that you want. This reinforces the critical role of all three capabilities in cultural change. Engagement not only provides a beacon through its pathfinding element, which lights the path to the desired future, but it increases the chance that the interactions among organisational members will shift the culture in the preferred direction. Performance Management reinforces those changes and provides support for changing and embedding new behaviours, values and skills. Without reinforcement they may well founder. Development provides the new skills, systems and relevant resources needed to support the new culture.

Managers therefore wishing to make cultural change should realise that action in all three reshaping areas is critical to success. Typically the organisation will be poorly placed to achieve what is wanted, and so considerable sustained effort is needed. Cultural change takes longer to achieve than most other changes, and needs to involve more people than other changes. The manager's own behaviour should also reinforce the new culture, and be sustained over time.

Change in public sector organisations

The last decade or two has seen considerable change in the structure and management of the public sector. It has faced growing pressure to lower costs and improve efficiency and effectiveness. There has been pressure for governments to privatise and move out of many activities, or to establish commercially oriented government business enterprises. There has been a pull back to what some see as 'core' government functions. Government policy on deregulation has seen the heightened review, both internally and externally, of the need for and operation of legislation. Cost recovery from beneficiaries of government services has taken shape in various forms, including user pays charges. This is not only between government services and industry users but also within government departments. Cross-subsidisation of services to different sections of the community has come under the spotlight as community service obligations have been costed and become public. Pressure to outsource operations has also worked to clarify costs and benefits of many services. As users pay for service they have stronger grounds for, and practice in, criticising the performance of that service.

Within the traditional public sector there are increasing changes in job security and career structure. Whereas there used to be standardised employment systems affecting job, pay, and promotion systems and structures, now these are varied on an individual workplace basis and, at senior levels, for individuals. There has been some increase, for senior posts, in the politicisation of the service.

So the public sector has seen significant, often system-wide, change over the last decade or two.

What our research shows

Public sector cases of change accounted for 46 per cent of the 243 cases in our study. The left-hand section of Figure 8.2 shows the *impact* each capability has on Change Effectiveness and the right-hand section shows the *average strength* of each capability in the public and private sectors.

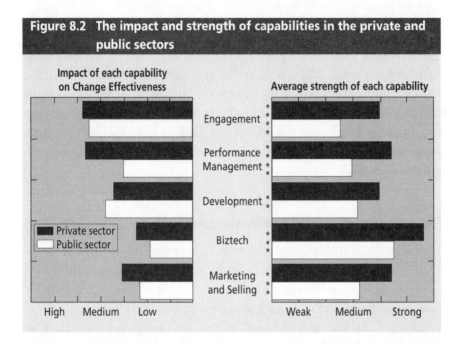

Figure 8.2   The impact and strength of capabilities in the private and public sectors

Public sector organisations—that is, those owned by state and federal governments—are represented by the white bars, and private sector organisations—that is, those non-government organisations owned by shareholders—are represented by the black bars.

Dividing the sample on the basis of private versus public sector ownership is not quite the same as dividing it between commercial and non-commercial organisations. Some government enterprises are run on commercial lines, and some organisations not owned by government—for example, charities—are run on a 'not for profit' basis. However, whether we split the sample between commercial and non-commercial, or between private and public sector, the findings are broadly similar.

As with Figure 8.1 on cultural change, whether the difference between two bars is significant is indicated by the asterisks at the base of the pair of bars. The more asterisks there are, the more significant the finding and the more certain the difference. If there are no asterisks, then the difference is not statistically significant.

The impact of the reshaping capabilities

The left-hand section of Figure 8.2 shows there is no significant difference between public and private sector organisations in the impact of the five capabilities on Change Effectiveness. The length of the bars shows that Performance Management has less impact in the public sector than in the private sector, and the impact of Development capability is a little higher in the public sector. However, in technical terms, the differences are not statistically significant.

The average strength of the reshaping capabilities

However, there are significant differences between the two sectors in the average strengths of all the capabilities. In all cases the capabilities tend to be weaker in public sector organisations. This is particularly true for Engagement and Performance Management, but also applies to Biztech, Marketing and Selling, and Development. Of course, it is important to remember we are talking of averages here. The data do not mean there are no public sector organisations with strong reshaping and operational capabilities. Nor is it saying there are no private sector organisations with weak reshaping or operational capabilities. In fact both exist. There are some public sector organisations with strong capabilities, just as there are some private sector ones with weak capabilities. But, on average, each of the five capabilities is assessed as significantly weaker in government organisations.

This puts the senior executives of the typical government organisation at a real disadvantage in achieving effective change. They face a situation where the corporate reshaping capabilities important to success are likely to be weak. That places much more demand on the personal reshaping capabilities of key individuals. Where senior managers have been promoted on their skills in policy advice, rather than for organisational and people management, the difficulties become compounded.

Every change that takes place in the public sector, as in the private sector, has its own unique and common features. While this is true of the changes described in Karen's story, which follows, it nevertheless serves to highlight some of the situations and differences public sector managers typically face in making changes.

Karen's story

'I'm currently in a personnel management role with our state's Department of Primary Industry. But the change I want to talk about started in a previous department, the Agriculture Department.

'The government at the time wanted an improvement in performance, by which it meant lower costs together with better targeted and more relevant services. An internal review team was established, assisted by some university academics operating as consultants. I was one of the team, as were a number of staff from various parts of the department.

'We looked closely at the organisation, consulted quite widely and came up with a new structure. It would involve reallocation of resources away from some of the more "high status" research and policy tasks into fieldwork and into more applied scientific analysis to directly support the fieldwork. There was structural change that went with this.

'There was to be a progressive reduction in staff numbers, but all through natural attrition. However, there would also be an adverse impact on career progression and salaries for a significant proportion of staff, mainly those who had worked in the more glamorous scientific areas.

'Our team briefed the head of the department, who had been kept well informed, and agreed with the plans and was willing to sign off on the changes as meeting the minister's intent. There was no problem at that level and we set to work on a high-level implementation plan.

'We also formally briefed the senior union representatives in the department. They were reasonably sympathetic to our intent. However, they had an election due in a few months. They did not want "the boat rocked" in that period.

'They approached the minister to delay the program. The minister, for political reasons, which had nothing to do with our department but involved other agendas the government was pursuing, agreed. He got our department head to sit on it. At the time we did not know this was what had happened.

'The department was alive with rumours. In campaigning, the union representatives, like their challengers, said they'd actively resist any changes with an adverse affect on their members.

'Those of us in the change planning team were very keen to get on with the change. We got pretty frustrated and began to doubt the sincerity of the attempt and our department head.

'The union election passed with the leadership retaining their positions. Our department head then gave the go ahead for the changes, briefing the senior management of the department. With some modifications, the original team was reconstituted as a change management team. Its job was to ensure continuous communication to all department members and to provide support to division heads as they developed and implemented detailed plans for their areas. It was also asked to monitor consistency with the overall plan, and to deal with any issues that emerged.

'The union became involved on some salary and career matters. That changed some of the detail of what was introduced and diminished its effectiveness and the cost reductions. However, these were not major in themselves—though they consumed a lot of managerial time and delayed implementation. The change was expected to take about eight months to complete. Because of the union involvement, it became longer.

'However, six months after we actually started, the government decided to combine our department with two others in a single Department of Primary Industry. It still wanted its cost and service requirements to be met. Most of the divisions of the old Agriculture Department survived largely intact in the new Department of Primary Industry, with a few bits grafted on or cut out. They still had to continue the thrust of the changes they had begun six months earlier.

'The central service units—like personnel, IT and laboratories—were amalgamated with similar units from the other two departments, reducing numbers and reducing integrated service to the line units. It has become something of a shambles. People's hearts have not been in it. We have become disillusioned trying to make it work.

'There has been a lot of community criticism of the results from the Department of Primary Industry. Now there is talk of recreating a separate Agriculture Department. I'm not looking forward to the effort, I can tell you.'

Differences in change in the public sector

External parties have a stronger impact on change in government organisations than in the private sector. This is particularly true of unions whose influence on change is much higher in government organisations. Karen's story will ring a bell with many managers in the public sector. Furthermore, the impetus for change often comes from external parties, such as commissions, parliamentary enquiries, performance and efficiency audits, and formal public reviews by relevant individual experts of one sort or another. When this happens, there is sometimes little or no direct involvement of internal staff who in the end have to respond to recommendations, usually already public, from outside the organisation. In these circumstances, where staff have not been part of the process of setting new directions, it is much more difficult to get effective Engagement at both a cognitive and emotional level. Pathfinding—developing, crystallising and articulating new directions or strategies—is a vital part of Engagement capability, and is especially important in public sector change.

Our study also shows that change communication, consultation and understanding the change have lower impact on Change Effectiveness in government organisations. Two factors may influence this. First, there is still a strong tradition of individual rights within the public service, which may make communication and consultation about proposed changes a less potent way of influencing motivation and commitment than in the private sector. Second, people may be less easily motivated and committed because of their previous experience of change failures. Like Karen's people they have seen it all before. They have learned that enthusiasm and responsiveness are likely to be frustrated. So higher past failure rates, in the public sector, become an additional barrier to the success of subsequent change initiatives.

Changes in government organisations are often focused on the internal workings of the organisation—for example, changes in top management, reorganisation of structures or cultural changes. In the private sector many changes are market related. Change Effectiveness tends to be lower when the change focus is on the internal workings of the organisation, and so this may partly explain why Change Effectiveness is lower in government organisations. Changes involving contraction, reorientation and new program developments are more common in the public sector, and existing capabilities are usually lower when changes of this kind are attempted. On the other hand, changes based on the incremental refinement and improvement of current strategies are generally supported by and strengthen existing capabilities, and this type of change is less common in the public sector

In practice, understanding of the change, empowerment and commitment (organisational states that are positive to Change Effectiveness) tend to be lower in government organisations. This may partly result from goals for change, sometimes set by external parties, which are not well articulated, and from the relative absence of hard measures against which to evaluate the progress made. Sometimes, as in Karen's story, the goal posts are changed.

While the strength of impact of top management and the workforce is much the same in public or private sector organisations, the impact of middle management tends to be lower in public sector organisations. This throws additional responsibility for action and energy on to top management who are already handicapped by lower general levels of corporate reshaping capabilities.

All these factors taken together—the difficulty of managing the influence of external parties, the stronger need for clear directions, the lower impact of communication and consultation, the internal focus of change, the types of change more commonly attempted, the lower level of positive organisational states, and the lower impact of middle management—go some way in explaining why Change Effectiveness is lower in government organisations than in private ones.

Change Effectiveness in government tends to respond more to systems and practices development and the existence of change champions—

individuals who champion the change within the organisation. Building and revising processes and systems embeds the change in the formal way the organisation works. This embedding is all the more important for the public sector, where the policy of frequent change in postings for executives lowers the likelihood of building many personal capabilities, particularly in Biztech and Performance Management.

The existence of change champions takes the impetus for the change outside the normal operational management structure. This is shown in the data to be more helpful for public sector change. Despite this there is actually little difference between public and private sector organisations in the use of change champions and the extent of practice and systems development. In other words, government organisations are no more likely to take actions that are particularly useful and valuable for them in achieving effective change. This again adds to the explanation for the lower Change Effectiveness found in government organisations.

Public sector managers sometimes envy the way in which their private sector counterparts can approach change and want to behave in a similar fashion. They are sometimes exhorted to do so by well-meaning, but ill-informed, commentators. In reality, they are normally constrained by regulatory requirements, and buffeted and limited by the demands and intrusions of elected officials—often a stream of them with short tenure and conflicting policies. They can also be hobbled by union involvement.

Often, as in Karen's story, public sector organisations have extensive experience of change that has not been constructive. It has often been driven by political masters whose aspirations for the public good are not matched by a real capacity for implementation. Such experience does not condition an organisation to be enthusiastic about new proposals for change. Nor does it help them to develop either the capabilities or the confidence that helps them to achieve effective change.

While this experience is relatively common in the public sector, private sector organisations also sometimes experience aspects of it. Imposed change is not uncommon for the junior partner in a merger or acquisition. At other times, when a firm is performing poorly, investors reasonably demand changes. Unfortunately, since investment analysts and investment journalists are rarely experienced managers, they are likely to publicly push for immediate visible changes that are not necessarily the most sound changes for the business.

What are the implications for public sector managers?

If you are a manager in the public sector it is important to remember that, in spite of some handicaps faced by public sector organisations, effective action in Engagement, Development and Performance Management is still the key to success.

In Engagement, action to develop new directions and to convey a credible vision is vital, even if external parties play a significant role in this area. Pathfinding, an important part of Engagement, is particularly important for government organisations. People need to be involved in the process and a clear vision for the future needs to be conveyed. The nature of external influences, and particularly the nature of the political process, imposes certain constraints. It also often makes a diagnosis of the changes needed more difficult. This requires managers to think through the political and other implications, as well as the managerial ones, of any proposed change. For example, are you fundamentally dependent on negotiating change with unions or other external parties? If so, negotiation and cooption skills become critically important. You may also need political or ministerial acceptance and support of your plans, not only at the beginning but also down the track when less palatable action may be required.

In the private sector three of the most critical stakeholders are customers, owners and suppliers. Usually their demands are about output: product characteristics, price and service for customers; profit for owners; and order behaviour and payment for suppliers. They do not typically try to impose on the organisation what it should do, and how it should be structured and operated. That is however the experience of many public sector organisations. So proactive management of the expectations and aspirations of key stakeholders becomes more critical than in the private sector. This evokes images of the TV program 'Yes Minister'.

Public sector managers often find that in order to change effectively and achieve good operational performance, they have to create some discretion and elbow room for action, for themselves and their organisation, by managing to constrain their stakeholders.

All of this suggests an environment in which change is negotiated with other parties, particularly unions and staff, and so while clarity of purpose is important, flexibility in approach may also be. In such a scenario, change is not executed through middle management, at least not to the degree that occurs in private sector organisations. It depends, at least partly, on individuals, such as change champions, who may be outside the normal management structure and who provide leadership of the change at different levels.

Where external forces are less powerful, or are in sympathy with the changes, and you can move outside a framework of negotiated change, you may be able to place more reliance on your organisation's more formal management structure. That means behaving more like a commercial organisation in the empowerment and use of middle management. However, since middle management's experience of such behaviour is likely to be low, there is a substantial initial task to build their confidence and ability to take on greater authority in change and their willingness to do so. Staff in the public service are more difficult to move than in the private sector, and so greater effort has to be made, in practice, to gain their commitment. They may also need to develop new skills. Action to train and develop them will not only help directly in this process but will make a contribution to achieving their Engagement.

This was an important element of the reorientation of NSW State Rail begun under Ross Sayers in 1988. Over five years, employment was reduced from 29,000 to 20,000 and output per employee was raised by at least 50 per cent. For many long-term employees it was the first time money had been spent on their development, and it helped them identify with their business unit. In many areas reductions in staff were accompanied by higher salaries for new multi-skilled positions for which staff were now being trained. They were offered greater career opportunities. Thus, among many of the staff who remained, there was both clear personal benefit and a sense of corporate interest in them and their development.[3]

When people develop new skills they are keen to use them. While technical skills may be needed, the changes will almost certainly need increased people and team management skills. Developing skills will help build a state of empowerment, which will help your change.

Lower assessments by public servants of public sector capabilities may not only reflect the reality, but may also reflect a lack of confidence on the part of public sector managers in their own managerial skills. A lack of confidence, as we have commented upon in earlier chapters, affects performance irrespective of the actual skill level. Building up confidence by training, goal clarification, effective goal setting, relevant feedback processes, and recognising and rewarding performance will begin to build much needed confidence at an individual, team and organisational level.

Change always involves some risk, especially for top management. Change in the public sector is always accompanied by the certainty of scrutiny and review. It is easy to play safe in such circumstances when bolder but more risky action is needed. Building confidence can help in encouraging appropriate action.

The identification and involvement of change champions will also be important. The individuals selected need to be both sensitive to the nature of negotiated deals and very good at proceduralising and systematising the changes. They may also play a strong role in achieving Engagement and Performance Management. Introducing new people can often be valuable provided they act as models for your existing people and have the culture needed for your new directions.

Performance Management may well be more difficult because of the relative absence and greater difficulty, at least in some areas, of measuring and rewarding performance in the public sector. It is therefore important to clarify your purposes, set goals, quantifiable wherever possible, and monitor your progress as fully as possible. This is much easier in the private sector where many measurements needed for operational performance are well developed. Developing new measures may well need training, but will improve every aspect of your change management performance. A number of public sector organisations have made progress in areas of measurement and the development of performance indicators. A benchmarking exercise may well pay dividends for you.

Performance Management plays a major role in changing behaviour, particularly when changed behaviour is publicly acknowledged and recognised. It will be important to follow through on the changes once you have begun and this will require a lot of personal follow-up action on your part.

There is also a need to put very conscious effort into the development of practices and systems that support the change, and to see that they are embedded in the normal day-to-day procedures and workings of the organisation.

In addition to managing change within the organisation, public sector managers often need to give a lot of attention to managing stakeholders. Thus, in trying to manage a major change to kindergarten services in Victoria in the late 1980s and early 1990s, Ann Sherry as Head of the Office of Pre-school and Child Care supported and gave substantial seed funding to the formation of an independent parent group, Kindergarten Parents Victoria. This body became an active participant in the debate about funding, service models, teaching hours and management. It was not a body that in any way Sherry controlled but in the debate and accompanying action it became something of a counter-weight to the Kindergarten Teachers' Union. It also became a relatively stable voice in a shifting policy-making domain that involved changing state governments and the federal government.[4]

In describing the NSW State Rail changes, Vince Graham, one of the senior executives remarked on:[5]

'... the enormous importance of ... issues management ... In implementing a process of change like this, there is a range of constituencies who are going to be impacted by it ... We put an enormous amount of time into not only identifying those constituencies, but into educating the constituencies as to how to handle the ultimate downside.'

Related to this Vince also observed that:[6]

'You have the ability to not only influence the government process (obviously no one is going to let you determine government policy) but, once you know what the policy framework is, you have the ability to keep a government at the political pain threshold. That is where change comes. Having the sensitivity to understand the differences between being at, and taking them through, that political pain threshold.'

Public sector managers frequently need to put a lot of effort into managing stakeholders as well as managing the change internally. This is a major addition to the task and the sustained effort that is needed. The task of 'issues management' is typically less important for the private sector, though there are occasions when it is also important for them.

Summary

In trying to make effective change in the public sector you will typically have less support from your organisation's corporate reshaping capabilities. You will need to focus on action in the areas of Engagement, Development and Performance Management, and develop personal skills in those areas to compensate, as far as possible, for any organisational weaknesses. You will be called on to make a substantial, sustained personal effort, sometimes with relatively little middle management support. While the task may be hard it is certainly achievable—the more so if it is better understood and prepared for by you and your team. Motivation to perform well is an important factor in success. The spirit of public service may well provide some of this for you.

Changes are usually complex

We have discussed aspects of cultural change and change in the public sector to identify and describe the role and importance of the reshaping capabilities. In doing so we have tried to isolate one change from others and one situation—public sector—from another. But of course changes and situations often occur together. For example, cultural change occurs within the public sector. And cultural change can be the focus of change in the private sector—for example, in a merger between two separate firms. We comment on aspects of cultural change in the public sector and follow this with some of the considerations managers dealing with mergers should take into account.

Cultural change in the public sector

If you are attempting some real cultural change in the public sector, you will almost certainly have weak corporate reshaping capabilities—both because you are in the public sector *and* because you are attempting cultural change. So you cannot rely on these capabilities. Instead, you must rely, in the first place, on your own abilities and on those you can quickly develop, or recruit, who will play a key role in the change.

As we have seen, Engagement and Performance Management are both especially important for cultural change. So, in working with the key individuals who will guide the change, you need to ensure a great deal of attention is given to actions that will engage your staff and will actually manage performance. Pathfinding, for example, will demand particular effort from you and other senior management.

Empowerment of middle management and staff is not common in public sector change. Yet cultural change is simply impossible unless staff have a substantial influence on the change. So you will have to encourage a level of involvement that is not normal for staff in your organisation. This means encouraging them to play a role with which they are inexperienced and uncomfortable. That, in turn, means providing support to them as they make the effort.

We also noted above that unions and other external parties typically have a strong impact on public sector changes. If that is the environment within which you are operating, there is no point wishing it would disappear. Unions will certainly affect the level and nature of involvement you can get from your workforce. So in this situation you need to coopt the union leadership to encourage constructive workforce involvement. In many public sector situations, if cultural change is the intent, then union cooperation is a precondition. Occasionally another external party may need to be given very special attention.

We have previously noted the valuable contribution that new people can make to cultural change. That is true for the public sector also, though it is sometimes harder to achieve. Remember that achieving Engagement is already difficult in the public sector, and so you need to be sure that any new arrivals support rather than impede Engagement. Consequently, they particularly need to be sensitive to the environment they are entering and to be able to work constructively and readily with members of the old culture.

Finally, we also know that practices and systems development is especially important for effective public sector change. Public sector cultural change will not occur just in changing the beliefs and attitudes of the organisation's people, though this is critical. It has to be carried into the practices and systems that are so important to the organisation in terms of its operational capabilities. So you will need to ensure sufficient resources and time are allowed for this, and that it is given a high priority.

All this reinforces that if you want to make cultural change in the public sector you face a very difficult though not impossible task. It will take a considerable commitment of time, energy and skill for you personally. You need to be motivated and committed if you want the change to succeed.

Acquisitions and mergers

The sustained effort and skill needed to achieve most types of change is often underestimated, but acquisitions and mergers raise the stakes in terms of the quality of change management required for success. Executives are often confronted with the need to deal simultaneously with two major changes rather than one. It is highly likely that changing culture in one, or both, of the organisations will be needed, as well as other changes in strategy and operations. So executives are often faced with making some extremely difficult changes, simultaneously, in two organisations.

Judgments about the desirability of mergers are likely to be made in some, perhaps most, cases, largely on financial and economic criteria. Little weight is given to the needs of effective change management because often those making economic judgments have little appreciation of what is actually involved in welding different organisations together.

A recent study of mergers in the nineties by Mercer Management Consulting looked at post-merger performance relative to competitors. It concluded that almost half have failed to create shareholder value. It also concluded that the likelihood of creating value is dramatically improved only by superior post-merger execution. In other words, it depends fundamentally on the quality of change management applied in actually merging the organisations and adjusting the businesses.

While the overall failure rate of mergers is about 50 per cent, the Mercer study showed that for major mergers the failure rate is actually around 75 per cent. In other words, three-quarters of major mergers do not create shareholder value, despite the strategic intent behind them. Major mergers are those where the acquired company is at least 30 per cent of the size of the acquirer. These are cases where the strategic intent of the merger is likely to imply significant change for *both* the merging organisations. It is interesting to note the similarity between high expectations of performance and high actual subsequent failure rates, found by the Mercer study, to those we quoted in the opening page of our Introduction to this book in respect of our own large sample of various changes.

The general capabilities framework we have outlined throws light on this and underlines not only the importance of Engagement, Development and Performance Management, but also the difficulty of effective action in these areas in mergers.

If both merging organisations are to be changed, to be welded into one, the reshaping capabilities of Engagement, Development and Performance Management need to underpin action in both organisations. Given their different histories, cultures and situations, the ways of achieving Engagement and effective Performance Management are likely to be different. Such differences may well not be appreciated. It is hard enough for a single organisation to achieve high levels of these capabilities. Inevitably it is much harder for senior management to achieve it simultaneously for both their own organisation and an alien one.

Management's difficulties are compounded by the fact that, as a consequence of the merger, the two organisations will typically differ in the form of change required. The strategies, agendas and the timetables for change may well be different in each organisation. Executives are confronted with the need to deal simultaneously with two major changes rather than one. The corporate Engagement, Performance Management and Development capabilities of the two organisations are likely to be weakened, or at least made difficult to harness, because of the merger. This is particularly the case for the junior partner in the merger. With diminished corporate reshaping capabilities, greater demands are thrown on senior management, as individuals, to act in a way that achieves high levels of Engagement, Performance Management and Development, and which is sensitive to the specific change situations applying to their two merging organisations. This will require really high-level personal Engagement skills to achieve commitment. Top managers with this level of skill may often not be available.

The most innocuous situation is an 'arm's length' acquisition, where change of ownership may provide a diversification for the acquirer and where no rationalisation is required. In that case there is normally little change for the acquirer, while the acquired organisation needs either mild change in the direction and operations of the business (reorientation) or better incremental implementation of current strategies (refinement).

At the other extreme is the acquisition of one competitor by another with a very different culture. In this case there are going to be substantial rationalisation and contraction, which are frequently the economic grounds on which the justification of the merger rests. While this contraction is likely to take place in the acquired firm, it sometimes rapidly spreads to both. The acquired organisation will probably also experience substantial reorientation, and this will often be accompanied by an attempt to remould its culture to match that of the acquirer. The acquirer may experience some reorientation or cultural change as well, or it may vigorously protect its own identity and culture so that for it there is little change. It is not difficult to see that in spite of an initial strategic intent to successfully combine the operations, some amalgamations and mergers end in a power struggle that requires high personal reshaping capabilities to resolve. These capabilities may simply not exist in the combined organisation, which almost certainly will have significant personnel changes and the merged business suffers as a consequence.

Additionally conflict is highly likely and, as we showed in Chapter 4, conflict has the strongest adverse influence on effective change.

Sometimes an acquisition is made of a smaller competitor that has displayed the type of culture a board wants to see in its own organisation. How the change works out in these cases depends on where operational power lies after the merger. If it is predominantly in the hands of a number of personnel in the acquiring organisation then they will act to protect the existing culture and impose it on the smaller partner, even if this is contrary to the strategic intent of the merger.

As mergers take place it is also difficult to build the key change-enhancing states of commitment, understanding, empowerment and esprit de corps. In the early stages there is often confusion and fear about what is intended. Management is often forced into premature action based on wrong assumptions, or there is a long delay to gather much needed information. But in any event the breeding ground for conflict, the state that detracts from Change Effectiveness the most, is fertile and frequently encouraged by poor management action. Building positive states will therefore be difficult.

Despite the difficulties, something like a quarter of the mergers meet economic objectives. Thinking through the merger in terms of the application of the capabilities framework allows you to plan for the change actions that are appropriate for both organisations. Conscious application of the capabilities in the framework and focus on the creation of change-enhancing states will substantially improve the chance of success. A failure in economic terms of the order of 75 per cent is too large either to ignore or accept.

Summary

In this chapter we have looked at the relevance of our findings to a wide variety of changes that were covered in our sample. We have seen their applicability to two particular situations—cultural change and public sector change—where our data show there are some significant differences in either the impact or the average strength of the capabilities. Even in these cases, which show the most marked differences in our general findings, it still holds true that effective action based on the reshaping capabilities is linked to the achievement of effective change. We also applied the framework to explain the high failure rate of mergers.

We are confident that approaching your own changes, and planning and taking action based on applying the framework to your own situation, will substantially increase your chance of success.

In the next chapter we are going to change our perspective and discuss *operational* capabilities. These are the capabilities that relate to achieving high Current Business Performance. Improving existing operational capabilities, or creating new ones that enable the firm to continue high performance into the future, is the prime purpose of change.

CHAPTER 9

Operational capabilities

I N THE PRECEDING CHAPTERS we have concentrated on the reshaping capabilities. We have described the framework and underlying support they provide for management actions that contribute to change. We have shown that in order to make effective change you have to manage only three fundamental activities: Engagement, Development and Performance Management. This does not underestimate how difficult this might be to do. Rather it emphasises that your chance of success is likely to be immeasurably strengthened if you can focus your efforts on the three key things that determine the effectiveness of change.

Yet reshaping capabilities are not an end in themselves. Ultimately they have no purpose other than to help you adapt, improve or in some way re-create and reshape your operational capabilities and the organisation and resources upon which those capabilities depend. Those operational capabilities need to be aligned with and support the positioning of your business in the marketplace in which it competes. Developing and maintaining your performance rely on a combination of reshaping and operational capabilities. Pathfinding, which is part of Engagement, is particularly important in finding new directions for positioning the organisation, while exploiting that position at any time rests on the organisation's operational capabilities

Our purpose in this chapter is to give a broad explanation and description of operational capabilities, and show how they complete the framework formed by the five key capabilities needed for long-term performance. Our exploration will also help managers think about their own organisation's operational capabilities and the linkage between them and the reshaping capabilities. Our discussion of them also establishes a base for the next chapter where we explore the notions of creation, renewal and embedding of capabilities, and how actions based on reshaping capabilities lie at the heart of this process.

Reshaping capabilities—Engagement, Development and Performance Management—have much in common across organisations, but operational capabilities, by their very nature, are specific to each firm. While Biztech rests upon some of the generic competencies in our survey—for example, financial—it also includes many that are firm specific, or industry specific. These firm-specific competencies could, of course, not be addressed in our survey. We do not therefore provide the same kind of systematic analysis of Biztech capability, or even of Marketing and Selling capability, as we have of the reshaping capabilities, although our study findings do provide some valuable insights into the nature of operational capabilities that help clarify their purpose and make-up. However, there are a number of important points we can make to help understanding and management of operational capabilities and their linkages with reshaping capabilities.

Since we were looking in depth at what makes change effective, it was necessary to collect information about generic competencies that might be relevant to both Change Effectiveness and Current Business Performance, and about actions involved in the change process. As we were not directly concerned in the execution or implementation of operational competencies we did not collect similar extensive data on actions involved in operational activities. Our focus in this chapter is therefore principally on capabilities and the competencies that contribute to them, and to a much lesser extent on the relevant organisational states and actions.

The three operational capabilities

As shown in Table 9.1 there are three operational capabilities—Biztech, Marketing and Selling, and Performance Management. We will focus on the first two since we have already written much on Performance

Management in Chapter 7. The primary contributing competencies are listed under each capability in Table 9.1. They not only give a 'flavour' of the key focuses of operational capabilities, but they stand in sharp contrast, particularly Biztech, to the principal competencies of Engagement and Development listed earlier in Tables 5.1 and 6.1, respectively.

Biztech combines many of those things that the firm does, and has, to create and deliver its products and services to its customers. Marketing and Selling capability enables the organisation to identify the needs of customers and events in its markets and broader environment, and respond and adjust to them in the light of its strategy. Performance Management essentially helps the organisation to control how well it does in creating and delivering the organisation's products and services. If these three capabilities are strong, in combination they enable the organisation to differentiate its goods and services from those of its competitors and meet both its customers' needs and its own.

Biztech capability

As our study shows, Biztech capability has the greatest impact on Current Business Performance. The study also shows that Biztech capability is not linked to the ability to change. Across the board, firms whose Biztech capability is strong are just a little better at managing

Table 9.1   Operational capabilities and contributing competencies

Biztech	Marketing and Selling	Performance Management
Technical	Marketing and selling	Performance control
Operational	Environmental	Resource application
Financial	assessment	Enaction
Environmental assessment	Pathfinding	Financial
Systems and practices	Integration	Planning
development	Resource application	Operational
Business-specific		
competencies		

change effectively than those with weak Biztech capability, but the difference is marginal. Indeed sometimes the very strength of the operational capabilities induces a sense of stability and breeds a complacency in the level of current performance that blinds people to the need to change. Some firms achieve excellent operational performance, as we will see in the example of McDonald's which follows, but the capabilities needed to change effectively are different from the capabilities required to perform well today. The firm may have the capabilities required to make effective change, but its performance in terms of 'end results' provides no guarantee of this. If it is to change effectively, it will need the reshaping capabilities of Engagement, Development and Performance Management.

The example of McDonald's provides a simple but powerful illustration of Biztech.

McDonald's

Frying hamburgers and serving them to customers are common, and seemingly uncomplicated, activities of thousands of small businesses across the world. McDonald's has developed a strong Biztech capability around those two activities (and others like procurement and property management), which has enabled it to build a truly global operation with over 15,000 restaurants in seventy-five countries with sales of over $25 billion. Its Biztech capability is based on (internal) common practices and policies and standardised systems and methods about every aspect of its business. These are imposed on, taught to, encouraged and practised by all its outlets, whether owned or franchised. It serves a very limited menu of world standardised products, by friendly smiling young people, in clean easily identified restaurants.

Every aspect of its operations—the computer-controlled fat content of its burgers, the standardised kitchen equipment, the potato chip specifications, the roles of kitchen operators, its training in making add-on sales, its cost control systems, and many others—combines to form a Biztech capability of great power. McDonald's Biztech capability has sustained very high business performance over a long period.

Making and selling hamburgers is not rocket science. Yet as McDonald's has demonstrated so well, even in that business it is possible to create an outstanding Biztech capability that produces consistently good results.

Of course, the success of McDonald's is due to more than its operational capabilities. Elsewhere we have stressed the importance of alignment between capabilities and positioning. McDonald's provides an excellent example of this. Its success stems from the alignment between its operational capabilities and its chosen positioning as an informal, inexpensive, family restaurant chain particularly oriented to children, and providing fast, friendly service in clean and pleasant surroundings. This alignment has allowed McDonald's to use the power of its corporate operational capabilities to service its chosen position and exploit it effectively, faithfully and profitably to the full.

If McDonald's is now running into problems in sustaining its profit growth, it is due to a weakening of its positioning in the market, rather than the failure of its Biztech capability. With the maturing of the baby boomers have come changes in their tastes and a declining proportion of young families, posing a challenge to McDonald's positioning. At the same time, the strength of its established positioning makes it difficult to create a new and different one. If the company does pursue a changed positioning, it will undoubtedly try to ensure it has a strong Biztech capability to match. Whether it can achieve that will depend on the quality of the reshaping capabilities it has available to it.

A multiplicity of business-specific competencies

By Biztech capability we mean commanding and understanding the technologies, processes and mechanisms through which the organisation produces and delivers its products and services to its markets. Biztech enables the organisation to efficiently create and deliver its products and services, drawing on its own body of knowledge, skills, technologies and processes. In doing so the firm differentiates its products and services—in design, price, delivery, service, or any aspect valued by its customer.

Our study shows that technical, operational and financial competencies are strong contributors to Biztech. These relate to the combination of skills, knowledge and know-how, which is important to performance and its commercial application in delivering value to customers and profit to the firm.

The capability also includes an ability to understand and monitor the environment within which the firm operates and to adjust to it. Biztech capability not only relates to the direct customer but also needs to take into account the wider environment. Dealing with regulatory authorities in many realms—for example, occupational health and safety issues, environmental pollution and equal opportunities—is part of a strong Biztech capability. It is not only about production, or logistics, or product creation, or service delivery. It includes an awareness of, and attention to, the environment, and therefore it needs to have a degree of external orientation.

While individuals are important to Biztech, so are the systems, practices and technologies that enable the business to leverage and integrate the work of many. A competence in systems and practices development is therefore needed for success in many of the operational activities that form part of Biztech.

Typically a Biztech capability depends on a range of generic and specific competencies. While these competencies can be described in generic terms—such as technical, financial, production, procurement, distribution, and so on—their actual form is varied and very business specific. So while generic groupings can be helpful for some purposes, they lose the specificity that is important to understanding the actual basis of the Biztech capability of each firm.

Boeing's Biztech capabilities are different from McDonald's. So are Motorola's, Sony's, Woolworths', StorageTek's or Du Pont's. So is the Biztech capability of the organisation in which you work. They are relevant to the specific strategies, purposes and needs of each. They are supported by the values and beliefs that the firm has about what is important to it. They become reinforced by the culture of the organisation—the way it does things, what it believes is important, and how people work together. Biztech may involve ways in which research and development is harnessed to business aims, the utilisation of specialised plant and equipment, the creation of particular roles, methods of training staff, the application of financial techniques or controls that sustain investment in the capability, and so on. It is an amalgam and integration of key factors in the technical, financial, physical, human and organisational aspects of the business needed to deliver performance. That amalgamation and its components will be different in some respects for every organisation.

For example, a road maker's crucial competence might be in contract management, or in managing relationships with local and federal authorities.

For a manufacturer, key competencies will include the basic ability to transform raw materials into its products, and these competencies are very different in firms producing steel, cars, computers, bread, petrol, explosives, aircraft, wine, furniture, and so on. Competencies in achieving short cycle time, or cost control, or in product innovation, or in managing the equity in its brands, may also be particularly important.

For a legal firm, important competencies might be expertise in intellectual property law, records management, or specialised recruitment and development of its personnel.

For a financial services firm, important competencies might be in systems management, economic research, risk management, or in behavioural analysis of customers and their management.

For a government taxation agency, being able to accurately assess the fiscal efficiency of different tax structures, information systems management to efficiently process tax-related returns and ensure visibility of attempted evasion, and the ability to consult effectively with the community and interested professional groups may be some of its important Biztech competencies.

For a transport company, key competencies might be in logistics, routing skills, warehousing or vehicle specification. For a water company, it might be in hydraulic systems or in environmental knowledge and management.

For the military, the ability to integrate the diversity of skills required by a military force, to instil discipline and cohesion, and the ability to provide effective logistics, communications and command during conflict, are some of many important competencies.

Our point is simply to illustrate the multiplicity of business-specific competencies that exist and the strong linkage between a firm's Biztech capabilities and its relevant markets and purposes. Biztech often takes a long time to build to the level where it becomes a competitive advantage. Usually it is a cumulative development, stages of which are triggered by particular events, opportunities or failures. Understanding the real composition of the best Biztech capability for a particular organisation thus requires insight into the specific type of business involved, and an understanding of how performance is actually achieved and its relationship to its market.

As the examples show, Biztech capability has a technical or expertise focus and content. But it involves and combines both technical and management elements. It is not just about the production function, though it certainly includes it. It results in application of business technologies by the firm to the service of its customers in ways that are commercially viable. It is relevant to any aspect of the firm's products and services and therefore may include aspects of those operations that directly cover procurement, design, production, distribution, financial control, and so on. It may well include aspects of the management of supplier relationships, or networks, or partnership arrangements, if these are an important part of the way the business differentiates and creates its products and services. At some level, the firm will need to be competent in many of these kinds of activities. Nevertheless, it will have particular strengths in some areas, or particular combinations of skills, or assets or systems, or know-how, which give it its own specific Biztech capability.

Executives of a firm will naturally have a feel for the competencies that underlie their Biztech capability. However, that insight may be deepened by analysing and understanding the various business-specific competencies that make up your Biztech capability so that you can improve and integrate them more effectively to provide a more powerful Biztech capability in future.

Biztech is more than 'core technologies'

In Chapter 1 we mentioned the varied use of the word 'competency' in the management literature and in discussion within companies. A similar varied usage surrounds the term 'core technologies'. We have used the term Biztech to describe the capability we are interested in because none of the current words and their current meanings cover our concept. It differs from a number of the terms used by others in this area.

Biztech, which we coined from our original description, 'business technologies', is much more than 'core technologies'. All firms employ some technologies. Some of these are in the public domain and available to other firms; others are proprietary and are used by the firm that owns them. Of course, the two kinds are frequently used in combination. Technologies contribute to a firm's competencies. However, a competence is far more than a technology. It also depends on the way technologies of different kinds are combined, the personal qualities of staff (for example, their intelligence, skill levels and energy), equipment, motivational factors applying within the firm, values, beliefs and behavioural norms. All these things may be part of a competence. Technologies are also part of a competence but they are not the competence.

Biztech is more than 'core competence'

'Core competence', a term in frequent use, is closer to Biztech than core technology because a 'competence' also involves the way the technologies are applied or managed. But Biztech includes more than just competencies that are judged by someone as being 'core' to the business. It includes things that are sometimes called 'complementary competencies'—that is, all those operational competencies that are needed to achieve good performance.

McDonald's and many, many thousands of companies do *everything* that they think will affect their customer and their business performance as well as they can. Some activities, of course, may be more important to that performance than others, and may take more development, investment or effort. But just as a chain is as strong as its weakest link, so Biztech relies on getting *all* the operational competencies functioning as strongly as possible. That may mean paying attention to many things that in themselves are mundane and ordinary—like a small hole on a tablecloth. There is no high technology involved in these, but get a number of what seem like relatively small things wrong and Biztech and the organisation's results can be seriously weakened—even if so-called core competencies are still strong. One of the weaknesses of talking about core competence is a failure to do many other, so-called non-core activities as well as possible.

Biztech is more than 'distinctive competence'

Lastly, a much older term, 'distinctive competence', is also used. Many organisations, perhaps most, do not possess a competence that is truly distinctive. Of course they may have many competencies, but they are not necessarily distinctive or unique. For example, there are tens of thousands of small individual businesses producing hamburgers. Even if we assume that most of them provide a fairly good product it would be hard to argue that many of them have a distinctive competence. But they do have a Biztech capability and they can work to strengthen it. What they generally possess is a competence at producing and selling hamburgers and related products, together with some form of an advantageous positioning. The positioning is likely to be based on physical location, convenient access for a good customer base, perhaps strengthened by a particular image and ambience such as a friendly proprietor. The combination of their competencies in a convenient location enables them to get enough trade and make a sufficient income to survive and perhaps grow. Their Biztech may be sufficient for performance and growth, but it clearly will not be distinctive in any meaningful sense.

It is not distinctiveness that matters. What matters is whether your Biztech enables you to meet your customers' and all your other stakeholders' expectations. Your Biztech should of course provide you with some competitive advantage in your relevant market. And you should be constantly trying to build and develop it.

Understanding your Biztech capability

Understandably, firms give a lot of attention to improving their Biztech capability or to adapting it to meet what they perceive will be a changed business environment. That is a major part of the way to achieve superior 'end results' performance and one of the ways in which Performance Management capability contributes to current and near term performance.

However, Biztech capabilities in large organisations are typically quite complex and how they actually work to deliver results and satisfy a market is not always well understood. In understanding your Biztech better it may be helpful to break it down into parts. It is important to keep two perspectives in mind. The first is what it actually is that the customer values and is willing to pay for. That has to be manifested in your products and services. The second is what you do that is important to achieving that. Identifying the competencies, therefore, that underlie a Biztech capability is a first step in simplifying the task of improving the capability. In this way, you begin to build up a picture of the competencies that constitute your Biztech capability and what action may be most useful to build up weak areas or combine and integrate individual Biztech competencies more effectively. It is the alignment between your competencies—what you are good at, and what the customer wants or will buy—that makes the competence valuable to the business.

Finally, ensure you also consider the relationship between your competencies and your corporate culture. The competencies have to be valued in the culture of the business or they will not be sustained when the business comes under pressure. As we will see in the next chapter, corporate culture can have a big impact on your corporate competencies and on efforts to improve them.

Biztech capability, states and actions

Organisations that have strong Biztech capability are typically also high in esprit de corps. Their results usually give them good reason to be confident in their abilities and in one another. Their staff also have relatively high workloads, their systems and practices tend to be good, the training of their staff is relatively good and their people generally feel empowered. We found that they are also less likely than other organisations to replace staff in key positions as part of corporate change. On the other hand, if they do make changes, our research shows they are no more or less likely to reduce the numbers of staff than firms with lower Biztech capability.

The finding that organisations with strong Biztech capabilities also tend to have systems and practices that are well suited to their activities is not surprising. Indeed we would have been surprised not to see this result. The strong use of training is similar in its implications and the links with a state of empowerment are similarly clear.

The fact that organisations with strong Biztech capabilities are less likely to replace people in key positions as part of corporate changes also makes sense. Key people often become very knowledgeable about what constitutes the Biztech of an organisation and play key roles during a major change. The ability to do this well depends on the integration of expertise, skills and assets. Much of that integration depends on personal interdependencies and relationships. Replacing key people interrupts this, potentially causing a hiatus in teamwork, collaboration and performance. Often it also causes the loss of tacit knowledge possessed by key individuals, which is central to their pathfinding and performance management roles.

Nevertheless, it is not something everyone would have expected or agreed with. Some people might reasonably argue that a continual infusion of 'new blood' at the top strengthens Biztech. Our results do not support such a conclusion. This may of course simply reflect the fact that when Biztech is high the level of personal competence in such organisations is also high, thus diminishing any pressure to change people. However, if Biztech capability is strong, it is not just because of the presence of people with high personal competence.

It is much more surprising to find that the likelihood of staff reduction during change is not related to an organisation's strength in Biztech capability. However, firms that are strong in Biztech are no more immune from the consequences of economic downturns than are others. Furthermore such firms can be strongly affected when environmental or market change affects the alignment between their strong and developed capabilities and their positioning. Even the most highly regarded firms across the world face such situations. While their Biztech capability may help them grow their market share and produce good results, their actions during change are not related to that. So they may take actions during change that generally do not contribute to its effectiveness. Staff reduction, of course, may also take place as a result of productivity improvements.

It is also interesting to find that strong Biztech tends to be accompanied by somewhat higher workloads. Some readers might reasonably have expected to find the reverse, that personnel in organisations with strong Biztech capabilities were able to get an easier ride. In fact, our data suggest the opposite. Organisations with strong Biztech capabilities also tend to have a demanding work ethic and a results-focused top management.

We mentioned earlier that firms with strong Biztech capabilities are marginally better placed to handle change than are other firms. This is likely to be linked with their much greater self-confidence gained from high levels of current performance. Their esprit de corps is very high and this reflects both confidence and trust. These tend to lower resistance and anxiety, which generally are detrimental to Change Effectiveness, and therefore help the change process to some extent.

The strength and management of Biztech

Our study shows that Biztech typically is by far the strongest of the five capabilities. There are a number of reasons for this. First, it is the most visible of the capabilities. When Biztech is weak, feedback on its failure is quick and certain, whether from inside the business or from customers. Its presence or absence is immediately evident. If Engagement or Development is not taking place effectively, it will not be noticed or evident for some time, perhaps a very long time.

Second, Biztech capability, or parts of it, are usually the direct responsibilities of particular managers. Although it combines many activities, each is often the definite focus and responsibility of managers of departments, units or functions. Targets, budgets and accountabilities are set for performance in these areas, and good or bad performance is usually appropriately rewarded. This supporting managerial framework influences and increases the development and strength of the capability. None, or little, of this supporting framework is provided for Engagement, the capability that has most impact on Change Effectiveness.

Biztech capability frequently has, unlike Engagement or Development, a strong base in specific disciplines or established fields of knowledge. The relevant disciplines—for example, engineering, physics, industrial design, metallurgy, statistics, finance, economics, geology, food technology, genetic engineering, biology and law—are different for each business. They nonetheless provide a sound base of established knowledge on which to build. This base is noticeably absent for reshaping capabilities.

Lastly, the causal linkage between Biztech capability and financial and other results is clear and recognised, which ensures that it is always a focus of top management attention. This is not the case with reshaping capabilities. For two of them, Engagement and Development, the link with Current Business Performance is very weak, and the link with change and long-term performance is often not well understood, and is therefore not reflected in management focus and attention.

For all these reasons Biztech is a central focus for much of management's work. There is great gain when top managers have a real understanding of their organisation's Biztech and how their business actually achieves its results. The deeper the understanding the better placed they are to contribute not only to performance but also to change. Whether they make that contribution depends however on the strength and use of action based on the reshaping capabilities. We illustrate this linkage in the following story of how an organisation developed a unique product, involving a new way of coating structural steel, which contributed to the development of its Biztech. This also introduces some discussion on the role Marketing and Selling capability, our last operational capability, plays in performance and change.

Silver for the price of steel

While writing this book, one of us went to Newcastle to talk with the top management of the Structural and Engineering Division of Tubemakers. Now a part of BHP, Australia's largest industrial company, who purchased it in 1996, Tubemakers had developed a world-class unique product, a new coating for steel pipes. This coating, which looks like silver, eliminates the considerable costs and time of shotblasting, cleaning and painting the pipe work after fabrication. The new coating, called Duragal, provides up to 28 per cent extra strength for no extra cost, enabling users to replace big heavy walled steel sections with lighter cheaper sections. Its development gave Tubemakers a competitive advantage in some of its markets.

Where did this unique product come from? Talking with the group general manager Leigh Daley and key engineers involved with the development of Duragal, some substantial discussion about 'technology' was expected. But technology was hardly mentioned as the prime cause of the development of Duragal.[1]

A new manager and a new vision

Tubemakers Newcastle had produced steel pipes in Australia profitably for over forty years, but during the mid-1970s began to face increasing local and international competition. Its market share became eroded and it moved into losses in the early 1980s. The plants had too many staff, were inefficient, and the influence of the unions was extremely strong. Its technology had stagnated.

A new divisional manager, appointed from inside, and a small team decided to set out with the vision of 'becoming a world leader of their products'. Since they knew from benchmarking studies that their productivity level was currently about 40 per cent of that achieved by the best plants in the world, this was some vision! But all the senior executives felt the vision helped to sustain them through the next decade until they achieved it. As one senior executive said:

> 'We thought we were doing something worthwhile. We had commitment from everyone. The superintendents were often champions. It's participative. We had technological expertise. We were a small group. All this gave us fire in the belly.'

Their first action was to establish measures for every process as a basis for improvement and to enable them to evaluate progress. They also established relationships with a few 'sister' plants in Europe and Japan for information and comparison. So from the outset, the vision was expressed not only in idealistic terms but also in hard numbers.

Major restructuring and investments

During the 1980s new managers, largely with technical backgrounds, were promoted into senior positions replacing people whose main skills had been in 'man management'. This action influenced the focus of senior management. There was a very substantial shedding of labour as new plants and methods were introduced and old plants closed down. Major investments were made in a new mill and new manufacturing and management processes. Flexible manufacturing systems were introduced. These opened the possibility of manufacturing for niche markets, but with the power, precision and reliability of modern production technology and at mass production prices. New manufacturing structures were introduced and the plant was reconfigured into cellular units. These stand-alone units were intended to function as 'market-oriented factories'. For example, one unit called the 'five minute mill' took five minutes from steel coil to finished product ready for despatch to customer. As general efficiency and productivity began to improve, profit began to be steadily restored. Each year produced regular, but hard won, improvements in general performance.

Everything out in the open

All of these restructuring and development actions took place over these years within a radical new approach to involve the workforce and unions in open discussion. Leigh Daley commented:

> '... everybody understood the challenge that lay ahead and had the opportunity to influence the final decision.'

All units were given all the data—financial, market and production—on their performance and the data from the sister plants worldwide which had been selected for comparison. The sister plant concept was extremely powerful and provided a tool for management to effectively talk to employees about goals that were demonstrably achievable. Negotiations with the unions and workforce were resolved by a series of agreements, each with a time frame of about one year. Leigh Daley, a key player in these discussions and the manager of one of the units, was appointed group general manager in 1991. He commented:

> 'The "indisputable" database of best world performance was always the reference point in all the agreements … No decisions of importance were taken without first having open discussion about them.'

The search for something extra

But while progress was sound and continuous, top management searched for other paths to improve performance. Steel pipes had largely become a commodity product with fierce price competition. Tubemakers looked for ways to differentiate its products from its competitors. The search for this, which took place over time as other improvements were happening, resulted in the development of Duragal. Daley says that Duragal came out of a process of looking.

Daley, and one of his senior engineers, explored the possibility of using a coating process being developed in the United States for the conduit and fencing market. Could it be applied to structural steel products? They believed that it could be altered and applied to their products. If so, it would differentiate their products from their competitors. The process was technologically advanced and would be capital intensive. They would need to design some of their own components to add to the highly specialised equipment involved. The resulting product would be expensive.

The marketing response

The initial market evaluation was not favourable. It was considered that the product would be too expensive. 'It's crap; they [the customers] won't pay for it,' was the general response. It was decided to carry out substantial market research in four key Australian states to find out how customers would react. The answer was similar. The advice from the survey was, 'If it costs 2 per cent more than the uncoated product *don't proceed.*'

Top management makes the path

Tubemakers proceeded. Management was convinced that Duragal represented a breakthrough and that once the product was available the market would perceive its true value. Commented Daley:

> 'We knew we had to move out of the box and do something that was qualitatively different, that was technologically advanced, that required investments at a level our competitors would not easily make. We had to jump the technology gap. Support from the Tubemakers board was absolutely vital, particularly when initial market research on Duragal's likely acceptance was negative. We needed a product that could change the market. The challenge was to educate the market.'

They educated the market and changed it.

All the advantages that Duragal has are now strongly marketed and it is sold for a variety of uses, very many not foreseen by its creators. New applications are continually growing. Duragal coated section is now used in custom-built coaches and in four-wheel-drive trucks, in replacing timber posts in garages and building structures in agricultural equipment and house flooring systems, and in countless other ways. In August 1997 a major new plant was commissioned in Melbourne to extend the Duragal range of products, opening further new opportunities for growth.

In the process of exploiting the new coating, the marketing team is working with engineers in the plants and potential customers in selling its virtues for existing applications and seeking new uses for the product. The ability to serve all these product markets is firmly rooted in the new Biztech competencies created as a part of developing Duragal.

Reshaping actions to renew operational capabilities

The events at Tubemakers show a series of extended and extensive action in the areas of Engagement, Development and Performance Management, which successfully reshaped and renewed the organisation's operational capabilities over time. First the top group and then the supervisors and workforce and their unions became *engaged* in the future of the business. States of *understanding* and *commitment* were developed and a new culture began to form. Daley commented:

> 'A key factor in the success was the realisation that took place that "We can change". It shifted the culture from one of surviving to one of winning.'

Another critical step was the development of new capabilities in flexibility and innovation. These major developments took place over time—an outcome of new investment, new approaches, new methods and new technologies. A completely new management system was developed for the new mill. 'The warehouse of the future' was built as part of the new approach. Tubemakers was strong in Development capability, not only in relation to physical investment but also in people. All the key people who renewed the operation were insiders. Commented Daley:

> 'We've got a few fifty-year-old guys who have run factories, are marketwise, energetic, know what it's all about professionally, who are highly motivated, with long service, who keep coming up with ideas. Separately we've also got some younger whiz kids who keep us up to date with new technology and help us take ideas and translate them into reality. They've come out of selective recruitment, maybe some by luck, but I think it's important how you identify people early in their careers.'

Daley had been identified very early in this way, recruited by Tubemakers, supported by them through a university degree and then moved successively through research management into increasingly more senior managerial operational roles to the top.

From the outset Performance Management was a major feature of the whole process. This was not only in relation to production and distribution and the technology, but also in the focus on performance measurement during the regular and open negotiations with its workforce and unions, which did much to achieve effective change.

The combination of reshaping actions taken by top management had created new operational capabilities, in Biztech, in Performance Management and later in Marketing and Selling. The Biztech capability included many competencies that Tubemakers' competitors would also have had, but when they developed and incorporated the new technology involved with the Duragal coating process, Tubemakers developed a Biztech that enabled them to position themselves in the market in a way that gave them considerable competitive advantage.

That advantage and positioning arose from action that developed new capabilities. It did not arise in response to market demand, any more than the computer, or the telephone, or the fax machine arose directly from demand. However, it satisfied an existing market more effectively and built markets for the product that did not exist. It stimulated demand.

Pathfinding competence, which its key leaders clearly possessed as they moved the firm continually forward in new directions, finally led them to Duragal as they considered the investment, technological and positioning aspects of their future. The Duragal coating gave them the chance of a superior positioning, of a new alignment between their capabilities and a new positioning. The new technology would have been less valuable if the firm had not already taken major measures over many years to improve its Biztech, Marketing and Selling, and Performance Management capabilities. Indeed it is highly likely that, without that basic improvement, Duragal may never have been sought, found or developed.

However, while, in this example, the product was not developed to meet a known market demand, the firm's capability in developing it further will be strongly influenced by its ability to refine and improve its product and develop new applications for it. Marketing and Selling capability will play an important role in this. It is to a discussion of this operational capability that we now turn.

Marketing and Selling capability

Marketing and Selling capability is about understanding the firm's markets and how external events affect them, identifying its customers' needs and selling its goods and services effectively to them. It is most strongly contributed to by marketing and selling competencies, fairly strongly by environmental assessment and moderately, but still meaningfully, by pathfinding. These competencies provide the firm with the marketing and selling skills needed for successful Current Business

Performance, and the ability to set and focus these skills in terms of both environmental changes and the longer term directions of the business. Competencies that contribute at a much lower level to Marketing and Selling capability include integrative and resource application competencies. These provide the firm with the ability to respond effectively to its understanding of the market.

However, while knowledge and understanding of the market is important, what the firm can actually do by way of responding to, or exploiting, the market does not rest on its Marketing and Selling capability. It rests fundamentally upon its Biztech capability—its actual ability to do what can be profitably sold in the marketplace. Without strength in its Biztech capability it will not be able to serve the market however much it may understand about it. Furthermore its development of significant new direction will be more influenced by the presence of pathfinding competence in the firm than by its Marketing and Selling capability.

This was clearly the case at Tubemakers. If Marketing and Selling capability had strongly influenced the decision to develop Duragal, the development would not have occurred. And, even if the capability had supported Duragal's development, pathfinding action by top management, with support from the board of Tubemakers, played the central role in its development.

Pathfinding relies on many factors other than marketing knowledge. Pathfinding has a strategic directional focus, including creating within the organisation an understanding of the chosen direction. Its horizon is usually much longer term than that of Marketing and Selling. Marketing and Selling became important thereafter in adapting the application of Duragal to a range of market opportunities. Marketing and Selling capability typically depends on a relatively wide group of staff within the firm, whereas pathfinding depends predominantly on a few key individuals in the firm's top management, and on their perceptions and judgments. This was what happened in the development of Duragal in Tubemakers. Some of the intervening developments in plant configuration in previous years may well have been in response to market demand. But the main drivers of the change that produced Duragal were reshaping capabilities and the primary driver of Current Business Performance will be the Biztech capability that produces it. Marketing and Selling is however likely to play an important role in product application and extension.

Marketing and Selling is one of the five essential capabilities that provide the basis for long-term performance. As Figure 3.4 showed, its impact is much less strong on Current Business Performance than the other operational capabilities. Its impact on Change Effectiveness is also less. Nevertheless it is still an important capability to have, particularly in some situations. Most organisations compete in marketplaces where relatively small differences in performance can make the difference between success and failure, or between being number one in an industry or number two or three. If an organisation is weak in Marketing and Selling it will be considerably handicapped in achieving high Current Business Performance. However, while the impact of Marketing and Selling capability on Current Business Performance for commercial firms is clear, the impact of Performance Management is stronger, and the impact of Biztech is stronger still.

Our research shows that Marketing and Selling is a more important capability for commercial organisations than for non-commercial and government organisations. This is, of course, not unexpected. Commercial firms operate within competitive markets, which are easily recognised, which they need to serve and which provide their income. This does not normally apply, or apply to the same degree, to most non-commercial organisations. Public sector organisations are typically much more dependent on the satisfaction of key stakeholders, principally the government of the day, than on the satisfaction of customers. For commercial enterprises, the bottom line relies on customer acceptance. So Marketing and Selling is much more relevant to their current performance. However, as government organisations are becoming increasingly privatised in many countries, Marketing and Selling becomes an important capability for them to develop. This does not just happen as an automatic consequence of being cut loose from government. It is a significant change that again depends upon the application of reshaping capabilities.

Marketing and Selling is not part of Biztech

Our survey data might conceivably have shown that Biztech capability actually includes marketing competencies. In fact our data show that not to be the case. Marketing and Selling is distinct from Biztech, just as Performance Management is distinct from Biztech. Consequently the strength of these capabilities is not closely linked. It is quite possible for a firm to be strong in all three operational capabilities. Equally, it is possible to be weak in all of them. But, importantly, it is quite possible, indeed common, to be strong in one or two of the three operational capabilities, but not strong in the other/s.

This is important to recognise. If your organisation has a strong Biztech capability, it does not follow that it also is strong in Marketing and Selling, or in Performance Management. Each of the three operational capabilities needs to be individually assessed and appropriately managed and developed.

Marketing and Selling capability and Change Effectiveness

Organisations follow different strategies of change. For example, the strategy may be one of 'reorienting' its business by changing its markets, products and services. Alternatively, a business might seek change by 'diversification, expansion or acquisition'. About 20 per cent of the organisations in our sample were following a strategy of maintaining their current direction, but seeking continual and gradual improvement in its implementation—a strategy we call 'refinement'. While Marketing and Selling capability is not generally a contributor to Change Effectiveness, it makes a significant contribution to change when an organisation is following a strategy of refinement.

In this situation, many small cumulative adjustments are required within the framework of the firm's existing direction. This requires close involvement with and response to customers, often within a number of different customer segments. Likewise it requires contact and interaction with the many micro-environments that are part of the firm's overall environment—for example, various groups of suppliers, developments in technology or distribution channels. Constant adjustment to market circumstances and responding to a great deal of feedback of all kinds is needed for refinement to be successful. The capability to understand and relate to the external environment is central to the effectiveness of the change process. The whole organisation should be involved in this process. Middle management has quite a strong impact upon the success of a strategy of refinement whereas top management's role is less central to success than in most other types of change. Empowerment and understanding the change is vital to success. Much depends on the creative support and compliance of many people and the effective working of relevant systems and processes.

Typically, organisations following a refinement strategy have strong capabilities and refinement continues to strengthen them. In this case the more embedded Marketing and Selling is in the organisation the better. In contrast, in some other strategies—for example, reorientation, when the organisation may be seeking new and different markets—key individuals play a stronger role.

The exploitation of Duragal has begun to take the form of continual refinement. There is a real need for constant adaptation to meet better understood market requirements rather than the development of a fundamental new competence to support a new product. In this situation, a firm's capability in Marketing and Selling is an important contributor to success.

Marketing and Selling capability can also support the repositioning of a firm as part of a change. In its contribution to current and near term performance, Marketing and Selling is concerned with important aspects of marketing, selling, advertising, promotions, brand management, price positioning, market research, and so on. While these activities are likely to help in short-term performance, some of them may also contribute to repositioning the firm in the mind of the customer. Not all positioning is, of course, perceptual. For example, physical location, alliances, geographic presence and cost structure are all positioning factors, which in themselves have little dependence on marketing expertise, though that expertise can help exploit them.

Other positioning factors, such as brand and corporate image, are far more dependent on marketing expertise and, in this way, can contribute to the outcome of change. Yet marketing alone cannot effectively reposition a company, except for very short periods of time. Unless Biztech and Performance Management capabilities enable the company to 'deliver the goods', the positioning it tries to establish with marketing expertise will be destroyed. For example, there is no benefit in a car manufacturer using its Marketing and Selling capability to create a luxury automobile brand if it is, in fact, unable to produce a consistently high quality, highly reliable and luxurious automobile.

Products and product service are also most influenced by Biztech and Performance Management. Though Marketing and Selling capability can make important input to this, if the product or service is not right, there is little that capability in Marketing and Selling can do to correct the situation.

Marketing and Selling supports other capabilities

In a general sense, Marketing and Selling capability acts to support other capabilities rather than being the primary force. For example, market awareness often helps identify ways in which an organisation needs to change. An illustration is the considerable attention now being paid to customer service. For many firms this has led to significant corporate change. Yet recognition that such a change is important to the success of the business and should therefore be adopted, and the actual achievement of such a change, is typically more dependent on pathfinding and reshaping capabilities than on Marketing and Selling. Furthermore, improving service to customers is often a matter of cultural change rather than product change. Cultural change—changing the way people see their jobs, the way they work together and the values they share—is most affected by Engagement, Performance Management and Development, not by Marketing and Selling capability, nor, for that matter, by Biztech capability.

Thus, within limits, Marketing and Selling capability has an important part to play in the long-term performance of a firm, through its impact on Current Business Performance and its contribution to positioning the firm and its products, and in its contribution to achieving incremental change.

The strength of Marketing and Selling capability

Marketing and Selling capability is typically much weaker than Biztech and about as strong as the other capabilities. As with Biztech, there are individual competencies that underlie Marketing and Selling capability for each organisation. Some of them, such as quantitative market analysis skills or marketing database management skills, are fairly generic and supported by knowledge, skills and a discipline base in the public domain. Others are more firm or industry specific. To make some simple distinctions, industrial marketing requires different skills and knowledge from consumer marketing. And in consumer marketing, there are important differences between marketing recurrent consumption products (for example, soap and breakfast foods) and durables (such as washing machines and cars). So Marketing and Selling competencies will in some cases be firm specific.

However, while most competencies that make up Biztech are seen as areas of specific expertise, many staff without any expertise in marketing still seem more than willing to suggest and influence what should be done in the marketing of their organisation's products and services. Part of this may flow from the difficulty of measurement of some aspects of marketing. Lord Leverhulme's comment about the enormous sums that his company, Lever Brothers, spent on advertising its soap—'half of it is wasted, but we don't know which half'—may belong to another epoch but still is too close to the bone for many businesses. The widespread intrusion of personal views tends to apply to marketing to a degree unmatched by most Biztech competencies. Some organisations measure and evaluate marketing initiatives very rigorously and hold the relevant managers accountable for their actual contribution. More commonly, the main focus of accountability for results spreads across many areas outside marketing. Furthermore since Marketing and Selling capability does not contribute as strongly to Current Business Performance as the other operational capabilities, it does not usually have the intense focus that is applied to Biztech.

Summary

Marketing and Selling capability generally makes a modest but still important contribution to Current Business Performance and a more limited one to Change Effectiveness with the important exception of 'refinement' situations. As a supplementary or supporting capability, it has value. But investment in it is of little value unless Biztech is strong and buttressed with strong Performance Management. That determines the products and services you can currently deliver well. They are the strengths in which you have previously invested. Of course you are then likely to use marketing expertise in promoting the products and services for which your existing Biztech capability is well suited.

If there are new markets, customers and product offerings that appear attractive, there may be a strong argument to pursue them. But, if so, first ensure your Biztech capability can deliver. That may mean important changes need to be made in your Biztech capability. Your ability to make those changes effectively, rather than your market responsiveness, then becomes the critical determinant of your success. It is likely to be easier to change your markets than your capabilities.

In most organisations, pathfinding competence and decisions about positioning tend to depend heavily on the judgments of a few key individuals in top management. Their personal competencies and knowledge are critical to correct decisions. Consequently, ensuring that top management is really well informed about markets, customers and opportunities, as well as the workings of the organisation and its operational capabilities, is vital to the organisation's future performance. This requires a real commitment of time and a process that informs top management about the organisation's markets, customers and products, and also potential developments in the broad environment.

CHAPTER 10

Building and embedding competencies

Larry Adler formed FAI Insurances in 1971. He was a man with very high personal competencies and abundant energy. FAI grew steadily for the next 10 years in a very competitive industry. By 1982 its premium income reached $47 million and its shareholder funds $59 million. Six years later, its premium income was $466 million, its shareholder funds were $468 million and its after-tax operating profit, which had increased by 50 per cent over the previous year, stood at $171 million. Growth had been, by any standards, quite outstanding. In six years, income had increased ten times, shareholder funds eight times and net operating profit thirty-four times.

Larry Adler was the mainspring of his organisation's success. FAI's control and motivation systems were largely in his own head. Supported by a small close-knit team, his style was intensely personal and entrepreneurial. The decision-making processes largely took place in his own head, heart and gut. He had a natural antipathy to systems, structures and bureaucracies. His world was informal, free-wheeling, unstructured and entrepreneurial. So was his organisation.

Profit in insurance comes principally from two related activities. The first is from the underwriting operations. For these to generate net profit, the income received must be greater than the costs and claims made under the policy over time. The second source of profit arises from the income generated by investing the funds received from the premium income. This investment income is usually the prime source of net profit for many insurance organisations.

Larry Adler applied his great personal competencies in using the premium income to make a whole series of entrepreneurial investments with high potential profit but also carrying high risk. Many of these investments met with spectacular success and transformed the profit position of FAI in the mid-1980s. In October 1987, the stock market crashed. The investment environment fundamentally changed. Just over a year later Larry Adler died. When this happened, the group lost not only the leader of its underwriting operations but also the prime source of the competence that had generated its substantial investment income. This investment activity had become the core business of FAI and Larry Adler was its major and virtually sole source of competence.

It is not at all uncommon for one person to dominate a part of an organisation, or even a complete organisation. This is frequently the case in small or young organisations, though by this time FAI had some sixteen hundred staff with sixty-five branch operations. We have earlier seen the impact Paul Simons had on Woolworths or Jack Welch on GE, both very large organisations. It is much more uncommon for one person to dominate the organisation's direction and operations, and also possess and use the technical competencies (in this case investment skills and the propensity to manage risk) upon which the organisation's total profit performance depends.

What FAI had was high personal competence, focused to an unusual extent on one person. It also had some collective competence, particularly in its sales force, but little embedded corporate competence, either in operations or investment. Its key competence was in fact not 'owned' by the company but by its founder. The company lost it on the founder's death.

A number of actions were taken over the following few years to build a stronger organisation. A relatively small and highly committed top team collected the information they thought they needed to change the organisation, and developed and ultimately set out to 'sell' their solutions to the organisation. In broad terms the changes were imposed from the top. Substantial downsizing was accompanied by major management changes. Most of the top sixty posts in the insurance operations changed hands. New specialists with personal technical skills to build skilled corporate services previously lacking—in budgeting, forecasting, product development, computerised underwriting and many other business facets—were recruited. To maintain the innovative and entrepreneurial culture they prized, individuals with these personal values were recruited. In an effort to change the culture from sales driven, which had provided money for the entrepreneurial investments, to profit driven, which was now needed for performance, new operational procedures were introduced and profit centres were established at branch, state and product level.

Corporate competencies, however, take a long time to build and competitors do not stand still. Profits dropped rapidly into losses, which continued until, in 1994, the company was able to report a small profit again. Previously its substantial and growing profit had depended principally on the personal competencies of its founder Larry Adler. As one of his senior colleagues put it:[1]

> 'The major problem was that Larry didn't leave any "how to do it" books.'

Forms of competence: personal, collective and embedded

Our example illustrates one of the three different forms in which competence exists within an organisation. These three forms are personal, collective and embedded. Normally organisations will have all three forms. Competencies, as we have shown earlier, are the building blocks from which the five key capabilities are formed.

Personal competence

Personal competence belongs to the individual. The individual brings the competence to the firm and when they leave the organisation, the competence leaves with them. The organisation has hired, but not owned, the competence.

Personal competence is very valuable to firms. For many very small firms it is their major source of competence. However it is important that the personal competencies of individuals are those that the firm needs and can use to perform effectively. This is particularly important for individuals at the top of organisations. For example, GE benefits from the personal skills of Jack Welch, as Woolworths did from Paul Simons, in Performance Management.

However, when firms, or an important part of their operations, become dependent upon the personal competencies of an individual (as in the following example), or a very few individuals, the greater the risk to the organisation and the more variable the results. Key individuals can deliver success. They can also deliver disaster.

A personal competence in visual merchandising

Janet had high personal competence in visual merchandising. She knew how to present and display merchandise in ways that created a powerful impact on customers and resulted in increased sales. She had flair. She was really talented. Although her original focus was fashion she had set out to become knowledgeable about everything the store sold from fashion to furniture, from men's wear to hardware. She read every magazine that featured or advertised goods. She was deeply interested in her own professional development. She talked her boss into sending her on an expensive internal display course in Switzerland. Although she was always up to date on fashion and colour trends she also understood how to display the selling points of a barbecue or a kitchen setting. She believed the use of accessories always made the difference. She regularly visited the stores with which her own store competed, and when she went overseas on holiday she returned with photographs of store displays or layouts from the country she had been visiting. It seemed that even on holiday she was interested in learning more about her job and how it could be done better.

Janet had a real understanding of the importance of store layout and of the right juxtaposition of departments to entice the customer to browse around the whole store. She provided attractive and interesting displays at the end of every walkway to stimulate the traffic flow.

She knew which fixtures would be best for certain types of merchandise. She understood how to segment the merchandise. 'The space you leave between items is just as important as the items themselves,' she used to say. She always blocked the colours and grouped the items in the most attractive and inviting way.

When the store was running special promotions, she could produce eye-catching posters and displays. She always talked to the selling staff about what was selling well and the best sellers were always featured in the most prominent positions. Janet knew that informative ticketing helped to sell goods. Departments often did not have good selling tickets for their goods although it was their responsibility. Janet would produce them by hand, to help the selling impact of the displays. With talent, energy and effort she always managed to make the place look full of interesting stock but not overcrowded and confused.

Part of Janet's role was to encourage the department managers to improve their own visual merchandising skills. She became a mentor to some of them, in spite of being about half their age, but many others simply left it to Janet to do all the work. Some seemed to resent Janet's effort and were critical if the displays didn't 'pull'. This never seemed to ruffle Janet. If something wasn't working, she pulled it down and tried something different.

While she spent her time and energy in making the store look attractive, she knew the purpose of her work was to sell more goods and use the space more profitably. She was always talking to the managers and selling staff about their sales results and looking for ways to help increase them.

Janet was a real asset. Unfortunately, one day she left. Regrettably, the store did not have a replacement. When they finally did recruit one, he turned out not to have the same level of personal competence as Janet.

Collective competence

Competence in an organisation can also be collective. Collective competence exists when there are a relatively large number of individuals with similar personal competencies. The particular competence is thus more widespread in the organisation, which is no longer so dependent, for that particular competence, upon a key individual (as in the examples of

Janet or Larry Adler), or on a few individuals. Partners in an accounting or consulting firm, or highly specialised salespeople, whose performance may be helped by, but does not fundamentally rest on, the firm's systems or processes are examples of this kind of competence. Performance is strongly dependent on personal abilities. While there may be some integration between individuals in their work, it is relatively small.

Management ability may be a collective competence in an organisation where there are a lot of good managers. Some of their work may become integrated to some extent, but essentially the competence resides in the individuals acting either on their own or as part of a group. Of course it is possible that the existence of a number of good managers may indicate the firm possesses a corporate competence in management development. But equally the skill in developing other managers may be an individual skill of a member of top management and will cease should he or she depart.

The lines between personal and collective competence are not, of course, rigid and definite. One merges into the other. Collective competence clearly gives an organisation more security in its capabilities because there are now numbers of people involved, and individual comings and goings are somewhat less damaging. The firm in this situation is likely to continuously maintain the pool of employees with the collective competence. Additionally, dependence on individuals usually causes the firm to develop some systems and practices to provide some consistency and standards in what the individuals do and how they do it.

Collective competence is very important to organisations, and countless organisations spend effort and expense in improving the competence of individuals who form its base. Collective competence nearly always involves systems to develop the competence of individuals, and standard practices to assist their performance, but it is primarily focused on the contribution, effort and skills of the individual within the overall system.

Embedded competence

Embedded competence occurs when the competence is owned by the organisation. This may have occurred because personal competencies have passed to the organisation, and become embedded, consciously or unconsciously, in practices, processes, systems, culture, technologies and capital assets. The competence has acquired a life of its own. Sometimes the embedded competence may be bound up with technical specialised assets—for example, a refinery for producing petrol incorporating firm-specific technologies—but this is not always the case. Embedded corporate competence may often exist without a strong investment in plant and facilities. We will illustrate the development and use of such competence in the next few pages. When a competence is embedded, people may come and go but the competence tends to endure. Individuals may still have valuable high personal competence but their presence is now less important to organisational performance.

We noted above that management is often a collective competence in an organisation. But management *development* can be an embedded competence. Organisations can, and do, develop practices, systems and processes—in recruitment, placement, training, job rotation, assessment, reward and career development—and support these processes with special structures and roles, and a strong culture of developing its own management. Such organisations, through these and other methods, have a corporate competence in management development. It is also one that is not highly dependent on investment in fixed assets. While individuals play a part in this process, essentially the competence that results in the supply of good managers is owned by the organisation. Many successful organisations have such an embedded competence and part of their success, often a substantial part, depends upon consistently high quality, largely home-grown, managers.

Woolworths' competence in, say, inventory management or store layout is embedded. So is McDonald's competence in kitchen operation or restaurant management, or Du Pont's competence in slitting film or an airline's in safety management or pilot training.

Often, an embedded competence becomes an extremely valuable asset of the business though it rarely appears in the organisation's balance sheet. Though it may have high value to the organisation, it cannot usually be sold, or bought by others, separately from the sale of the business. Its integration in the business, and the fact that it combines a large number of factors in its composition, makes it very much the property of the business. Corporate competencies are sometimes difficult to identify, even for some people in the business who do not understand how the business actually works. They are difficult for competitors to identify, imitate or match. They frequently take many years, or sometimes decades, to develop. They can erode or disappear. They are sometimes very difficult to change. They are often a major source of competitive advantage.

Signposts to the rest of this chapter

In the rest of this chapter we are going to explore a number of aspects of competencies. We start by describing how an organisation developed an embedded corporate competence in an area of operations in which it was previously dependent upon the personal competencies of a few individuals. We will use this as a base to describe what a competence consists of, how it can be built and embedded in an organisation, and some of the benefits of this.

We then examine the different ways in which organisations develop competencies that are part of a reshaping capability. We look at an example of the development and embedding of a competence in communication, which is an important part of Engagement capability. Lastly, we describe a situation where an organisation allowed an important competence to erode, how this happened, the damage that resulted, and how the organisation rebuilt the competence in a new form.

Each of these examples throws light on different aspects of the development, sustaining, operation, erosion and benefits of corporate competencies. This should help you in identifying and exploring your own organisation's competencies and deciding how you can develop, embed or use them more effectively.

An embedded corporate competence in visual merchandising

Unlike Janet's organisation, Robert's organisation, which we met first in Chapter 1, had developed an embedded corporate competence in visual merchandising. When Robert's visual merchandising manager, Clifford, left, the problem was relatively quickly overcome. A few years before

Robert's appointment as store manager, the group had been concerned about the enormous differences in the effectiveness of their internal layouts, merchandise displays and promotions. A new store's group director started a series of actions to develop an embedded corporate competence in visual merchandising as part of a drive to increase the profitable use of space. He discussed his aims with his department store managers who quickly shared his vision for upgrading and invigorating the somewhat dated and conservative approach of the group to visual merchandising.

Consequently, following Clifford's departure, Robert found a great deal of embedded competence in existence to help him maintain his store's performance in this important area. Some of it was in numerical and pictorial knowledge in hard copy documents, some was in processes to develop and motivate managers, some was in management structures and systems to develop skills and disseminate knowledge, and some was in the culture and reputation of the organisation.

Sharing knowledge about visual merchandising

A regularly updated manual contained pictures showing the best examples in store and department layout. The various types of fixtures were illustrated. The way different sorts of merchandise should be displayed on the available range of fixtures was detailed. Lighting intensities and colours were described for differing departments. All of the pictures were accompanied by reasons that gave the rationale that lay behind the various recommendations so that people could build up their own knowledge of why things worked well.

There was also a great deal of data about how best to use space to generate profit. Each year, each store had to send to head office details of the space given to each department. Sales and profits per square metre being achieved in each department by each store in the group were circulated. This provided achievable benchmarks for departmental and store performance. Robert also received a monthly list from head office of the top ten best sellers in each department, and so it was easy to check that the best sellers were being strongly promoted in his store.

Creating a visual merchandising culture

The processes for point-of-sale promotion were altered. New goods were accompanied by merchandise information sheets, written by the central buyers, outlining the key selling points with suggested ticket wording. Point-of-sale materials for major group-wide promotions arrived simultaneously with the goods from a central display and ticketing studio.

Each store held a competition every six months to choose the best displayed department within the store. It was judged by two general managers from other stores in the group. This resulted in an improvement in merchandising impact and focused the attention of store managers, both as judges and as judged, on improving store display. The competition was then raised to store level and judged by the store's group director and other senior group executives. The prizes for the best displayed store in the group were handed out by the group's chief executive at a six monthly meeting when all the key managers of the group were present. In this and other ways, a culture was created in which visual merchandising was of vital importance, was something on which managers would be judged and rewarded, and was a competitive advantage to be fostered.

Embedding the growth and management of visual merchandising

As the combination of knowledge, skills and action grew, managers became more confident of their ability and more motivated to carry out the work of visual merchandising, which had so often been left to the overworked specialists. The visual merchandising managers were encouraged to see their role as helping managers to improve the displays rather than doing most of it themselves. Some managers had natural talents, which were developed by access to the new initiatives and in turn increased the quality of their competence over time. Others, to whom the ideas and skills were new, were still able to benefit and learn. All managers were able to enhance whatever level of skills they previously possessed. The developed ideas and practices became a new standard segment in the training program of all departmental managers.

Over time, the tacit skills, knowledge and accumulated experience in the heads and hands of the visual merchandising managers, line managers at all levels and key executives at the centre were, bit by bit, turned into explicit and codified skills and information that large numbers of people in the organisation could use themselves. The group added to its internal knowledge by gathering all the information and skills it could from overseas department store groups. It joined an international network of department stores, which exchanged not only practices and policies, and enabled training visits to take place, but also shared the figures on which sensible decisions about the use of space could be based.

The management structure was changed to integrate aspects of visual merchandising that had previously been separated. The store's layout department, which previously reported to the group's building director, now reported to the store's director. A central manager was appointed to take responsibility for the continued growth and effectiveness of the visual merchandising competence in all stores. So both the planning and implementing aspects were brought together reporting to the store's director.

Management effort was put into training the specialist managers responsible for this activity in each store and helping them see their role in a wider context. There were some problems in this area as these people were often very artistic and used to working on their own. However, care was taken to involve them closely with developing ideas for use round the group as a whole. Some were sent overseas for specific training and exposure to new ideas. Over time most grew into their new roles. They began to see an improvement in the level of visual merchandising in the stores and in the value placed on it, and their work, by senior management. They conducted their own visual merchandise training for their own department managers, enabling and encouraging many managers to practise and develop skills. Their role had changed, to some extent, towards training and development, but they still did specialist display work to maintain their personal presentation skills. A balance was maintained between central direction and local initiative. The competitions fostered continuing interest.

As a result of actions taken by the management of Robert's group, competence development, maintenance and performance became an ongoing, continuous and managed process. *The organisation had developed a corporate competence it did not have before, which was now part of its embedded Biztech capability.*

To do this it had *engaged* individuals and groups in the process, and conveyed a vision of what they might achieve. The managers and central buyers had become involved in the process. It had amassed and distributed an enormous amount of information in a form that was useful to a wide range of people. It had put a major effort into *developing* the knowledge and the skills of managers and specialists across the organisation. Training had taken place at many levels. It had established benchmarks as a basis for *performance management* and competitions to motivate, and rewards to recognise good performance. It had established new positions and altered roles to maintain focus on monitoring and managing performance. As a result the competence was largely embedded in the organisation and remained despite the turnover of individuals. The organisation now owned a corporate competence, which was an important part of its Biztech capability.

Summary of key points and linkages

Table 10.1 summarises elements of the competence, the actions that management took to build it and the mechanisms, media, systems, processes, structures, technologies, relationships and culture in which it was embedded.

The structure of competence

There are three aspects to the structure of competence. The first two are:

- knowledge and understanding
- technical skills.

The third aspect is the managerial ability to *integrate* the knowledge, understanding and technical skills, and *apply* them in the range of different situations that a person encounters in the case of a personal competence, or that a firm encounters in the case of a corporate competence.

Table 10.1 Embedding visual merchandising competence		
Competence consists of knowledge and related skills in areas such as:	Built by actions in Engagement, Development and Performance Management, such as:	Embedded in a combination of:
Use of fixtures	Conveying a vision	Physical records
Store layout	Involving all managers	Databases
Lighting	Involving central buyers	Systems
Merchandise grouping	Developing manuals	Processes
Use of accessories	Creating new promotion methods	Structures
Use of colour	Training at all levels	Roles
Ticketing	Developing central services	Forums
Sales/promotions	Creating new benchmarks	Relationships
Sales per square metre	Circulation of performance	Technology
Space allocation	figures	Plant/facilities
Profit per square metre	Six monthly competitions	Organisational culture
	Competence performance rewards	Large numbers of people
	Appointment of central manager	

Knowledge and understanding

The first requirement of a competence is knowledge and understanding about the task or activity to be performed. This includes knowledge about the task or activity itself and also includes how that knowledge can be applied, in various situations and environments, to produce intended outcomes. The knowledge may be formalised and taught, or at the other extreme it may be so intuitive and tacit that its owner may not understand, at a cognitive level, how or why the results are actually achieved.

In Janet's case she had a good understanding of what made displays and presentations successful. She understood intuitively the impact of colours and designs. She appreciated how to bring out the selling points of goods. She understood how fixtures or position focused the customer's attention. She understood the need to draw on the experience of the selling staff. She knew what she had to do to be a successful visual merchandiser, and that the final purpose was to sell more goods.

A corporate competence needs knowledge about the activity, its purpose and how results are achieved. That knowledge needs to be in a form that many people can access and understand and apply to their tasks. Considerable work may be needed to develop tacit knowledge into the explicit knowledge that can be taught to others. The knowledge will have to be communicated to many through training and education.

Technical skills

Janet's technical skills were in placing and grouping goods, in her ability to choose and arrange accessories to bring the displays to life, in her skill in siting displays in relation to walkways, in her ability to produce informative selling tickets, and so on.

A corporate competence similarly requires technical abilities and assets in whatever is needed for its business. The skills of individuals and collective skills of groups will be harnessed by abilities embedded in the organisation in systems, practices, policies and structures. The skills too need considerable integration if the outcome is to be productive.

Technical assets usually play a very much larger and more obvious role in corporate competencies than they do in this particular example. This applies particularly to competencies that contribute to operational capabilities, though it is less true of competencies that contribute to reshaping capabilities. Corporate competencies often require major investment in assets and resources and many of the skills and know-how are linked to and often locked up in plant, equipment, facilities and physical resources. The management of the performance of these assets is part of the corporate competence.

Managing application in differing situations

The third aspect of competence is the managerial ability to integrate the knowledge and technical skills and apply them in a range of different situations. For example, Janet needed to manage her performance. She had to focus her efforts, and motivate herself to perform. She also had to manage a wide range of working relationships with the store's managers, some of whom were difficult to deal with. She had to do a lot of her own information gathering and skill development. But she organised it and did it. Janet's performance therefore not only needed her knowledge and skills but it depended on how she managed herself in applying these.

Getting our own act together in terms of our own personal performance in any activity is substantially influenced by our own motivation and confidence. It is also influenced by the vision we have of what we want to do. This vision guides our learning process as well as our actions when we perform. When that vision is strong, it tends to have a continuing impact on our motivation and consequent behaviour. However, our actual performance will also be influenced by our state at the time and the situation when we perform. As we discussed in Chapter 4 our management of our personal state is therefore also important to our personal performance.

A competence cannot therefore be separated from its owner. It is much more than knowing what to do and having the skills to do it. *It also means doing it*—doing it when things are going well or badly; doing it all the time, or whenever it is needed, not just when you feel you want to; doing it under pressure and in competition; and doing it because you believe in it. A personal competence is you in action.

Similarly, corporate competence cannot be separated from the attributes and characteristics of the corporation. Corporate competence involves and requires integrating knowledge, skill and action. Sometimes that integration has to occur in a particular part of the organisation. Sometimes it has to occur across the world. This will require systems, practices, mechanisms and networks. But it will also need motivation and energy. Just as an individual needs motivation and self-management to perform, so does the corporation collectively. Control and reward systems, and training people, will contribute to that, but so will a sense of vision and a belief that what people are doing is worthwhile and valuable. A corporate competence is manifested and visible in the corporation in action.

So the performance of the corporate competence will not only depend upon knowledge and skills but also on the extent to which the corporation can harness the energy and motivation of its people. Strong motivation and commitment supplies a relatively stable source of effort and energy. But action will also be influenced by the state of the organisation—how the organisation collectively responds to any given situation. This is considerably affected by the actions of managers to influence organisational states as we illustrated in earlier chapters.

How are corporate competencies embedded?

Organisations embed competencies in a number of different ways, and in a number of different mechanisms and processes. Action to embed in one area provides a base, or reinforces embedding in other areas. For example, embedding knowledge or data in a manual of procedures provides a base for skill development in those areas. Embedding them in many complementary aspects and mechanisms of a business makes them more robust, since they do not rely on limited bases of support and are more likely to be stable and enduring.

Physical records and databases

Competencies are embedded in physical records and in documents of many kinds. Procedure manuals for skill application or guidelines for customer treatment are typical basic examples. At a more sophisticated level the information and method application stored in the computer network for use by all its consultants worldwide at Andersen Consulting combines aspects of knowledge and skill integration and embeds them in software. McDonald's checklist of behaviours for employees serving customers is a much simpler example, but still very powerful.

In Robert's group, illustrated visual display manuals and databases built from the effective allocation and use of space in all stores are examples of this.

Systems and processes

Standard operating procedures, safety processes, performance appraisal systems, management information systems, market research routines, strategic planning processes, and meetings and forums are typical examples of what is an enormous range of ways in which knowledge, skills and actions are made explicit, embedded and distributed in systems and processes. Often the competence only comes into existence through the creation of the system or process. Such systems and processes are frequently the outcome of considerable experiment and development by individuals and groups over long periods of time. They provide a basis for increased effectiveness in action. They can be relevant to both operational and reshaping needs.

In Robert's group, new systems for the collection and distribution of visual merchandising data, new training at all levels in the organisation and new merchandise promotion processes all helped to embed the competence.

Technology and capital assets

Corporate competence is embedded in technology and in specialised capital assets and equipment. A fully automated manufacturing plant embodies much of the competence and know-how in the equipment itself, but the highly skilled operators embody another level and special product features yet another. In less sophisticated plant, the processes, skills, training and commitment of the staff combine to capture and embed the competence. Specialised technology and assets are just as applicable to the service sector, which is highly capital and technology intensive. In retailing, for example, corporate competence can be captured in shop construction design, checkout design or automated warehousing. In banking, it could be embedded and retained in specialised systems used to gather, store and retrieve customer information. The interaction of people, systems, technology and capital equipment locks the competence ever more closely into the ownership of the organisation. Competence also exists in proprietary knowledge, which is often further secured in patents and technical agreements.

In Robert's group, collaboration between the two central departments of store layout and visual merchandising enabled the group to design its own fixtures capturing its developing knowledge of visual display in them. The growing technology ultimately influenced the way new stores were designed and built. Previously the layouts were secondary to the design of the building. The layouts now influenced the design of the building. New equipment to manufacture tickets centrally and new processes for collecting information about the selling points of the goods, and new ways of designing and presenting tickets, enabled ticketing standards to be raised across the group.

Numbers of people and collectivities

Individuals and even very small groups can leave an organisation and take a competence with them but, once the number spreads beyond a small group, the competence is likely, in practice, to become increasingly collective and finally largely corporately owned. Human resource management or other policies that encourage long service in employees—such as meaningful jobs, career development, high rewards and allocation of equity—can all help to retain employees and their skills for long periods. Multi-skilling, job design and job rotation widen the skill base of those retained and minimise loss from the departure of individuals.

In Robert's group what had previously been the focus of a few became part of the work of the many. Managers at all levels were given access to information and received training in relevant skills. Of course some individuals still focused entirely on visual merchandising, but it was now within a framework of much wider and more explicitly based knowledge. As the contribution to results of improved visual merchandising became increasingly recognised more resources were put into the activity. The buying side also became involved. As skills and knowledge became more widely distributed, the organisation became less and less dependent on the skills of a few individuals.

Organisational structures and roles

Competencies can also be embedded in organisational structures and roles. For example, one feature of the matrix structure is to try and maintain a functional competence with a divisional structure. Many organisations have central staff whose focus is very much on a particular competence—for example, marketing or product innovation—while other responsibilities are dealt with on a unit or divisional basis. The central unit becomes the guardian of the competence and the network accesses it as needed.

The establishing of special posts may help to capture a competence. In Robert's group changes in management structure, and the establishment and change in reporting of central departments, became vital to the growth and embedding of the competence in visual merchandising. Woolworths improved performance management in the stores by establishing a special post in store review and back-up processes to ensure action. Most banks have a chief credit officer responsible for credit policy, practices and compliance with them, even though actual credit decision making is normally widely dispersed in the bank.

Organisational culture

Competencies are often embedded in and supported by the values and culture of the organisation. A culture that is strongly focused on customer service will support the embedding of competencies directed at producing customer satisfaction. Likewise a corporate value of sharing information encourages and supports competencies that rely on wide information sharing. The importance that the culture places on the competence will do much to ensure its retention and use. This will be strikingly illustrated later in this chapter when we look at the loss of credit management competence in a bank. In Robert's group the part played by store display competitions, the focus on them by the store's director and the public rewards all played a symbolic part in building a supporting culture. The heavy investment in the training of people also signalled the priorities of the group. When an organisation demonstrates the importance of an aspect of its business by top management focus and supporting investment, it helps to build a culture that values, rewards and supports that activity.

Relationships and alliances

Competencies are more loosely but often enduringly embedded in special relationships with outside organisations and networks. Foremost among these are relationships between organisations and suppliers. Just-in-time inventory management is an example of this. Marks & Spencer, the British retail chain, has had close, integrated relationships with its suppliers for more than fifty years. These have stretched into mutual design, production management, inventory management, and so on. For many high-tech companies working relationships with universities or special research institutes have captured knowledge and skills. Automobile manufacturers capture competencies in design through their relationship with their distributors. The British oil industry has made major improvements in reducing costs and improving performance by establishing alliances with suppliers where both partners share the benefits. Sometimes relationships are formalised into joint ventures or partnerships to retain competencies. The electronic, telecommunication, computer and automobile industries have hundreds of these involving the strongest companies around the world.

Robert's group competence in visual display was strongly aided by its joining an international association of stores that exchanged information, facilitated visits and training. As a consequence of this, relationships with particular stores became strong at the formal and informal level. Ongoing collaboration developed across many activities involving many executives.

Combination of embedding methods

While we have highlighted a number ways of embedding a competence so that it becomes the property of the organisation, many competencies are captured and embedded simultaneously in all or many of these ways. The example we gave earlier, of visual merchandising, was embedded in almost all of these ways, though they took place over time. Real strength comes when the competence is embedded in a number of different, mutually reinforcing, ways. This makes it extremely difficult for a competitor to identify what the competence is or understand how it actually works. It is therefore hard or perhaps impossible to match, or copy.

The benefits of embedded corporate competencies

The establishment of a corporate competence has the potential to deliver a number of major benefits. An embedded competence provides a platform of skills and knowledge on which every manager can build. Each manager in Robert's organisation was enabled to increase his or her level of visual merchandising, increasing the total power of the organisation to perform in this area. Because the competence was commonly available and used by many, the performance became better, and at the same time less variable across the group.

Knowledge that is in a form to be widely disseminated needs to be changed from tacit knowledge to explicit knowledge. Tacit knowledge is the knowledge in a person's head from innate understanding, learned skills and experience. It is the basis of professional judgment. This kind of knowledge must be understood, codified, structured and captured on paper, in computer systems or processes before it can be disseminated, taught and learned. This process often increases the quality and applicability of the knowledge through analysis, understanding and codification. When people know what to do, they do not have to spend time in finding out, and their energy can be focused on doing.

As people begin to apply this formalised or explicit knowledge, they develop their own tacit extensions of it. This increases the amount of knowledge and the way it can be applied. Such knowledge and skill are usually very relevant to business performance as many managers seek to solve the real business problems that confront them. If the process is managed, this new tacit knowledge is, in turn, made explicit and fed back into the knowledge and skill base, thereby increasing the potential power of the competence. If not all the knowledge remains, there is a continual sedimentation effect, as what is more valuable is kept and what is less valuable atrophies. This is what happened in Robert's group as the input from many managers and specialists became incorporated into the knowledge and skill base.

Once a firm has developed embedded competence, it is possible to use less skilled and costly staff to carry out work that was previously the responsibility of more highly paid people. This is one of the purposes of Andersen Consulting's computerised Knowledge Exchange. It enables them to use lower cost consultants to do what more experienced and costly senior consultants did before. This was not a benefit in Robert's case. The costs of specialists would not have changed much. But the quality of most of the managers would have risen for little extra cost, and so organisational productivity rose.

Embedded corporate competence does not depart with individuals. It remains as a resource of the business. Although not directly reflected in the balance sheet, it may well be the corporation's most valuable asset. The Janets of the world are relatively scarce and, unfortunately, ultimately leave. Once a business has developed embedded corporate competence in activities important to its performance, it becomes more secure in its ownership, control, development, extension and exercise of the competence.

Firms with high corporate competencies attract high quality individuals who are interested in the competencies it exhibits. This is not only true for organisations that have generated reputations of corporate technical excellence, but also applies to organisations that have developed corporate reputations in management generally.

Building and embedding reshaping competencies

We have described the actions that took place in Robert's organisation to build an operational competence in visual merchandising. We saw actions in Engagement, Development and Performance Management to build and embed the competence in a variety of mechanisms, processes and other aspects of the business. We focused on the actions of managers, but, of course, action will have taken place at every level in the firm. We also focused on successful action, though learning also takes place through failed action. Frequently in discussion with executives about a change in which they have been involved they say, 'If I only had known at the beginning what I now know at the end I would have done it differently.'

While the example was of a retailing competence we could equally well have chosen to describe the building of a competence in credit management, metal extrusion or hydraulic systems. From our study we know that to be successful, managers will have typically taken action to *engage* their organisation, or the relevant part of it, in the building of the competence, they will have *developed* whatever was needed in resources or skills for the competence and they will have *managed the performance* of the change process to ensure it had a successful outcome.

If the individual managers involved in the building process learned from their actions and experience, they will have developed a personal competence in some aspect of managing the changes that resulted in improved competence in visual merchandising, credit management, metal extrusion or whatever. That is to say they have developed two kinds of competence. They will now have a new *operational* competence—in our example visual merchandising—and in the process of building this competence they will have learned a *reshaping* competence. Faced with making a similar change they may well be able to say, 'I've done something like this before. I know what has to be done and I believe I can do it.' They will be able to apply some, or much, or all, of their new reshaping competencies to a future change. They did not set out to learn the reshaping competencies, but learned them by doing them, through action, because they were important to the success of the main task, which was to improve the operational competencies of the organisation.

It is likely that a number of managers will have been involved in the change. This means that the organisation has now acquired some collective reshaping competencies. Should the organisation decide to make further changes, managers will have an understanding of the key things they have to do to make the changes successfully.

If, as a result of their experience of successful change, the managers embed some of these competencies in their organisation, then they will get some, or all, the benefits of these embedded reshaping competencies for future changes. For example, we have seen that communication is an important contributing competence to Engagement capability. If the organisation embeds some communication competencies in its systems, practices, mechanisms and culture, the power of that corporate communication competence will be available to help the organisation in continuing or future changes. As we have seen earlier in this chapter, the development of a corporate competence brings many potential benefits.

Individuals' personal communication skills will be leveraged, the process of communication will be better understood, its use more widespread, the communications more effectively carried out and the outcomes will be better and less variable across the organisation. We will shortly give an example of such an embedded communication competence in Robert's store.

As action takes place to make effective change, individuals begin to acquire reshaping competencies, collective reshaping competencies begin to emerge and the possibility of embedding some of the competencies also arises. So as organisations attempt change and gain experience and competencies in taking change-related action, they also have the option to decide how much of the competencies they will try and embed in their organisation. As more of the reshaping competencies are embedded, the three reshaping capabilities themselves become more firmly entrenched in the business.

However, most attempts to improve operational competencies *are taken consciously with an end in view.* Some opportunity, or need, is identified, or some weakness is revealed, and the firm's management decides to do something about it. The change that takes place may be quite small, or it may transform the organisation over a long time. But what is done is usually consciously done, and if it is done well, the firm develops an improved or new operational competence that will contribute to one of its three operational capabilities.

Reshaping competencies are not improved or developed in the same way as operational competencies. Managers do not usually set out to develop reshaping competencies, particularly in Engagement or Development, *as an end in themselves* as they do with operational competencies. They are a means to an end. The end is better operational competencies. Reshaping competencies and the actions based upon them are means to that end.

Consequently reshaping competencies are often not seen as competencies in the same way as operational competencies. Once the new operational competence is in place all, or much, of the focus and action is put into exploiting the advantages it gives to the firm. This often means that the reshaping competencies used to develop it begin to erode and may soon be lost. If reshaping competencies were not important to the change process that leads to the development of operational competencies that would not of itself matter. But our data show they are absolutely crucial to success in effective change.

Why reshaping competencies are often not embedded

In many cases reshaping competencies are not embedded, or even retained as a collective competence. Each time a new change has to be made, a new saviour is needed and the wheel is reinvented with the consequent highly variable risks of failure or success. Why is this so?

There are three reasons why some managers are not motivated to embed reshaping competencies. First, managers may not see that effective change stems from actions based upon particular competencies, in the way they normally see, say, visual merchandising, credit management or metal extrusion as based on relevant competencies. Because they do not conceptualise what is needed for effective change in terms of specific competencies or capabilities, they have no understanding, basis or motivation for action to develop or embed them.

Second, they have little or no information for linking particular competencies, even if they conceptualised them, with achieving effective change, nor indeed would many see that achieving Change Effectiveness needs different competencies from those needed to achieve Current Business Performance. This lack of understanding is demonstrated by the way some firms approach the task of change. People are expected to be able to make successful change without understanding or commitment to the new directions, with lack of development of resources, systems, practices or training, and with unclear goals, inadequate monitoring or reward. This happens not only in firms that are currently performing poorly, but also in those whose performance is high. Since there is no identification of the competencies needed, there is no action to embed them.

And yet the link between particular capabilities and the changes needed for future performance is clearly understood by many successful companies who invest considerable sums and effort in activities that are essentially those of Engagement, Development and Performance Management. Examples of these were given in the preceding chapters.

Our study provides answers to both these first two major problems facing managers. It describes the capabilities and key competencies needed for Change Effectiveness, how they differ from those needed for Current Business Performance, and what states and actions are typically linked to them.

The third reason for not embedding reshaping competencies is that the costs of embedding and maintaining them are immediate, continuing and can be significant, but the pay-off is largely down the track in circumstances that cannot be foreseen, and when current managers may no longer be there. Our study shows that two reshaping capabilities—Engagement and Development—add little to Current Business Performance. Essentially they are about changing and renewing organisations, and so their pay-off is in the future—perhaps a distant future. For managers whose horizons are short term, and often encouraged by the reward systems to be so, the motivation to invest in these reshaping capabilities is very low.

Performance Management, on the other hand, contributes to both Change Effectiveness and Current Business Performance, and so there should be less inhibition in developing or embedding the competencies that form this capability. Some firms attempt to make change with very heavy emphasis and reliance on Performance Management. This was the case at GE in the first stage of Welch's tenure. But change based on Performance Management alone is unlikely to succeed. Without real Engagement, the most important reshaping capability, which generates commitment and motivation, change lacks the most powerful generator of action and support. Without Development, people may not be sufficiently empowered to achieve the changes and the very mechanism of creating new competencies is missing.

Costs of not embedding reshaping competencies

While decisions to embed competencies have costs, decisions not to embed reshaping competencies also incur costs. These are not so immediately visible but they can be very heavy. They take place down the track when the organisation has little embedded competence to help it make needed changes. Such organisations have no alternative when change is needed but to look for a saviour, frequently from outside. The costs of saviours are often high. They may well come with even shorter term agendas than those they replace. The costs are often borne by members of the organisation, who are jettisoned when the newcomers want to make a quick impact. Many of the organisation's real assets may well be reduced or destroyed in the process. Furthermore, unless some corporate reshaping capability is then built into the organisation, the process is likely to be repeated.

There is also a major investment in learning afresh each time change is attempted. Mistakes made while learning can be costly. If change is likely to be very infrequent a manager may well believe that it is not necessary to incur the costs of maintaining reshaping capabilities. But unhappily we have no reliable way of knowing when we will next need to change. Change is currently taking place frequently and seemingly, in some areas, almost continuously. Managers who do not embed reshaping competencies may well find that when they need them most they have them least.

Managers therefore need to make judgments about what and how to embed reshaping competencies in their organisation. The costs between embedding and not embedding may not, in the end, be very different. *But the outcomes are likely to be considerably different.*

You cannot learn to swim in bed

Since reshaping competencies usually arise out of action to develop operational competencies, it is difficult, perhaps impossible, to develop them consciously, unless the organisation is actually facing or trying to achieve change. To learn a new skill without action, practice and feedback in real situations is difficult. While training in some related skills may be helpful, it is not possible to learn to swim in bed. At some stage you have to get into the water. For example, communication to be effective has to be about something of substance and importance. Development has to be in skills, resources or systems that are to be used in the new situation or for the new strategy. Performance Management must be related to real performance that has to be changed or achieved.

Goals, monitoring and rewards have to be real to be meaningful. So reshaping competencies are likely to be best developed when firms face reshaping needs, and action has to be taken. Preparation, training and knowledge will be valuable but the doing, in real time in the real world, will be crucial to the learning.

It is important therefore for managers to see change not only as a need to develop improved and new operational competencies, but also as the opportunity to develop improved reshaping competencies. Each change, even quite small changes, is an opportunity for individuals to develop reshaping competencies. These will be developed more effectively if they are accompanied by training, coaching and feedback, and if they can be given within an overall framework that enables people to see what makes change effective. The capabilities framework in this book is suitable for this.

Many organisations take effective action to develop managerial skills by moving managers into different situations to encourage the development of a number of particular skills. However, these are often built round the need to acquire operational capabilities rather than reshaping ones. The latter may be more important, in the long run, especially for managers who are likely to reach the top, or near the top, of an organisation.

Motivation to embed reshaping competencies

Although many firms do not embed reshaping competencies, many managers do take action to embed them. Some of that embedding may well be a random event—driven by individual managers who feel a personal responsibility for the firm's long-term performance and what happens to it after they leave. But a more substantial and less random reason is likely to be managers identifying with the purposes, values and goals of the organisation. When people believe in the worthwhileness of what they are doing, they are much more willing to promote the organisation's long-term health. This commitment is often seen most strongly in organisations with purposes which, in fact as well as theory, go beyond the making of money.

Such organisations therefore are more likely to develop managers who are willing to take a long-term view and who are more motivated to embed, or maintain, reshaping competencies that enhance the organisation's ability to change and thus achieve its long-term objectives. Such organisations often develop their own senior management and chief executives, thus successively reinforcing and maintaining the long-term purposes of the organisation and the continuous renewal of its performance over time. Robert's organisation had such long-term aims. One of its corporate competencies was in communication and we now describe some aspects of this as an example of an embedded reshaping competence.

An embedded reshaping competence at Robert's store

When Robert arrived at his store he found a number of past actions by management, in most cases by its founder and senior group management, had established a range of processes, activities, meetings, mechanisms and a very strong culture, which had embedded a communication competence in the organisation. Because of the nature of some of the communication processes, which we will shortly describe, they provided also a strong monitoring process so that they contributed not only to Engagement but also to Performance Management. Robert found both were valuable to him, and they leveraged and enhanced his efforts to make effective change.

There were required meetings, practices and forums that facilitated communication. There was also a strong culture of open communication that was part of the group's vision about how it should share information. The culture had become established through the practices, and the commitment of senior management to them. The practices and processes had been set up over time as corporate policy and were a feature of all stores in the group.

There was a weekly store newspaper. It published the store's and every department's weekly sales results. This was available to all of the store's 300 staff. Everybody knew how sales in the business were going.

Additionally, the daily sales results were written up on a board in the store's canteen, and so everybody was up to date. Robert had added this embellishment and, as the increases started coming in, some staff cheered as he chalked them up at lunchtime. There was also a staff suggestion box in the canteen. A small bonus was given for *every* suggestion and a much larger one for the best each month.

There was a section in the store newspaper in which letters were printed about the store—comments, queries, complaints, anything. Signed and anonymous letters were accepted and printed unless they were legally libellous. The letters were received by the editor of the newspaper, who did not report to the store manager, but to an executive in head office. All letters were answered by the store manager at the same time as the letter was printed. This had to be within three weeks of receipt. A copy of any letter not printed had to be sent to the chief executive of the group with reasons for not publishing it. Very few were sent to the chief executive. Even fewer were not published. As a consequence of publishing all anonymous letters, virtually anything that anyone wanted to air was aired.

A similar process went on at corporate level. Here the results of each store and each central buyership were published weekly with comments. There was a similar section that published all received letters, of which there were many. Robert's people therefore had detailed information not only about their own operation but also about operations throughout the group. If anyone anywhere had a point to make, it could be made, anonymously if needed. It would be published and would be fully answered. The organisation felt the benefits of exposure were greater than the problems such comments sometimes caused.

A range of regular meetings in the store aided communication, including:

1 The store opened half an hour late one morning each week. In this half-hour, department managers held a meeting with their own staff to discuss their results and action for improving them, and to deal with any other issues raised.

2 A regular weekly meeting between the store manager and the department managers was held to discuss results and matters of importance to future performance. A record was taken and circulated to those present.

3 The store had a store council with elected representatives of the store and a few appointed management members. This council met eight times a year. Representatives could and did raise any matter for discussion—for example, store performance, strategies for development, opening hours, pay rate issues and training. Minutes were published and displayed in the store.

4 An elected committee was given a substantial sum of money each year to distribute, in the form of loans or gifts, to any staff facing personal financial difficulty. Consequently people, elected by their colleagues, were given the financial resources to help minimise personal difficulties, which often affect performance, but in the normal course of events would not become known to the store manager.

5 Another elected committee within the store was concerned with direct communication between staff and the chairman in head office. This group, which met six times a year and did not include any local management members, tended to function principally as a grievance settling body. Chaired by a specialist from head office, matters were raised by this chairperson after the meetings directly with the store management and settled promptly. The minutes were published together with the action taken by management to resolve the issues raised.

6 Robert addressed the whole store on its results and opportunities twice each year and answered any questions.

Robert found a strong structure in place that facilitated open and frequent communication, not only within his store but also between it, the rest of the group and top management. This was buttressed by a series of prescribed meetings, a dissemination of information on a major scale, and the involvement of many of the people in the store and groups in the interactive processes that were set up for communication. Communication was horizontal and vertical within the store and across the organisation as a whole.

Communication was further developed and embedded by the establishment of specific posts in the organisation's structure. For example, store and group newspapers were edited by individuals as part of their paid work. The central managers who chaired the committees in all the many units in the organisation were full-time appointments.

The values about sharing information and widespread communication were not only espoused, they were real. Because of the group's values, people became more open in communication and felt free to discuss things. Many were long-serving members and consequently a lot of the skills became collective. Robert found that his views about the future of the store were not only a matter he discussed with his managers but that the staff also discussed them in their regular meetings with the chairman's representative. This enabled staff who had concerns to raise them with a neutral party. Robert was interested to learn how well the neutral party handled such matters and, though he felt somewhat uncomfortable to start with, he discovered this was a valuable process.

As a result of the shared public information about results, and public discussion of actions of any kind, the group simultaneously developed a monitoring process. Our study shows that monitoring is an action that is linked to both Engagement and Performance Management. Of course, a particular and unusual feature of this monitoring process was that it took place in public. All results, all comments and all questions, anonymous or otherwise, were printed and shared by everyone. The store knew what was happening in the group. The group knew what was happening in the store. The chairman, through a multiplicity of mechanisms, knew most of what was happening everywhere. The pressure to perform when all performance is publicly known is very strong. It became a very powerful control and influencing system, but one conducted in public, with some of the checks on power that public exposure brings.

Many of the aspects of corporate communication took place because they were part of the founder's beliefs. But even so they were not ends in themselves. They were focused ultimately on improving the operational capabilities of the organisation. They enabled the chief executive to continue to influence operational performance by his considerable involvement in the process.

Of course particular corporate values and processes never suit everyone, and so these particular approaches to communication and monitoring attracted some and repelled others. This strengthened the competence because people who believed in the level of open communication and monitoring were attracted to the group and maintained the corporate competence. Those who were uncomfortable with it left. It is little surprise that the corporate competence endured. Such a system might seem bureaucratic or cumbersome to an outsider, but to insiders who had grown accustomed to it, it became a quite normal way of corporate communication and monitoring. Other organisations have developed their own corporate competencies in communication with very different features. Our illustration is simply one example.

Losing a competence

Because an organisation has an embedded corporate competence, it does not mean that it cannot lose it, or indeed that it should not be changed. The following section describes the erosion and loss of an important operational competence in a bank, the impact this had on the organisations involved and the steps taken to recreate the competence in a new form.

When the chickens come home to roost

Harry knew it was time for him to go. He was getting towards retirement anyway and the bank had offered him, reluctantly, its chief executive had said, a reasonable early retirement settlement. Credit management had been Harry's life. He had been one of the best in his field. He had lived through the booming eighties trying hard to maintain the standards and skills in lending that had been inculcated in him by years of training. But he had watched as these skills and standards were downplayed, criticised as dated, and their impact marginalised. And then the late eighties and the nineties had come. It was cold comfort for him as the bank's bad loans steadily began to mount and then raced to enormous sums. And his bank was not alone. He watched as a competitor bank recorded the largest corporate loss in Australia's history. The chickens had truly come home to roost.

Now, he appreciated, it was the era of technology in credit decision making, with computer programs systematically and efficiently analysing every case and deciding to whom to grant credit, the conditions and how to manage their case. Harry knew this was the future for credit management. He understood the quantitative mechanisms involved, their strengths and their limitations. He had overseen their introduction into his bank. He had recruited and fostered the specialists in this new kind of lending. But somehow it was foreign to his nature.

For Harry, credit skills were still personal skills and attributes. These were developed over many years of making loans. He remembered how, as a young man in the bank, he had served his long apprenticeship in lending, under the ever-watchful and stern gaze of his tutors and managers. He recalled explaining his actions and reasons to the loan inspectors who regularly visited his branch to report, with great thoroughness, on all aspects of the way the loans were being made and managed. He remembered worrying about customers having difficulty with their repayments where he had to make gut-wrenching decisions—should he extend further credit to a customer in difficulty, or call in the loan and maybe destroy the customer's business or force the selling of the family home? Harry had lived through many of these tough and difficult decisions for years before he became a senior loan inspector. His skills had been hammered out on the anvil of experience and shaped by the culture, practices and standards of his bank.

Harry remembered the tales he had heard as a young loans officer in the bank—tales of employees who had laboured for the bank for decades and on retirement had seen their expected gratuity reduced to nothing to compensate for loan losses for which they were held responsible. In truth, Harry had never met such a person and, as he had risen to ever more senior roles, the story seemed unlikely. Yet it was part of the folklore that surrounded the work and formed its culture. 'To be a good banker you have to be a good lender. Everything else is secondary.'

Harry believed it. So did all his colleagues. So did the bank. And so did other banks. They became self-renewing repositories of collective skills in lending and credit management. These were enshrined in their practices, drummed into their staff and a major source of their pride. If there was one thing banks knew how to do it was to look after the money of their depositors and shareholders. They treasured and nourished their collective competence in lending.

Harry remembered how things began to change. The booming economies of the seventies and eighties generated ever-increasing profits and deposits. He had done his best to maintain standards, writing reports on the bad quality of lending decisions, loan documentation and loan management. So had other inspectors who had grown up in the bank with him. But the reports made little impact. Most lenders in the bank were, in fact, not losing money. Instead they were being praised and rewarded by the bank's top management for the volume of lending they were doing and the profits the bank was booking on their loans. Harry felt his own people were being marginalised.

The stars in the bank were now the people who built new ventures, and who grew the bank's business through aggressive lending or through their marketing skills. The emphasis had changed from 'husbanding' the bank's money to aggressively competing with other banks to make loans. Harry could remember when sales and marketing were rarely talked about in the bank. Now they were talked about all the time. The bank ran courses in selling skills as part of its training program. This widened the types of loan the bank became involved in, taking it into areas where it had little real knowledge and skill to make the right judgments. But in an era when it was hard to lose money, lending skills and credit management lost their place in importance in the bank's operations.

Harry remembered the late eighties when, one by one, the bubbles began to burst. He thought of the many times he had to write back, as losses, the large sums that the bank had earlier booked, as profits, on these many loans. Where were the stars who had made these loans and received the bank's accolades and bonuses? They had gone.

Harry felt a sense of loss, not for the stars, with whom he had little in common, and who had rejected his warnings as negative and dated, but for the bank. He felt it had somehow let him down. It had let itself down. Deep down he felt it was a matter of values. Perhaps that was why he felt it was time to take an early retirement.

But Harry was a professional to the end. He was proud to have played a key role in supporting the introduction of the new system. Many thousands of past cases had been analysed and coded to give every piece of possible information about what was involved in successful loan management. A new system of loan management had been created by the statistical analysis of these past cases. Developing the software for using all this had required real expertise, and Harry had been interested to watch its development. New people, without Harry's vast experience, had been recruited to apply it. The early trials of the system had shown up a few defects but these had been overcome and it was now working well. Harry knew its real test would be some years down the track. And it would not just be a test of the new system but of the people who were setting the standards and influencing the culture.

One thing that did please Harry, who deep down had some reservations about whether the system could ever replace the personal skills of the trained lender, was that it did encourage consistency in lending decisions. This would be important as the new recruits did not have that wealth of training and development that Harry and his colleagues had built up over many years, nor the strong culture that had supported their decisions. And the system did allow for greater central control of adjustments in lending standards. That could be valuable, particularly in times of future change. Of course, Harry mused to himself, the systems alone would not be enough. The culture to support it was vital, and so were the values and standards of responsibility of those at the very top.

Not only in Harry's bank

Harry's experience was replicated in many banks and in many countries. In the United States, which, unlike most countries, has thousands of banks, the failure rate for banks averaged two a year in the 1970s but rose to around 130 a year for the 1980s. It reached 188 in 1987, 233 in 1988 and 193 in 1989. While the failures were mainly among the numerous smaller banks, the actual loss rates of the largest banks (loan losses relative to assets) were substantially greater than those of the smaller banks.

Yet though many banks reported massive losses in the late 1980s and early 1990s, others did not. There were some common features in the loan portfolios of banks with large losses, particularly highly leveraged transactions and commercial real estate. This commonality provided a basis for those banks to suggest the problems were macroeconomic and not their fault. While macroeconomic conditions made some contribution, the success that other competitors had in avoiding these same traps suggests the actions of the banks themselves was what made the difference.

This is shown very clearly in the results of the major banks in Australia in 1992. In that year the total profit of Australia's four major banks, which together accounted for about 80 per cent of the market, was close to zero. Yet two of them had combined losses of $1.6 billion and two had total shared profits of $1.2 billion. The most successful of these, National Australia Bank, through maintaining a strong credit culture and practices, surpassed its previously larger rivals to become Australia's biggest and most profitable bank.

In some cases, the bank's failures accompanied attempts to enter risky fields for which the organisation had little prior experience or competence. Deregulation, booming conditions and competitor action also encouraged many US savings and loan companies (S&Ls) to follow this path, with an ultimate loss of hundreds of billions of dollars, much of it borne by taxpayers. Two major banks in Australia, owned by different state governments, failed in this way. They extended from strong local retail franchises, in which their competence was high, into large commercial loans where their competence was low. They lost billions of dollars leaving huge costs for their local taxpayers to meet.

In other cases the losses were effectively the consequences of the institutions being pillaged by individuals and groups to serve their own interests. In the United States property developers and investors gained direct control of many S&Ls and virtually looted them for their own benefit. In Japan the *yakusa* (organised crime) became the beneficiaries of enormous failed property loans made by a number of *jusen* (mortgage lenders) who were ultimately bailed out by the taxpayer for hundreds of billions of yen. Even the greatest banks were not immune from a deterioration in credit practice and culture. Citicorp, the largest bank in the Americas in the early 1990s, saw its provisions for loan losses zoom from $1.2 billion in 1988 to $3.9 billion in 1991. The Citicorp experience was typical of the time, played out, in different forms and different intensities, in numerous other banks around the world—but not in all of them.

Corporate competencies insights from banking

A number of important aspects of corporate competencies are illustrated in the story of Harry and the banks. We will focus on three aspects:

- the importance of values and culture in building and sustaining the use and value of a competence
- the key role that the actions of top management make to the operation of a competence
- the role of Performance Management in maintaining a competence.

The importance of values and culture

This case illustrates, in somewhat dramatic form, because of the billions of dollars involved, the importance of the values and culture of the organisation in sustaining a competence. For very many decades the banks had placed great value on, and invested enormous sums in, building a competence. It was a vital part of their Biztech capability. Its strength did not rest solely on competencies—whether personal, or embedded in systems and practices—but in a number of other things that supported them. The culture of the bank gave great weight to the importance of credit management. It was central to its activities. Its operation was professionally reviewed. The bank's training priorities, career structure and reward practices supported it. Its top management espoused its virtues. When these things began to change, the foundations of the competence began to crumble. When practices—for example, the reporting on bad loan management—did not involve corrective management action and support, the signal was read clearly by all those involved. The motivation given to individuals to acquire, develop and sustain those skills was undermined. The impact and standing of those who wished to maintain them was devalued.

An operational competence, thus, is not just a matter of the possession of particular skills, or technologies, though these are, of course, vital. Its practice needs the support of the organisation's culture and values to build and maintain it.

The role of top management

Top management actions have an important impact upon a corporate competence. Top management needs to understand the importance of the competence to the organisation's performance and it needs to be able to recognise when it is eroding. Retrospectively, it is apparent that a collective personal competence, which was widespread throughout the banking industry, largely disappeared during the seventies and eighties. Few people in the banking industry would have been aware, certainly in the early stages, that a major business technology was being eroded and would be emasculated or indeed, in some banks, die.

In the earlier decades there were real mechanisms, practices and a supportive culture at work in most banks, continuously renewing and embedding the skills and values upon which the competence depended. These, for example, had been central to Harry's development as a banker. In the latter decades, these supporting factors were seriously weakened and yet this went largely unrecognised by senior management. They did not set out to incur a higher loss rate or lower their competence in credit management. And yet this is what happened. The competence steadily evaporated without the recognition that this was occurring.

Part of this lack of awareness of what was happening was undoubtedly influenced by the booming external environment of the times. Sometimes there is a period when strong business performance occurs without any apparent contribution from a particular competence. This is often the case in boom times, and applies to many businesses. Cost estimating in the construction industry, service quality in retailing, or marketing competence in many businesses, often get less attention when sales and profits come more easily. So the actions of top management and others can weaken them because of complacency. This behaviour is not confined to bankers.

This is compounded where top management lacks knowledge of the importance of the competence. They may not always know enough about how the business actually achieves performance to appreciate the true value of the competence to results. This is one risk with appointees from outside who may inadvertently damage important competencies. Alternatively, they may appreciate the value of the competence but are out of touch with the extent of its current strength. This was precisely the situation that took place at Woolworths in relation to its pricing. Being price competitive is as vital a competence for a mass supermarket retailer as good credit management is for a bank. And yet when Paul Simons, at his first meeting with his top management, asked them to estimate the difference on a number of articles between their strongest competitor and themselves, it became apparent that the collective view of their real price competitiveness was unbelievably mistaken. Woolworths had policies, systems and practices to ensure its competence in competitive pricing but they were just not being acted on and its top management did not know.

Top management also affects the value of a competence by the balance it holds between competing requirements for performance. Banks clearly saw the benefits of developing stronger competence in selling as important to performance. It is unlikely that many saw this would lead to a weakening in competence in credit management. In some it did not. But in others the actions taken had this effect. The different reward systems for lenders and credit managers that operated in some banks were an example of this. In some cases bonus plans were introduced for lending officers based on the volume of money lent, not on the quality of the loans. Bank officers who voiced their concerns at this were labelled as negative, weakening further the position of those who wished to maintain the competence. Balance between competing needs is one of the responsibilities of top management. Where the balance was wrong, the competence in credit management began to erode. Actions by top management, particularly in what they signal as to the value and importance of a competence, have profound effects on the growth and maintenance of a competence or on its erosion or destruction.

The role of Performance Management

The strength of a firm's capability in Performance Management affects not only its results but also the maintenance of its competencies. The banks' competence in credit management was, in many cases, linked to weak Performance Management capability.

Performance Management in the delivery of a product or service usually receives strong feedback from two sources. The first is internal where observed problems—costs, design, production, delivery or other problems—signal that corrective action is needed. Internal feedback from the many Harrys in their banks gave them some warnings. However there is normally a long lead time between granting loans and bad debt, and the sales volume was continually rising so that many banks paid insufficient heed to it before it was too late.

The other source of feedback is the marketplace where sales, customer reaction or competitor progress signal that action is needed. If a firm's product quality or service drops off their customers will tell them or go elsewhere. Often this feedback gives quick signals that a competence is eroding and stimulates quick response action to maintain it. But the banks did not have external negative feedback at the time when it mattered. Sales rose and customers were generally happy. Nothing dire appeared on the near horizons. Many at the top would have assumed, without checking, that normal loan management constraints and behaviours were operating as usual. Those who might have checked may well have come to accept that some of the previous disciplines were no longer as necessary.

New generations of bankers were reaching top positions in the industry. These bankers had never lived through the tougher times that had given rise to many of the credit disciplines once thought essential. Some thought the rules of the game had changed, as they had in some industries, and success would be achieved in different ways than it had in the past. Some, unhappily, may simply have taken a shorter term outlook, 'swinging' along with the external environment of the times. But, whatever the reasons, the competence suffered, in many banks, in the absence of early feedback on its weakening.

A strong Performance Management capability does not focus just, or even primarily, on end results. It focuses on the precursors to bottom line performance. That, of course, depends on a good understanding of the relationships between various factors today, and future bottom line results. Feedback was possible for banks that understood their business and designed their Performance Management systems to reflect that understanding. Some did. Others did not.

The damage caused to some organisations when competence is eroded lies a long way down the track. This was the case with the banks, but it applies in many cases. Although the erosion is steady and often unnoticed, its consequences are not. Many of the airline crashes that occur can be traced to eroding competence in safety management, visible to some, particularly in the enquiries that follow, but sadly though not to the victims. Loss of engineering competence or safety management is reflected later rather than sooner, in falling bridges, collapsing residences and mining disasters. Failure in competence in cost estimation hits the firm sooner but is recognised too late. Where time lags are long, the firm is ultimately dependent, in the absence of effective external regulation, upon its Performance Management capability and the quality of its standards set and accepted by its senior management.

Lags not only occur where the outcome is failure but also where it is a success. Research and development is an example where competence will only be apparent in success in the future. That future may be five, ten or many more years hence, in industries like pharmaceuticals, consumer electronics, software development or automobile development. The long track record of success of some companies in these fields suggests the presence of a strong Performance Management capability. This is likely to be buttressed by the organisation's core values and commitment to purposes beyond the making of money. It may well be supported by the motivations and personal competencies of its leadership, who tend to be promoted from within and are thus carriers of its culture and believers in its purpose.

While banking is an example from the private sector, the public sector is frequently faced with decisions about investing in competencies that have a pay-off a long way down the track. Competence in air-traffic control, customs inspection, health care or the police service are just a few instances of the many areas of the public sector where competence can erode over a period before the impact is felt. In the case of the military, the lack of hostile action over long periods creates conditions where, in the absence of effective management action, the erosion of competencies may go undemonstrated for many years. It has become commonplace to discover, in times of conflict, that the military is well equipped now to fight the battles of the last war.

So developing or sustaining competencies and preventing unplanned erosion, particularly for those where outcomes are down the track, requires real knowledge of the business, a strong supporting culture, care in actions that could signal lack of support, a willingness to take a long-term view, high standards of consistency and integrity, particularly in top management, and strong Performance Management capability. This is true whether the competencies are operational or reshaping. In many banks unhappily this did not occur. But in some it did.

CHAPTER 11

Planning for action

T HE PURPOSE OF THIS CHAPTER is to provide a structure to help you think through, develop and check your plans for change. Of course everything cannot be covered in a plan. Some of the knowledge you need and the actions to take will only emerge as you engage with your organisation as the change gets underway. Your ability to deal with the dynamics of the change process as it unfolds is likely to be strengthened if you have done a great deal of preliminary thinking of your own within a framework that works.

Effective change is ultimately about building new and improved operational capabilities, which provide the basis for renewed performance. These capabilities will be strengthened in their application by the way the organisation's state is managed, and by the culture that values and supports them. So it is useful to start with some initial thinking about your current operational capabilities and why they are important to your success even if, as is likely to be the case, you will develop and alter your views about future operational capabilities as a result of going through the Engagement, Development and Performance Management process.

Operational capabilities

Think through aspects of your organisation's operational capabilities from two perspectives. What competencies are the most important contributors to your current performance? What are likely to be the most important contributors to your performance, say, five or so years from now? You will identify many of your operational capabilities more easily and reliably if you think about your products and services and work back from them.

Current performance

What are the key products or group of products/services/outputs your organisation sells or provides to its customers? It will help to write them down.

What do you think are the particular attributes of your products/ services that the customer values?

What are the significant things your organisation does well (competencies), which enable you to offer these products/services in ways that your customer values? In answering this look separately at Biztech, Performance Management, and Marketing and Selling capabilities. Make this list as comprehensive as you can because it may reveal things that are necessary to satisfying your customer but to which you give relatively little attention. You can reduce it later to the most important factors.

Future performance

What do you judge will be the demands from customers/users of your organisation's output in, say, three or four years' time? List the key competencies you think will need most improvement, or transformation, or will need to be created, to meet the shape of that product/service demand. In our work with organisations on change, competencies that firms believe they need to build for better future performance are frequently those relevant to their own business-specific operations that will provide innovativeness, quick responsiveness to market changes, improved personnel, high quality in customer service, and improved customer knowledge, product excellence and promotional skills. These in turn will provide the organisation with its new key success factors. While, of course, you may not yet be sure what competencies you need to improve and for what purpose, thinking them through and deciding what are the really important ones will sharpen your focus on what you need to do. Also ask yourself if these competencies are likely to be significantly dependent on one or a few key individuals.

A supporting culture

As we have stressed in *Change Power* competencies need to be supported by the organisation's culture or their impact will be weakened. Here you should think about the cultural changes your organisation most needs to support the competencies that will be valuable to you in the future. In our work with executives, organisational cultures often identified to support the competencies they wish to develop include building a culture of reward based on performance, commitment to continuous improvement, emphasis on teamwork, acceptance of corporate responsibility to develop people, focus on customer service and satisfaction, organisational innovativeness and the importance of personal initiative. There is considerable agreement between private and public sectors about what cultures are desirable to develop. Your own shortlist will have other cultural changes appropriate to your needs but some, no doubt, will be common with other organisations working or competing in the same environment.

The structure and organisation of work

Thought needs to be given to changes in structure and the organisation of work in your business. You can better judge this when you have clarified in your mind the future operational competencies and the cultures needed to support them. Changes in this area often relate to reducing the number of levels of responsibility between top and bottom, movements of resources between central and operating units, reduction in staff numbers, and changes in job design and responsibilities. More generally you also need to think about changes in the distribution of power in the organisation, methods and processes of decision making and the redesign of key operating processes.

Your key change intents

You have now begun to clarify some of the future competencies you need to develop, aspects of the culture you believe are needed to support them, and some elements of your structure and operations that may also need change. We will call these your 'key change intents'. These will form the focus for your action and the centre of the message to your organisation. There is, of course, no magic number of key change intents but since part of the purpose is to focus the organisation's energy on achieving them you do not want many. One may be enough if it is important and central enough. Two or three, maybe four, will also provide a clear sharp focus for attention, but if you have many more you are likely to find it much harder to get that focus, or the understanding or commitment from your organisation you need. Most changes develop over time, and so as you make progress and get results with the main changes you will be able to add other change intents more sensibly.

Organisational states

Lastly before you think about actions in the areas of Engagement, Performance Management and Development you need to remind yourself of the role that organisational states plays in effective change. Part of the purpose of your action should be to build up states of commitment, understanding, empowerment and esprit de corps. You should now ask yourself what are the current strengths of those states in your organisation at this time in relation to the key change intents you have been crystallising.

Engagement action

What you have been doing so far in working through this chapter is, of course, a personal pathfinding activity, making up your own mind about the way forward. At this stage it is worthwhile to review the key change intents you have developed in the light of your organisation's purpose and key values. While you could have started from an examination of your organisation's purposes and developed your change intents from them, most organisational purposes are not sufficiently clarified or developed to make that the best practical approach.

Pathfinding and corporate purpose

What do you think is your organisation's corporate purpose—that is, 'what do you want your organisation to do beyond making money'? We suggest you put it in words. It will strengthen your understanding if you also clarify your key values and those of your organisation.

Check your key change intents against your own view of your organisation's purpose. Do they advance the current purpose or do they in some degree change its purpose? If there is some difference, you need to get alignment between your view of your organisation's purpose and your change intents. In considering this alignment you may well find that you will clarify both. Similarly, when you involve others in path-finding work, you need to achieve alignment between the intended changes and the shared view of the organisation's purpose.

Part therefore of the Engagement action that you need to take has to result in shared views about both organisational purpose and intended key changes. Do your members have *a shared understanding* of your *corporate purpose*? Your corporate purpose should provide an accepted, meaningful, motivating and enduring vision for the strategies and new directions that need to be built.

If there is not a shared understanding of your corporate purpose, what action will you take to develop one and put it in place?

There is no effective shortcut to working out where your organisation's future lies. It usually needs the collection of a great deal of information internally and externally, a lot of dialogue, developing and exploring a number of options, experimentation, time and hard work. The process may well be accelerated by critical events, workshops, external business consultants, and just occasionally academics! Remember the fundamental point that pathfinding in itself is not Engagement—

it is part of it. A brilliant strategy devised by someone else is not going to work in practice unless and until the organisation, or a critical mass of it, has become engaged in the change.

Further improving understanding and commitment

In addition to pathfinding action you need to take other actions to help achieve Engagement. What other actions will you take to:

- more effectively *convey a vision* of the new directions
- *consult* with and *involve* your people more productively in the change
- *monitor the changes* you are making more effectively so that people have feedback on progress towards your new directions
- *recognise your people's contributions* to the changes or use other ways to increase *commitment* to your intended changes?

Positive states

Part of the purpose of your action is to develop change-enhancing states. Actions, of course, affect more than one state, but when focusing on Engagement action, it is a relevant time to ask what further action you should take to develop states of commitment and understanding of your key change intents.

Development action

Most changes need new or improved resources and systems of all kinds to build the new operational competencies for the business. This typically involves Development and action in some, or all, of the following areas:

- management skills
- workforce skills
- systems, processes and practices
- physical facilities

- business technologies and know-how
- other areas special to your situation.

You can think about these areas from two perspectives. The first is action that is needed in each of these six areas to improve current performance. The second is to look at the key change intents you have set yourself, and which hopefully by now have been improved and are shared, and see what Development action is specifically needed for each area.

When you have considered both perspectives you can review what actions you have already taken, and what now needs to be done. It is worth checking which of the remaining actions are very dependent on a key individual and what you can do to strengthen the organisation's position so that it becomes less dependent on a particular individual.

Positive states

Action in the Development area is strongly linked to creating a state of empowerment. As a further check on creating positive states, ask yourself what further Development action you should take to give your people the resources, competencies and authority they need to bring your shared key change intents to life.

Performance Management action

Performance Management contributes strongly to both Change Effectiveness and Current Business Performance, but here we will focus on its role in Change Effectiveness.

Key areas for action in Performance Management include goals, resource management, and monitoring and evaluating performance and rewards. Much of the action here is business specific but in each area we suggest a general question or two to start your exploration of what actions will help your change to be successful.

Goals involve aspects of clarity, standards, expectations, priorities, understanding and motivation. A key opening question is: What action will you take to set goals in ways that motivate the strongest performance from your people to achieve your key shared change intents?

Resource management includes planning, providing, focusing and applying resources most effectively. How and where do you want to see your resources used differently to meet the new objectives? What actions will best achieve this?

Monitoring performance includes an understanding of the critical factors in getting results, developing realistic measurements, providing timely, valid information and taking early action when performance is not on track. When new directions are being attempted, any or all of these things can themselves change. An opening question is: Are we measuring and providing the things that matter to achieving our new directions?

Evaluation includes giving feedback on performance in ways that develop better performance. While one aspect of it includes the role of a judge, evaluation is much more than judging performance. It is fundamentally a managerial competence that is focused on getting improvement. Do people really understand how they are doing in relation to the goals that have been set? What needs to be done to make that knowledge motivating for them to achieve the key change intents?

Rewards need to be, as far as practicable, performance related. Performance can be measured and rewarded at many levels—individual, team, unit, divisional, and at the total organisational level. It is important to reward not only in terms of meeting objectives but also in ways that individuals value. Unless the recipients value the rewards, the power of the reward system is weakened. Here the key opening questions could be: What actions can be taken to ensure people are consistently rewarded for their performance in achieving the objectives of the intended changes? What variety and scope are offered in rewards that enables individual needs to be met?

Positive states

Before we leave actions in the areas of Engagement, Development and Performance Management, check on actions that would improve the organisation's esprit de corps, another state that is linked to Change

Effectiveness. What other action could you take that would increase the firm's collective self-confidence and its belief that it can achieve the key change intents it has developed? What can you do that will increase mutual trust, openness and unity?

Building and embedding competencies

As a starting point for thinking about building and embedding reshaping capabilities in your organisation we suggest you revisit the many actions you have decided to take in response to the questions in this chapter. List them in the order in which their effectiveness will depend most upon your own personal competencies. Starting where there is the highest dependency on you, think through the actions you could take to embed some of that competence in the organisation's systems, processes, mechanisms, technologies and values.

Next, move your perspective from yourself, and ask: If you were to leave the organisation, what particular embedded competencies would you like a successor to have available that would give your organisation more power to influence its own renewal?

These two perspectives give you a useful starting point to think about the corporate reshaping competencies that would be valuable to embed in your organisation. In consolidating these two perspectives you could ask: What actions should and could be taken to embed Engagement, Development and Performance Management capability more strongly in your business?

Developing your own competencies

To play the role that is needed you may need to develop some of your own reshaping competencies to deal with the challenges you will face. As outlined in Chapter 10, reshaping competencies are best built by action in dealing with real situations of change. If you are about to embark on changing your organisation it will be a real opportunity to build some personal skills.

At a fundamental level, to develop a competence you need to:

- increase your knowledge and understanding of what the competence consists of and why it works
- practise, practise and practise the subskills that make it up, integrating them and getting continual feedback on your performance
- get support from others, both in the learning and application processes, to help you in managing your confidence and state throughout the process.

However, before you take any of these actions you need to be sure you are truly motivated to put in the hard work involved, or you are likely to give up when things get difficult and other agendas clamour for your energy. You may need to change some values you have about what is actually important to achieve performance, and you may need to deal with the barriers, sometimes practical but often embedded in your own mind and emotions, which have prevented or hindered you in acquiring this competence before.

Now revisit the competencies you have identified where success will depend on your own personal competencies. Choose one of these that you are motivated to develop.

We provide you with an organising framework of four areas for your action:

1 Describe the competence you would like to build in positive and specific terms. What is it that you want to be able to do more effectively? Write it down. Set yourself a goal that will stretch you, but which is achievable with real effort.

2 Recognise and list the reasons that have prevented you so far from building this skill. Perhaps you have felt it was unimportant. Perhaps you were not confident you could actually learn it or do it. Perhaps the organisation erected barriers. Perhaps you were not willing to give it the time and effort. There will be other reasons, but you need to understand and face them. To develop the competence you have chosen will almost certainly mean some change in your current

behaviour, actions, use of time, beliefs, priorities, and so on. It is because of this that you must really be motivated to build the new competence or you will not overcome these existing hurdles.

3 Gather the knowledge and understanding about this competence, how it works, and its subskills. Watch others who do it well. Seek their help and support. Read about it. Watch videos about it. If you approach it purposefully you will find that a great deal of information exists about it, and how and why it works. Some of it may be within your organisation. Much more may be outside.

4 Practise the appropriate behaviours and actions. Get feedback on what you are doing as a basis for continually improving your performance. Monitor your own performance. Find a model, or a mentor or a coach, or better still all three. Watch people doing it well. Seek their support and involvement. Practise wherever possible in situations appropriate to your level of skill. As your success grows so does your confidence. If you want to learn mountaineering you are going to fail if you think you can start by climbing Mount Everest. What builds success is the constant achievement of stretching but achievable goals. Practising failure does not achieve it.

There are of course many actions you can take to develop your own skills. The aim of this framework is to enable you to tackle it as a task to be achieved, like any other task. Having used the framework as a basis for organising your own action you can now choose another competence to develop. Learning is a skill, and if you are motivated to learn your opportunities for continual growth will be enormous.

Look at change through a new and powerful lens

Plans have great benefits in helping to generate relevant information, in the creation of options and in finding and clarifying direction and responsibility, and in focusing energy. However, some, perhaps many, of the best actions for you to take will unfold as the changes unfold. If you have thought deeply about alternatives and options as part of developing your plans and not become too fixed in your thinking you will be well placed to take sound decisions and actions as things around you evolve.

You can have great confidence that if you focus your attention on Engagement, Development and Performance Management you will be able to see what you need to do through a new, powerful and different lens. You should be able to focus your actions on the things that really do make the difference between successful and unsuccessful change, and enhance the prospects of making your own changes, both at a personal and at an organisational level, a real success.

Your leadership of change

I F YOU ARE A MANAGER with responsibility for change your actions are pivotal to its success. In our view, you can have the biggest positive impact on the success of your change by ensuring that Engagement, Development and Performance Management actually take place. Myriad things will clamour for your attention but you should focus on the key things that matter. It is essential to take a strategic perspective of what you are trying to do, to think through your strategies for Engagement, Development and Performance Management, and to make sure they happen.

If you are new to the organisation and want to make changes it is important to remind yourself that the appropriate actions in the key areas of Engagement, Development and Performance Management will, in some ways, be different from those you may have successfully taken in your old organisation. There is sometimes a tendency for managers to replicate successful actions of the past that worked in other organisations and other situations. But as you will have seen in innumerable illustrations in *Change Power*, the actions you choose must be the right actions for your new firm and in some, perhaps many ways, it and its situation will be different. Even if its industry is the same, your new firm's culture is likely to be different, and changing culture is a difficult job. So there is likely to be some unlearning and learning for you. It is very easy for newcomers who are anxious to make changes to unintentionally destroy corporate competencies that in the early days of their leadership they do not recognise. All too often organisations are set back by the wrong changes or die the death of a thousand initiatives.

So, whether you are in your existing or new role and in a new organisation or in one you have worked in for some time, you may not only need to change your organisation but also yourself. You may need to change the use of your time and the focus of your effort, or even some of your values about what is important and how best to get results. You may also need to consider ways to develop yourself to increase your abilities to influence change.

In terms of your organisation, assess what you need to do. Assess the levels of personal and corporate competence your organisation commands and try, where possible, to build on them. Think through aspects of the changes you are attempting. We have outlined in Chapter 11 a structure to help you do this.

While there are a number of ways in which you can contribute to Engagement, three are likely to be particularly powerful. The first is your individual contribution to pathfinding competence—an important aspect of Engagement. The second is in setting an atmosphere that encourages others, particularly other managers, to be engaged. The third is by embedding Engagement competencies within your business so that people can become engaged not only in your current changes, but also in those that will be needed in the future. In doing the latter you are likely to pass to your successors a stronger organisation than you inherited.

Helping develop a realistic vision for your business and playing a key role in conveying it to all your people will be a significant endeavour. The contribution you can personally make to pathfinding will clearly depend upon your individual competence but, whatever your personal competence may be, you can also set the atmosphere and framework that enables other individuals, who may well be able to make significant contributions, play a valuable role in this. Part of your responsibility is to make sure that happens. Real Engagement may provide a vision for your business that will motivate its people to do great things. If you can convey that vision, by your personal actions and example, you will make a major positive impact on the success of your organisation's renewal.

In the area of Development you are uniquely placed to contribute to your organisation's renewal and long-term performance. Development capability consists of two related sets of competencies. The first is about the way resources can be developed—for example, training people or creating new systems. The second is recognising what skills and systems, or other developments, will be the right ones for your future. The latter relies on resource application, pathfinding and planning competencies. This latter area is where you can make a real difference. The technical aspects of training or system development, or other resource development, can be done by someone else, although you need to ensure the organisation is making sufficient allocation in its budgets for these. But you should have a primary influence on the direction of Development. You have the key vantage-point as its manager to have this perspective. You need to ensure Development is focused on action to achieve your shared vision and new directions.

Ensuring your managers and workforce develop their own skills is very important. While your personal contribution will have some impact on individuals, particularly those with whom you work closely, your key role is to make certain you develop and embed in your organisation the practices, processes, systems and values needed to ensure management and workforce Development occurs and endures over time.

And of course you should always remember that your people are looking at how you develop yourself. It is not easy to develop an organisation that will be going strongly into the future if you, as its manager, are standing still yourself.

In Performance Management you can make a major contribution to your organisation's Change Effectiveness in the standards you set, the priorities you signal and the ways you monitor, support, evaluate, recognise and reward performance. Since action based on Performance Management capability contributes both to Current Business Performance and to Change Effectiveness your pay-off for action in this area will be high. Performance Management is about doing things better. While, of course, this involves thinking and planning, it also needs action. Your personal example in action can be critical to progress in this area.

Setting the level of performance you want the organisation to achieve is one way you can influence performance, whether of the change process or of current performance. Setting it at a level where people are really challenged, but are capable of achieving if properly led, is one way you can influence results. That level is not fixed. You as leader can substantially influence what people believe they can achieve. The level of performance will be affected by the levels of motivation, support, feedback and recognition about performance that you and your organisation give its people.

When people are engaged and developed and when their performance is effectively managed, their commitment and motivation are strengthened. Your action is central to increasing their performance, and in providing this leadership you can play the defining role in helping your organisation achieve successful change and renewal.

APPENDIX A

The sixteen competencies in the survey

1 **Performance control:** setting goals, monitoring what happens, taking action to keep performance on target.

2 **Resource application:** obtaining and applying resources to best achieve the firm's aims.

3 **Motivating and enthusing:** getting people motivated about their work and the firm.

4 **Integration:** achieving coordinated action throughout the firm.

5 **Enaction:** taking timely and effective action, not just planning and talking about things.

6 **Communication:** throughout the firm, communicating on matters relevant to people and their work.

7 **Achieving commitment:** achieving widespread commitment to carrying out decisions.

8 **Pathfinding:** identifying, setting and spelling out new directions for the firm.

9 **Developing resources:** developing the firm's resources (for example, people and facilities) to improve effectiveness.

10 **Systems and practices development:** instituting systems, processes and procedures that result in efficient and effective work.

11 **Environmental assessment:** monitoring events external to the firm and anticipating and adjusting for their consequences.

12 **Planning:** development of comprehensive, realistic and useful plans to guide action.

13 **Marketing and selling:** understanding of the firm's markets and customers; ability to identify their needs and sell to them.

14 Financial: effective control of funds and business finance.

15 Technical: knowledge and command of the technology used by the firm.

16 Operational: efficient, timely and quality procurement, production and distribution of products and services.

Table A.1 provides an overview of the sixteen competencies and indicates the competencies that are most strongly linked to each of the five capabilities.

Table A.1 The sixteen competencies and the five capabilities

Contributing competence	Engagement	Development	Performance Management	Biztech	Marketing and Selling
1 Performance control			X		
2 Resource application		X	X		X
3 Motivating and enthusing	X				
4 Integration	X		X		X
5 Enaction	X		X		
6 Communication	X				
7 Achieving commitment	X				
8 Pathfinding	X	X			X
9 Developing resources		X			
10 Systems and practices development		X		X	
11 Environmental assessment				X	X
12 Planning		X	X		
13 Marketing and selling					X
14 Financial			X	X	
15 Technical				X	
16 Operational			X	X	

APPENDIX B

The organisations in the survey

Quantitative data for the research were provided by 243 cases of change as detailed and described by executive staff. The organisations represented in the sample are listed below, using the names by which they were known at the time data were collected:

3M Australia Pty Ltd
ACT Electricity and Water Authority
Activon Scientific Prod. Co. Pty Ltd
Advance Bank
AGC Limited
AGL
Agtec Pty Ltd
Alcan Australia Ltd
Alcoa of Australia
Altona Petrochemical Co.
AMP Society
Ampol Ltd
Anglican Retirement Villages
ANZ Banking Group Ltd
APM
Argyle Diamonds
Andersen Consulting
Association for the Blind
Atlas Steels
Attorney General's Department (Commonwealth)
Austrade
Australia Post
Australian Centre for Unisys Software
Australian Defence Industries
Australian Government Health Service
Australian Maritime Safety Authority
Australian Overseas Telecommunications Corporation
Australian Taxation Office
Barclays Bank
Baulderstone Hornibrook Engineering Pty Ltd
BHP Petroleum
BHP Steel
Brella Pty Ltd
Caltex Oil (Australia) Pty Ltd
Cashcard Australia Limited
CBFC Ltd
Chemical Cleaning Ltd
CIBA–Geigy New Zealand Ltd
Civil Aviation Authority
Cobar Mines Pty Ltd
Commonwealth Bank of Australia
Commonwealth Department of Tourism
Conaust Ltd
Control Instrumentation
Coopers & Lybrand

CSIRO
CSL Ltd
CUB Ltd
CUNA Mutual Insurance
Department of Defence
Department of Education
  (Commonwealth)
Department of Education
  (Queensland)
Department of Health (NSW)
Department of Health, Housing &
  Community Services (Tasmania)
Department of Industry, Trade &
  Technology (South Australia)
Department of Primary Industries &
  Energy (Commonwealth)
Department of Primary Industries
  (South Australia)
Department of School Education
  (NSW)
Department of Transport &
  Communications
  (Commonwealth)
Dulux Australia
Elders Ltd
Electricity Trust of South Australia
Export Finance and Insurance
  Corporation
F.H. Faulding & Co.
FAI Insurance
Federal Airports Corporation
Freehill Hollingdale & Page
George Weston Foods Limited
GMH Automotive Ltd
Golden Casket Art Union
Great Barrier Reef Marine Park
  Authority
Hamersley Iron Pty Ltd
Hilton Bonds New Zealand
Hunter Area Health Service
IBM Australia Ltd

James Hardie Industries Limited
Kemcor Australia
Ken Everett Pty Ltd
Kilpatrick Green Pty Ltd
Kodak (Australasia) Pty Ltd
Koppers Australia Pty Ltd
Legal Aid Office (Queensland)
Leigh Mardon Pty Ltd
MacNaught Pty Ltd
Melbourne Parks and Waterways
Ministry of Maori Development
  (New Zealand)
Ministry of Science, Technology &
  Environment (New Zealand)
MM Electrical Merchandising
National Australia Bank Ltd
National Mutual Society
NCom Services
Neville Jeffress Advertising
New Zealand Dairy Group
New Zealand Post Ltd
New Zealand Treasury
Northern Territory Treasury
Novacoal Australia
Office of Public Service
  Commissioner for Northern
  Territory
Omicron Pty Ltd
OTC Ltd
Pacific Coal Pty Limited
Pacific Power
Pasminco Metals—BHAS Pty Ltd
Perpetual Trustees Qld Ltd
Pipeline Authority
Police Department (South Australia)
Precision Valve Australia
Property Services Group
Prudential, New Zealand
Public Transport Corporation of
  Victoria
Qantas Airways Limited

Queensland Alumina Limited
Queensland Corrective Services
Rainsfords Pty Ltd
Reserve Bank of Australia
Roads & Traffic Authority (NSW)
Rockmans Stores Pty Limited
Rothmans of Pall Mall NZ Ltd
Royal Australian Navy
Royal Blind Society
S.E.A.S. Sapfor Ltd.
Schwarzkopf, NZ Ltd
St George Bank Limited
State Bank of NSW
State Electricity Commission
    (Victoria)
State Electricity Commission
    (Western Australia)

State Rail Authority of NSW
State Services Department (South
    Australia)
StorageTek
Telstra Corporation Limited
The Law Book Co.
Tower Life Ltd
Trust Bank Bay of Plenty Ltd
Tubemakers Ltd
V/Line Pty Limited
Valuer General's Office (NSW)
Water Authority of Western
    Australia
Westpac Banking Corporation
White Wings Foods
William Brooks & Co.
Woolworths Limited

ENDNOTES

Introduction

[1] N. M. Tichy and S. Sherman, 1993, *Control your Destiny or Someone Else Will*, Doubleday, New York, p. 245.

[2] B. Saporito, 1991, 'Campbell Soup Gets Piping Hot', *Fortune*, 9 September, p. 95.

[3] Scott Paper, 1996, 'From the Outhouse to the Penthouse', *Fortune*, 15 January, p. 15.

[4] D. Turner, 1994, 'The Girraween Story, Du Pont Australia', CCC *Working Paper No. 040*, Centre for Corporate Change, AGSM, University of NSW.

Chapter 2

[1] D. Turner, 1992, 'The Revitalisation of Woolworths', CCC *Working Paper No. 028*, Centre for Corporate Change, AGSM, University of NSW, p. 16.

[2] Ibid., p. 12.

[3] Ibid., p. 21.

[4] Ibid., p. 17.

[5] Ibid., p. 12.

[6] Ibid., p. 23.

[7] Ibid., p. 29.

[8] Ibid., p. 22.

[9] Ibid., p. 22.

Chapter 3

[1] D. Turner & M. Crawford, 1995, 'The Impact of Corporate Competencies on Long Term Performance', CCC *Working Paper No. 051*, Centre for Corporate Change, AGSM, University of NSW.

[2] We also collected data from participants who had been on other executive programs that did not cover this topic.

Chapter 4

[1] D. Turner, 1992, 'The Revitalisation of Woolworths', CCC *working Paper No. 028*, Centre for Corporate Change, AGSM, University of NSW, p. 18.

Chapter 5

[1] C. Smitton & A. Cottam, 1993, 'Achieving Fundamental Change in Nuclear Electric', company publication, p. 10.

[2] N. M. Tichy & S. Sherman, 1993, *Control your Destiny or Someone Else Will*, Doubleday, New York, p. 73.

[3] Ibid, p. 160.

[4] J. Quinn, 1994, 'What a Work-Out', *Sales and Marketing Management (Performance Supplement)*, November, p. 58.

[5] Tichy & Sherman, op. cit., p. 196.

[6] C. Kennedy, 1995, 'The Company that Jack Built', *Director*, 49(3), September, p. 45.

[7] Ibid., p. 47.

[8] Tichy & Sherman, op. cit., p. 92.

[9] Ibid., p. 92.

[10] Ibid., p. 209.

[11] Ibid., p. 211.

[12] Ibid., p. 210.

[13] M. Loeb, 1995, 'Jack Welch Lets Fly on Budgets, Bonuses and Buddy Boards', *Fortune*, 29 May, p. 146.

[14] D. Stace & D. Dunphy, 1991, 'Beyond Acquisition to Access: A Case Study of the NSW Library', CCC *Working Paper No. 005*, Centre for Corporate Change, AGSM, University of NSW, p. 4.

[15] Ibid., p. 9.

[16] Ibid., p. 5.

[17] Ibid., p. 11.

[18] Ibid., p. 8.

[19] Ibid., p. 16.

[20] J. C. Collins & J. I. Porras, 1994, *Built to Last*, Century, London.

[21] Ibid., p. 82.

[22] D. Turner, 1994, 'The Girraween Story', CCC *Working Paper No. 040*, Centre for Corporate Change, AGSM, University of NSW, p. 6.

[23] Ibid., p. 2.

[24] Ibid., p. 3.

[25] Ibid., p. 3.

[26] Ibid., p. 4.

[27] Ibid., p. 4.

[28] Ibid., p. 4.

[29] Ibid., p. 5.

[30] Ibid., p. 5.

[31] Ibid., p. 7.

Chapter 6

1   J. C. Collins & J. I. Porras, 1994, *Built to Last*, Century, London, p. 70.

2   1997, 'The Motorola Story: An Interview', *Training and Development*, 51(8), August, pp. 26–7.

3   Ibid.

4   T. A. Stewart, 1996, '3M Fights Back', *Fortune*, 5 February, pp. 44–9.

5   J. B. Quinn, 1992, *Intelligent Enterprise*, The Free Press, New York, p. 215.

6   Collins & Porras, op. cit., p. 50.

7   D. Garvin, 1993, 'Building a Learning Organization', *Harvard Business Review*, July–August.

8   Quinn, op. cit., 1992, p. 321.

9   Discussions with Jeff Hodgins, then CEO of StorageTek Australia, and colleagues.

10   Ibid.

11   D. Turner, 1994, 'The Girraween Story', *CCC Working Paper No. 040*, Centre for Corporate Change, AGSM, University of NSW, p. 8.

12   Ibid.

13   Ibid.

14   Ibid.

15   Ibid., p. 9.

16   Ibid., p. 3.

17   Ibid., p. 6.

18   Ibid., p. 15.

19   T. A. Stewart, 1995, 'Mapping Corporate Brainpower', *Fortune*, 30 October, p. 151.

20   R. Henkoff, 1993, 'Inside Andersen's Army of Advice', *Fortune*, 4 October, p. 85.

21   Ibid.

22   Ibid.

23   Quinn, op. cit., p. 266.

24   Ibid., pp. 266–7.

25   M. Ryan Garcia, 1997, 'Knowledge Central', *Information Week*, 22 September, p. 252.

26   Quinn, op. cit., p. 125.

Chapter 7

1   N. M. Tichy & S. Sherman, 1993, *Control your Destiny or Someone Else Will*, Doubleday, New York, p. 81.

2   J. C. Collins & J. I. Porras, 1994, *Built to Last*, Century, London, p. 173.

3   J. Bowles, 1994, 'Beyond 100 Percent Satisfaction at Rank Xerox', *Fortune*, September, 'Quality 2000' section.

4   Ibid.

5   J. D. Duck, 1993, 'Managing Change: The Art of Balancing', *Harvard Business Review*, November–December, p. 109.

Chapter 8

1   S. Spriggs, 1997, 'Transforming the New South Wales Railways: Focusing on Economic Performance and Results', *CCC Working Paper No. 083*, Centre for Corporate Change, AGSM, University of NSW.

2   S. Spriggs, 1997, 'Transforming the PreSchool and Child Care Sector in Victoria', *CCC Working Paper No. 082*, Centre for Corporate Change, AGSM, University of NSW.

3   Spriggs, 1997, *CCC Working Paper No. 083*, op. cit.

4   Spriggs, 1997, *CCC Working Paper No. 083*, op. cit.

5   Spriggs, 1997, *CCC Working Paper No. 083*, p. 26.

6   Ibid., p. 27.

Chapter 9

1   Information and quotes in this chapter on Tubemakers were from discussions with Leigh Daley, group general manager, Structural and Engineering Products Group, Tubemakers of Australia Ltd, and colleagues.

Chapter 10

1   D. Turner, 1993, 'Ensuring the Future at FAI', *CCC Working Paper No. 034*, Centre for Corporate Change, AGSM, University of NSW, p. 4.

INDEX

Access *Change Power* on the Internet

You can exploit our tools and insights in dealing with change in your organisation.

Point your web browser to the *Change Power* site *Change Power on the Web* (http://changepower.com) to build on the ideas in this book.

Through the *Change Power* site you can access:

- our questionnaire and database to measure your organisation's change capabilities, change states, corporate culture, and more;
- ideas about using them to help you in your own situation;
- further developments in our research and its application; and
- a focal centre for literature and ideas on corporate change.